John Bryant's passion for motorcycling started at age 15 when he bolted an old motorised wheelchair engine to his pushbike. Half a century later he has owned and ridden them all: mopeds, scooters, dirt bikes, sports rockets, cruisers and tourers. His two-wheeled escapades have led him into the volcanoes of New Zealand, over the mountains and prairies of the USA, and across a lot of Australia. John started Australia's first motorcycle wedding escort service when he imported six of the world's largest road bikes, and dressed his riders in tux jackets, bow ties and white gauntlets. After surviving a few wipe-outs, he is now growing old disgracefully, still on two wheels, and still succumbing to the lure of the blacktop.

# GREAT AUSTRALIAN MOTORCYCLE STORIES

## John Bryant

ABC
Books

The ABC 'Wave' device is a trademark of the Australian Broadcasting Corporation and is used under licence by HarperCollins*Publishers* Australia.

First published in Australia in 2014
by HarperCollins*Publishers* Australia Pty Limited
ABN 36 009 913 517
harpercollins.com.au

**HarperCollins*Publishers***
Level 13, 201 Elizabeth Street, Sydney NSW 2000, Australia
Unit D, 63 Apollo Drive, Rosedale, Auckland 0632, New Zealand
A 53, Sector 57, Noida, UP, India
1 London Bridge Street, London SE1 9GF, United Kingdom
2 Bloor Street East, 20th floor, Toronto, Ontario M4W 1A8, Canada
195 Broadway NY, NY 10007, United States of America

National Library of Australia Cataloguing-in-Publication entry:

Great Australian motorcycle stories / John Bryant.
  ISBN: 978 0 7333 3266 1 (paperback)
  ISBN: 978 1 4607 0108 9 (ebook)
  Great Australian stories.
  Motorcycling — Australia.
  Motorcycling — Australia — Fiction.
  Motorcycles — Australia.
  Motorcycles — Australia — Fiction.
  Australian wit and humor.
  Australia — Social life and customs.
  Bryant, John Richard, 1946– editor.
629.2275

Cover design by Hazel Lam, HarperCollins Design Studio
Cover image © David Freeman
Author photograph by Peter Rosenhain
Photograph of the Axe on page 156 by John Bryant
Typeset in ITC Bookman Light by Kirby Jones
Printed in Australia by McPherson's Printing Group
The papers used by HarperCollins in the manufacture of this book
are a natural, recyclable product made from wood grown in sustainable
plantation forests. The fibre source and manufacturing processes meet
recognised international environmental standards, and carry certification.

*To my beloved pillions:*
*Benn, Kris and Tam*

# Contents

# Riding with Pope Paul VI

John Bryant
Bilpin, NSW

I think most blokes remember their first motorcycle the same way they remember their first girlfriend — she may not have had all the equipment, but man she was exciting!

Mine was a 1960 BMW R27, a 250cc single-pot engine with 18 almost-invisible horsepower, boasting a rubber-mounted powertrain and shaft drive. She came complete with a little metal prong that had to be inserted into the top of the headlight to start her, which acted as the ignition key. This was handy because whenever I misplaced the prong I would start her with an old nail. Back in 1964 when I bought her I paid £110, a steal, but one in original condition today would probably be worth 10 times that. Underpowered, ungainly and as ugly as sin, but I loved her!

As the 1960s turned into the 1970s, I was living a carefree life on Sydney's North Shore, supported by Mum and Dad, pretending to go to university while cramming in as much social action as I could physically handle. The BM took me to uni as well as parties, beaches, stomps, footy matches and any event that featured girls, beer or motorcycles. In those odd moments when nothing else was happening, I indulged myself in a new sport that I had stumbled upon almost by accident.

I need to mention that when I was a little kid, maybe 10 years old, my hero was a motorcycle policeman who lived down at the end of my street. I would often see him going to or from work, sitting majestically astride his black Matchless police motorbike. Every kid in the neighbourhood worshipped him. The two things that have stuck in my mind were the huge red M logo on the bike's gleaming fuel tank and his neat cop uniform, which included a chromed police badge on his helmet and leather leggings attached to his shiny boots. Once when he stopped to bawl me out about my dog, which was always running around loose on the road and barking at his bike, I noticed that he had several pens tucked into the top of his leggings. I thought about those pens a lot and decided that he probably used them for writing out his victims' speeding tickets. Whenever he was passing and saw me standing outside my house, he would wave then give the bike's throttle a crack, causing the machine to accelerate with a burst of thunder from the parallel twin cylinders. I suspect he was just a young rev-head at heart, one who could do just about anything he liked simply because he was wearing a police uniform.

Looking back, my choice of a black BMW as a first bike may have been made at a subconscious level, although I must admit that most bikes of that era were that colour anyway. What wasn't coincidental was my gradual acquisition of a black riding outfit. I scored a black duffle coat from an unfortunate mate. He had snapped the kick-starter on a Vespa motor scooter that I had owned previously, but didn't have the money to pay for it, so he offered his duffle coat as compensation. Underneath the coat, like 99 per cent of my friends, I sported a pair of black stovepipe jeans, which dropped down into my black suede ripple-soled boots. Those boots were super cool at the time, often referred to as BCPBs — Brothel Creeping Poo Boots. And to top off my black clothing, I bought myself a shiny black open-face helmet. I used to enjoy pulling up on my black BM dressed in my black outfit in front of large shop windows. I would sit there admiring my own reflection — I thought I looked fantastic.

One day I rode over to a mate's place decked out in my black gear. As I pulled into his driveway, I noticed that his dad and another man were sitting on the front porch, having a smoke. They took one look at me, jumped up and ran inside, slamming the front door behind them. It wasn't until I had dismounted and gone inside to see my mate that I was confronted by the two men who glared angrily at me, one of them yelling, 'You nearly gave us a heart attack! We thought you were a copper!'

That was my eureka moment!

When I stopped and thought about it, they were right. To a casual observer, I looked exactly like a motorcycle policeman; the only thing missing was a chromed police badge on the front of my helmet. That was easily fixed by a trip to a motor wrecker's where I was able to buy a chrome-plated V8 badge about the same size as the police badge (I think it came off an old Chevy). After bolting it to the front of my helmet, the illusion was complete and thus began my career as a de facto motorcycle cop.

On those slow midweek evenings when there was absolutely nothing happening, when all my mates were doing something else, I would climb into my black outfit, mount the BM, and slowly patrol the Pacific Highway between North Sydney and Hornsby. When I came across a speeding driver I would draw alongside and motion for him to pull over. I would do the same thing whenever I came across a carload of young hoons regardless of whether they were speeding or not, because I knew from experience that they were always feeling guilty about something. After my unfortunate victim had pulled over and stopped, I'd simply accelerate off as fast as I could, fuelled by an enormous adrenaline rush. On the one hand I was excited by the sheer stupidity of what I had just done, but on the other I was terrified. If the driver caught on to what I was up to, I would have a lot of trouble outrunning anyone who decided to give chase to my underpowered BMW 250. Fortunately, I was never challenged and my only regret was that I was unable to book my victims and collect the fines, but it gave me one hell of a buzz anyway. Once I was safely clear of the scene of the crime, I never failed to laugh.

It was during the time that I was riding around in my copper's outfit that I scored an historic opportunity to get a motorcycle ride with Pope Paul VI. It happened back in late 1970 when the whole of Australia was in a state of excited frenzy, anticipating the first ever pastoral visit to this country by a pope.

It was a hot Saturday morning in December when I took one of my regular rides into the city to check out the motorcycle shops around Central Railway Station. I loved drooling over all the new machines, none of which I could ever afford to buy. I had just left the city and was on my way back home when I came up the Cahill Expressway and wound my way towards the southern approach to the Sydney Harbour Bridge. As I was about to emerge from the tunnel, the traffic was at a standstill, which was a bit unusual in those days. Like every good motorcyclist, I split the lanes, riding between the stationary cars until I came to the head of the queue. There I discovered the source of the problem: a police roadblock preventing all northbound traffic from entering the bridge. As I sat there at the front of the queue, a traffic policeman wandered over, so I asked him what was happening. He told me that the Pope's motorcade had left the city and was due to cross the bridge at any moment, heading for a papal appointment at a church in North Sydney. The words had only just left his mouth when there was a throaty rumble of engines and the Pope's white convertible, flanked by more than a dozen police motorcycles, roared into view.

And there he was! Pope Paul VI, the man himself! He was sitting serenely in the rear of the open-top limo, waving majestically to the throng of spectators who were crammed into every nook and cranny on the bridge walkway, many waving banners and flags. I must admit it was a pretty impressive sight.

After the motorcade had passed us and was about halfway across the bridge, the coppers removed the barricades and waved the traffic on. Being at the front of the queue, I gunned the BM and went hell for leather to catch up with the motorcade. I wanted to get another look at Pope Paul VI from close quarters; I would never have an opportunity like this again. With the Pope sitting in the back of the open-top vehicle, the motorcade wasn't travelling all that quickly, so I caught up with him just before he reached the northern end of the bridge. No one seemed to notice me coming up at the rear and I tucked myself in behind the last two police motorcycles, figuring that I could simply ride along and enjoy the spectacle from a totally unique perspective. I reckon I wasn't more than 10 metres behind the Man in White, so I got a very close look — if he had sneezed, I would have been sprayed with papal snot!

As the motorcade reached the northern end of the Sydney Harbour Bridge, it swept off to the left, into the North Sydney bypass. I kept following. It wasn't until I glanced in my rear-vision mirror that I realised that another bunch of coppers had pushed barricades across the road behind us, preventing unauthorised traffic from getting tangled up with the Pope's official party. There I was, a fake cop dressed in a fake police uniform, riding my old single-pot BM, now part of the greatest show on earth!

As the motorcade wound its way majestically through the streets of North Sydney, there were literally tens of thousands of cheering spectators waving flags and holy objects. The only ones waving back at the crowd were me and the Pope; all the police motorcyclists sat stiffly in formation, staring dead ahead like stuffed dummies.

I got so caught up in the excitement of the moment, waving and shouting back at my fans, that I nearly ran into the rear of the motorcade as it halted outside the Catholic church. My bike came to a standstill wedged in between the last two police motorcyclists. They looked at me and I looked at them. They both shouted at once and almost instantly I was surrounded by half a dozen uniformed police and a couple of plain-clothes blokes who grabbed me quite roughly and dragged me off my motorcycle. I didn't even have time to push the BM's side stand down; the bike fell to the pavement with a nasty clatter.

After a quick trip in a paddy wagon, I spent the next few hours in North Sydney police station answering questions. Who was I? What was I doing? How did I get so close to the Pope? Who else was involved? What was my intention? Had I been in trouble with the police before? After strip-searching me for weapons, they finally figured out I was simply a teenage jerk who hadn't actually broken any laws. With much ranting and raving and a barrage of threats, they let me off with a stern warning, telling me never to try a similar stunt again. To be honest, I was scared stiff and extremely relieved when they took me to the back of the police station and pointed me to my bike, which they had trucked over and left sitting in their parking lot.

By the time they let me go, the Pope was long gone and there wasn't a single spectator to be seen anywhere, just the North Sydney streets covered in rubbish. As I headed the BM up the Pacific Highway towards home, I was feeling strange. My hands trembled as they gripped the handlebars. I was still shaken by the rough-house tactics of the cops, but I also felt a huge thrill at having pulled off a ride in the Pope's motorcade.

I was winding my way up Pymble hill when I saw them. A couple of young blokes on a smoky, noisy, ratty old Honda Dream, and they weren't wearing helmets. They were weaving all over the road so I concluded that they were unlicensed novices, or perhaps they'd had a couple too many at the Pymble pub. The cop in me surged to the surface. I felt honour-bound to pull them over; after all, if I didn't protect the community from riffraff like this, nobody else would.

I'll never forget the look of dismay on the blokes' faces as I pulled alongside them and pointed towards the kerb — both their mouths hung open. But then to my horror the driver was so nervous, or maybe terrified, that he forgot to watch where he was going. As their bike slowed it developed a fatal wobble, suddenly crashing into the Telecom telephone box that sat next to the road, the Honda's front wheel wedged through the timber wall. As I accelerated away, I watched them in my rear-vision mirror. I saw them both scramble to their feet — they were okay.

Bloody irresponsible kids!

# A Close Shave

As told to Jen Scanlan
Kurrajong Heights, NSW

It was one of those very hot days in western Sydney when the tar on the roads starts to melt. The plants droop as you watch and the grass browns before your eyes. The garbage in the gutters seems too tired to move as the traffic swishes by. People's tempers fray quickly and the haze in the air seems to settle on people's minds. On such a day, roadworks and lane closures cause motorists' patience to wear thin.

The heat was providing me with a very busy morning in my job as a paramedic with the Ambulance Service of New South Wales. I had attended a man with chest pains, an old lady who had fallen over in a shopping centre and a child with dehydration. A hectic six and a half hours into my shift, I was sitting in the ambulance station lunchroom, taking a well-earned breather while having a quick bite to eat. As usual the phone rang just as I had settled down to relax; I leapt to answer.

'Cars 986 and 970 on air for a cas ... motorcycle accident, under the railway bridge.'

Both cars were intensive care ambulances and we responded with the utmost swiftness. Motorcycle accidents are usually serious, so much so that ambos have a nickname for riders: 'Temporary Australians'. Coming off a bike or into contact with another vehicle with only leathers and a helmet for protection, well, the results are usually not pretty. I recalled previous jobs. I had images of bones piercing through leather and possible paraplegia all running through my mind.

Both cars arriving at the scene in unison, we found a rider and a pillion passenger spread-eagled across the road.

The first patient I reached was the pillion passenger. As an ambo, I am trained to assess things very quickly, taking in many aspects at once. The patient was dressed in skin-tight black leathers, like Catwoman. She was beautiful, drop-dead gorgeous, real model material, with blonde hair and vivid blue eyes, still looking good despite the accident. She was even wearing high-heeled boots and a gold chain around her neck, adding to her movie-star appearance. It was a hot day and she was hot, alright! The ambos from the other car were equally quick with their assessment and the senior officer directed me to the other patient.

So over I went to the male rider. He was dressed in tight black leathers too with his helmet still in place. If she was Catwoman, this young bloke must have been Batman. My impression was confirmed by a quick glance at his bike — a bright red Ducati 1098 Superbike. The two had been ejected from the bike and were spread between a series of three concrete barriers that had been erected to close the lane.

With the police guiding traffic, it was safe to attend to my patient where he lay. After my initial assessment for obvious injuries and his level of consciousness, I asked the rider, whose name was Ryan, 'Where does it hurt?'

Ryan's responses were: 'Is my girlfriend okay?' 'Is my bike okay?' and 'My balls are on fire!' In that order.

'What happened?' I asked.

'The two lanes were merging because of the lane closure. I was in the left lane, heading for the barriers. This car wouldn't let me in; he just wouldn't give way although he could see me quite clearly. The lane was about to end so I kicked the car's side passenger door. Then the lane ran out and I hit the concrete barrier with the bike. We were catapulted over the handlebars — I snagged the bars on the way over.'

Ryan was lying behind the first barrier, but his girlfriend had been hurled over the second barrier. I started checking him from head to toe and repeated, 'Where does it hurt?'

He again said, 'My balls are on fire!'

After removing Ryan's helmet and checking his spine, I applied a collar to his neck. Even though we were under the railway bridge, the tar was so hot we put him on a spine board, then loaded him onto a stretcher and into the back of the ambulance. While I was certain that there was no spinal damage, I explained that I needed to remove his leathers to continue assessing his injuries. He begged me not to cut his leathers as I carefully took off his jacket. Three times he pleaded, 'Don't cut my leathers!' I really struggled to get him out of his tight pants without cutting them, but after a mammoth effort I finally did so — he was ever so grateful. Underneath, his T-shirt and shorts needed cutting off, revealing a pair of magnificent satin boxers. They were red, to match his Ducati.

After removing his clothing, I noticed that he was as hairy as, from neck to toe, amazingly hairy by anyone's standards. He appeared not to have any other injuries; neck, chest and arms were all clear. Ryan was still complaining that his balls were on fire, so I put it to him delicately: 'Then I'll need to have a look at your fire pit, mate.'

When I sliced off his red satin boxer shorts, a look of astonishment must have come over my face, because Ryan gasped, 'What's the matter? What's wrong?'

'Nothing, mate, everything's in place ... one, two, three. No swelling at this stage, just a bit of bruising starting to show.' I hesitated. 'Just one question: do you wax or shave?'

Ryan was as bald as a badger, as smooth as a baby's bottom, from bellybutton to mid-thigh. His response stopped me in my tracks. 'Neither! My girlfriend waxes me 'cause it turns her on.' His jewels were obviously her pride and joy!

I was intrigued. In all my years in the ambulance service I had seen a few Brazilians, but never had I come across an explanation like this. I chuckled to myself for the next 20 minutes, the time it took to transport Ryan to hospital and hand him over to the nursing staff. By then, his pride in his girlfriend's handiwork had grown to the point where he loudly informed the nursing staff, 'My girlfriend waxes me!'

Following the handover, I met up with the other crew, who happily related that after thoroughly and carefully checking over their stunning Catwoman patient, she was uninjured. Some people get all the breaks.

Looking back, I realised that Ryan and his girlfriend got a break too. They got to be Australian residents for hopefully a lot longer. But when I went home and made a suggestion about waxing to my wife, it didn't turn out quite as well ... Happy waxing, Ryan, and take it easy on that Duke.

# The Wild One

## As told to John Bryant by Mark O'Carrigan
## Bell, NSW

In our small country town only certain types of people were drawn to the infamous Dipstick Theatre during its brief heyday back in the 1950s. The premises had hosted a motor wrecker for more years than anyone could remember, but old Ces had shut the business down when he turned 80. Although he had spent his working life breaking up wrecked cars, selling their innards and packing grease under his fingernails, he had another passion: watching movies. So endeared had he become with this form of entertainment that in his later years, long before TV came on the scene, he started his own movie collection. With nothing else to do in his retirement years, he decided to screen his movies at his disused wrecking premises, just to have a bit of fun and make a few bob on the side.

Old Ces only ever screened movies about cars and trucks and motorcycles and anything else propelled by an engine. Most of the movies tended to incorporate violent disasters where the machines were incinerated or blown to bits, or the characters were punched senseless before meeting a sticky end. Movies incorporating romantic love stories and the like were never on the program, which tended to determine the type of clientele that was drawn to the Dipstick. The only women that ever turned up were usually reluctant girlfriends trying to please their men.

The Dipstick was open once a week, Saturday night, with upcoming attractions scrawled on a chalkboard nailed to the front door. It was an open-air theatre where patrons sat out under the stars, which wasn't too bad during fine weather, although the mozzies could get a bit ordinary at certain times of the year. It was easy to find, being located on a half-acre block of sump-oil-soaked industrial land on the edge of town. For years the two-and-a-half-metre-high corrugated-iron fence around the perimeter had stopped people pinching old Ces's car parts, but now it stopped anyone watching the movies without paying to enter. Inside the Dipstick the yard was scattered with an assortment of seating, ranging from rat-infested lounges and folding chairs that Ces had picked up at the local tip, to a variety of steel drums and benches. Needless to say, it was a good idea to arrive early in order to get a decent seat, literally. Old Ces had made the movie screen himself. It consisted of a number of flattened 44-gallon drums welded to a large frame, painted dirty white and bolted to the inside of the fence at one end of the property.

The Dipstick was particularly popular with the young blokes around town because they had little else to entertain them; they were absolutely desperate for something to do, especially on Saturday nights. While there was also a more conventional movie theatre in town, the Dipstick was half the price and twice the fun. It was also the only place where anyone, underage or legless, could buy a glass of beer, no questions asked. The town copper tended to turn a blind eye to the place unless he was called out to a brawl. Everyone knew that once he turned up that was the end of the evening, so the patrons tended to resolve their differences peacefully.

It was in the middle of summer in 1955 that the Dipstick's chalkboard announced that it was about to show the motorcycle cult movie, *The Wild One*, featuring Marlon Brando. No mention was made of ticket prices because everybody knew that the one-shilling entry fee got you through the door with a glass of warm beer thrown in. The word quickly spread to bikers in surrounding towns, so the following Saturday night saw a pretty big line of motorcycles outside the Dipstick, all parked pointing outwards, ready for a quick getaway. Inside, the place was jumping, with old Ces run off his feet collecting entry fees while pouring glasses of beer from the warm DA longnecks that he zealously guarded under the counter.

Amongst the crowd were Neville and his two cousins who had walked in from the Koori settlement half a mile out of town. At 16 years of age Nev was motorcycle mad. He had thrashed about on an old AJS 18 his cousin had 'borrowed' while it was unattended outside the feed store, but he dreamed of planting his bum on his own bike as soon as he could get one, regardless of whether or not he got his motorcycle licence.

Nev had already scoffed his warm beer before the movie got under way, but he was unprepared for the profound impact that it would have on his life. As the images danced on the dirty white screen, he sat there with his mouth open, awestruck, watching Marlon Brando play 'Johnny', sitting astride his magnificent Triumph Thunderbird motorcycle. Long before the movie ended Nev had decided that a Thunderbird was the ultimate motorcycle, and that he wouldn't rest until he got his hands on one. After the film finished, Neville and his cousins lingered outside the Dipstick to watch the blokes kick-start their motorcycles, rev the guts out of them, then roar off into the night in showers of gravel. It was then he spotted it, one of the last bikes to leave — a shiny new Triumph Thunderbird just like the one in the movie he had watched only minutes earlier!

Over the next couple of weeks Neville kept coming across the new Thunderbird with its well-dressed, wealthy-looking owner. Outside the grocer shop, at the service station, ripping along the main road, and always it was parked outside the Dipstick on Saturday nights. Nev's fascination turned into envy, which morphed into lust. It was driving him nuts. He could think of nothing else. Finally he could stand it no longer and decided he had to do something about it. He desperately needed that Thunderbird. He would knock it off!

The following Saturday night, while the fella with the Thunderbird was inside the Dipstick watching a dirt track demolition involving a pair of modified 1919 Saxon Roadsters, Neville and his cousins quietly pushed the Thunderbird a hundred yards down the road. They had had plenty of practice hot-wiring the AJS, so getting the Thunderbird started didn't present a problem. After a brief argument between the cousins as to which one would ride pillion, the younger one lost, so Neville and his other cousin kangarooed off into the night. Neville had learned to ride in a paddock on an old 350 with a jockey shifter and suicide clutch before the AJS had come along, so he figured he was a bit of an expert. Added to that he had watched the fella with the Thunderbird take off a few times, and it sure looked like an easy bike to ride.

Within a couple of miles Neville's confidence was soaring, as was his speed. Paying more attention to his jabbering cousin on the back than the road, Nev was rapidly approaching a creek where the road did a big dogleg before going over a timber bridge. Up to this point Neville had not used the brakes, but as the 90-degree bend in the road neared he was too low on the learning curve to have any chance of slowing down. As the bike reached the sharp bend, Neville made a pathetic attempt to follow the road. He was too upright to take the bend and too inexperienced to use the brakes. Heading almost straight ahead, the bike crashed off the road into the pitch-black bush, ejecting both Neville and his pillion into the scrub. The Thunderbird continued its trajectory, slamming into a mature red gum, taking a three-metre strip of bark off one side of the tree. The bike died a silent death, its innards scattered around in the dark.

Shaken but unhurt, Neville and his cousin started the long walk home, unperturbed by either their brush with death or the demise of their stolen Thunderbird, excitedly chattering about the bike's awesome acceleration. Nev was more convinced than ever that he was destined to own a

Thunderbird and possibly become one of Australia's most famous riders.

The Thunderbird's owner reported his precious bike stolen, but since everybody had been inside the Dipstick watching the movie that night, no one had seen anything that could help identify the thief. About a month later a DMR worker found the remains of the wrecked Thunderbird when he walked into the bush to have a pee. The police were unable to locate the culprit and the case was closed.

Forty years later Neville still lived in the same town, but by this time he had a wife and five grown-up children. Sadly, a Ford dealership stood where the Dipstick had once entertained the town's youth. Old Ces and the open-air movie theatre were gone forever; hardly anyone remembered either of them.

During the intervening years, Nev had owned a variety of motor vehicles, including a couple of motorcycles, but somehow he just never managed to get his hands on a Triumph Thunderbird. He was now a respected member of the community, the wayward days of his youth a mere memory. He had almost forgotten the little caper that had occurred outside the Dipstick that night long ago, until a notice in the local paper caught his attention.

OzHeritage, an archaeological firm, advertised that it was about to conduct a survey on behalf of the roads department prior to the construction of a new bridge over a local creek. Their role was to establish whether the area contained any items of heritage significance, including possible evidence of indigenous habitation or artefacts. The article made particular mention of a large mature red gum next to the creek, one that carried a significant 'scar', the type that was sometimes found where the indigenous landowners had removed the bark to make a canoe. Interested parties were invited to contact the archaeological firm because, if nobody came forward, the tree would be removed to make way for a new bridge to be built straight over the creek, thereby eliminating the dogleg in the road.

Nev smiled to himself as his mind drifted back 40 years to that hot summer night when, on youthful impulse, he had stolen the Triumph Thunderbird. Since then he had driven past that tree often, seldom noticing the large scar that was now almost overgrown by new bark. He felt a pang of nostalgia, so severe it nearly hurt. They were great days when he and his mates had gathered down at the Dipstick. The warm beer, the screams of hilarity as the machines in old Ces's movies exploded and ruptured, fists smashing into faces as heroes lived and died, and afterwards the excitement as cars and motorbikes fishtailed and executed doughnuts before smoking off into the night. It would be a huge shame for that red gum, which bore testimony to the impact of the stolen Triumph Thunderbird and all that it stood for, to be chopped down just to make way for a new bridge.

The next morning Neville, greying hair at his temples and wearing collar and tie, walked into the archaeological firm with a copy of the newspaper clipping in his pocket. He was ushered into the manager's office and offered a coffee, which he readily accepted with five sugars. After some pleasant chitchat, he announced the purpose of his visit and placed the newspaper clipping on her desk.

Yes, he told the lady, he was a member of the local indigenous community who had lived in the district all his life, as had his forebears as far back as anyone could remember. And yes, he was aware of that red gum with its unique markings. Not only did it have special meaning to his People, he explained, but it was in fact a sacred site that should not be disturbed. The archaeologist listened with fascination as Nev described with a great degree of emotion, which surprised even him, how the large scar bore testimony to a bygone era, the Dreamtime, when he and his People lived a different life, when they had been guided across the flood plains by the

Great Spirit. He finished by emphasising how the removal of that majestic tree would not only be a gross injustice to his People, but it could be a possible harbinger of imminent disaster for him and his descendants.

The archaeologist carefully noted down Nev's comments, nodding solemnly as she empathised with his love of the land and his earnest desire to protect and preserve his timeless culture. Yes, she agreed with great determination in her voice, that old red gum must be preserved no matter what the cost! As Nev left the archaeologist's office, he was surprised that both of them had tears in their eyes; it had been a very convincing performance.

And so it is, if you drive along that road today, you can thank Nev that an old battered red gum stands untouched on the bank of the creek, proudly displaying a large scar inflicted by a Koori way back in the Dreamtime — a Koori riding a yellow Triumph Thunderbird motorcycle.

# Ego Tripping

John Bryant
Bilpin, NSW

Like a lot of kids, it was my dad who got me interested in motorbikes.

When I was 10 years old, about a decade before the Yamaha PeeWee was invented, Dad bought me a beat-up Honda Step Through. Being a simple four-stroke air-cooled single with four-speed transmission and auto clutch, Dad figured we could work on it together so I could learn a few basics about engines. For quite a long time after that we'd spend most Sundays in the garage pulling the CT-90 apart, then putting it together again. One of the most memorable days of my life was when Dad kicked it over. It started third go! After that Dad and I spent most of our Sundays riding our bikes out at Pacific Park near Maroota, northwest of Sydney.

By the time I got my motorcycle licence I had mentally locked in Sunday as motorcycling day. Some folks went to church, I rode motorcycles. While I've never lost my love of dirt bikes, I also discovered the joy of road riding, owning quite a few different models during my younger years. When I got married I saw no reason to change my habits, so most Sundays saw me fiddling about with my motorbikes. The majority of the time I was too busy riding them to think much about maintaining or washing them, but every now and again I'd bite the bullet and spend the day catching up.

After two years of marriage, my garage contained a BMW K100, a Gold Wing, two Harleys and an old Yamaha DT 360 trail bike. One Sunday I was in the process of draining the oil out of one of the Harleys when my lovely wife came into the garage with a coffee. Sitting there, watching me as I worked, she suddenly asked how much money 'we' had sitting there on the garage floor invested in motorcycles.

The nature of the question and the tone of her voice warned me of danger. It was obvious she expected a sensible response because I knew from recent experience that being flippant or evasive could take the conversation in an ugly direction. I think that it's moments like these why the male species has been equipped with the ability to think at the speed of light, to come up with a solution that ensures preservation when seemingly trapped in a dead end.

'Well, my love, I had been hoping to keep this as a bit of a surprise, but since you ask I suppose it's time to reveal my plan. Put succinctly, I intend to use this fleet of motorcycles to launch a new business. This new venture should allow me to convert my spare time into cash so that we can afford that trip you've always wanted — over to Europe to visit all those famous gardens.'

I held my breath as I waited for her response, hoping she didn't realise that selling half my motorcycle fleet right now would easily fund her dream overseas adventure. She just rolled her eyes and walked off. I could see from the expression on her face that she had sort of half bought my explanation, but maybe not quite. So far, so good, but like most wives she had a memory like a steel trap. At some stage she would follow up and unearth my porky if I didn't cover my bases. To have any chance of wriggling out of this one, I now had to make an effort at establishing a 'business' with my motorcycles; something tangible that would produce a bit of cash, no matter how meagre.

The following Sunday I met up with some mates at the Pie in the Sky cafe near Brooklyn, north of Sydney. As we sat there munching pies, I threw the problem on the table and asked for suggestions. Rory reckoned that I should advertise myself as a stunt rider for TV and movies, but I'd already broken a leg once in my biking career and quite frankly I wasn't impressed with the pain. Alfie thought banging a sidecar on one of the Harleys to carry a coffin for funerals would be a great money-spinner. He even offered to prepay his own last trip. Not a bad idea, but at the end of the day anything that involved spending yet more money on motorcycles or accessories would go down like a truckload of manure. Nigel, who was a local GP and well known for not ever having had an original idea in his entire life, proposed that I establish a motorcycle courier service around the city. Yeah, Nigel, there'd be a big demand at weekends, which is the only time I had available to devote to my proposed motorcycle business!

As my burbling Road King carried me home late that afternoon, I was feeling anxious and depressed; I knew sooner or later she was going to conduct a further interrogation. Other than confessing that I had been engaging in wishful thinking, I was pretty short on ideas. It was with such negativities floating around in my head that I pulled up at a set of traffic lights, and there, next to me, were two white stretched Mercs covered in ribbons. Inside one, a bride and groom sipped champagne. Behind them in the other Merc was their wedding party. At the same instant the lights turned green I suddenly saw my way of escape, and one that my dear spouse would surely accept!

I would set up a motorcycle escort service for wedding cars!

I don't remember the rest of my ride home while my mind massaged the possibilities. I'd smother the bikes with white ribbons and deck the riders out in white dress shirts, tuxedo jackets, bow ties, matching black leather pants and black boots. By the following weekend I had written my business plan, registered the business name 'Ego Trip Motorcycle Escorts' with the Department of Fair Trading and sourced white gauntlets from the supplier to the NSW police force. I dreamed up a humorous business card, which screamed my mission statement: 'Have Bikes, Will Escort — Anything Except Volvos'.

On the back of the business card I listed the type of people who needed to consider a motorcycle escort to enhance their image. They included war heroes, rock stars, celebrities, eminent persons, chief executives, pensioners, politicians or anyone simply needing an ego trip. I offered pensioners a 50 per cent discount and threatened politicians with a 50 per cent premium. My plan was to provide a flexible service that was solemn, sophisticated or outrageous, with bikes and outfits to match my customer's mood.

My enthusiasm skyrocketed as I realised that I was no longer just devising a plan to appease my wife, but was now embarking upon a seriously fun-filled quest to turn my love of motorcycling into a cash cow. I couldn't wait for her to ply me with trick questions, because for once in my life I had all the answers ... but to my utter disappointment, nothing. She never raised the topic again.

The next Sunday couldn't come quick enough because without a few mates to ride escorts with me I didn't have a business. As I revealed my plans to my buddies, I could detect their growing excitement. Alfie just sat there, his mouth open, with a semi-masticated egg and bacon pie hanging from his lower lip. 'I'm in!' he yelled, transferring some of the egg and a bit of bacon to the front of my T-shirt. The euphoria quickly gave way to concern as my mates realised that I only needed two or three escort riders at most; there was now subtle but anxious competition to be amongst the chosen few. In the end it all got down to the bikes and their colours — we needed to offer our customers colour-matched bikes for maximum impact.

Although I had budgeted some dollars to advertise and promote my new motorcycle wedding escort service, fate took me on a different route. I had a friend whose daughter was getting married the following weekend, so I offered to do a motorcycle escort free of charge, just to see how things would work out. Alfie and I wore our quickly cobbled together but classy uniforms, hid our identities behind sunnies and, with white ribbons all over our bikes, rode two abreast in front of the wedding cars from the bride's home to the church.

Two things became very clear. The first was that as we rode along, pedestrians simply stopped in their tracks and stared at the motorcade. Whenever we stopped at traffic lights people came running up to ask, 'Who's getting married?' They obviously expected that the wedding cars were carrying royalty or some big-time celebrity! This immediately became a good opportunity to hand out our newly printed business cards. The other significant factor was that in every group of guests at a wedding there were always several young people who were also anticipating matrimony in the near future. So from that very first wedding escort we began taking bookings from other couples without having to advertise. Each time we did a wedding several more bookings emerged, which meant our order book escalated exponentially. We started off by offering two motorcycles for two hours for a cost of $200, but as demand exceeded our ability to supply the market we jumped our fee to $250, then $300 and finally to $400. It got to a point where Nigel's hourly rate as a motorcycle escort almost eclipsed his hourly rate as a general practitioner, and without the overheads.

Most people working second jobs tend to get sick of them fairly quickly, but we found the opposite. Some weeks we would do an escort for a Jewish wedding on Friday, then squeeze in a couple of other weddings on Saturday, plus we'd attend the occasional job on a Sunday. Apart from being paid handsomely to ride our bikes short distances, it was great being around the wedding parties and their guests as everybody was in good spirits, often offering us drinks. The brides and grooms were always keen to have their photographs taken with the bikes, which meant more free advertising for our services when they showed their albums to their friends and relatives. We even added a tasteful sign to the rear top box of each bike that discreetly identified us as 'Ego Trip Wedding Escorts' — subtle advertising!

Pretty soon the demand for our motorcycle escorts saw us booked solid. Not only were we doing weddings, but word of mouth saw us escorting high-school kids to their Year 12 formals and 50-, 60- and even 70-year-olds to their birthday parties and wedding anniversary functions. On one occasion our local federal MP hired us to help him make a grand entrance to a community event where he had to give a speech. The locals loved it so much that he subsequently sent us a letter of thanks on federal parliamentary letterhead!

After we'd been operating the business for about a year, we decided to upgrade our motorcycles, which gave us an opportunity to buy matching models and colours. This made the service even more attractive in the marketplace and demand continued to grow. By this time my wife had accepted my motorcycles as a bona fide business venture. I once overheard her boasting to her girlfriends about how our escorts added a marvellous touch of romance to weddings and how we often brought tears to our customers' eyes. Yesss!

Most of the weddings we attended went off without a hitch, as evidenced by the warm letters we received afterwards, usually from either the bride or her mother, thanking us for our contribution to their memorable celebration. While many of the weddings were reasonably modest affairs, we sometimes had the privilege of escorting the bridal cars of genuine celebrities. One very large Italian wedding that was celebrated in St Mary's Cathedral in the city had a motorcade that comprised eight stretched Mercedes Benz, escorted by eight of our motorcycles. I'll never forget the procession as the motorcade proceeded from Hyde Park through the city, down Parramatta Road to Leichhardt, stopping frequently at traffic lights. Bystanders stood and stared and clapped, while motorists in both directions tooted their horns and waved madly. Alfie put his finger on it when he said afterwards at the pub, as we were divvying up the $3,200 fee between us, 'I simply can't believe that people pay us to do this. It's obscene!'

Another notable wedding occurred when a young couple booked us to escort their bridal cars to their reception at the Sydney Opera House restaurant. The wedding ceremony took place in the Sydney Botanic Gardens, after which the bride insisted on spending 45 minutes driving around the streets of the city in her escorted motorcade, enjoying the stares and applause from passers-by. When we finally pulled into the Opera House driveway a huge mob of tourists crowded around our parked vehicles, taking I don't know how many thousands of photographs.

After the bride and groom had gone into the restaurant with their wedding party for the reception, we were about to leave when Alfie decided there were still a few dollars to be made on the day. He motioned to an Asian tourist who seemed particularly intrigued by our motorcycles, inviting him to sit on the bike while he used the tourist's own camera to snap his photograph. Using sign language, Alfie indicated that the fee for the Asian to sit on his motorcycle for 30 seconds was five dollars, which the tourist readily paid amidst much bowing, smiling and unintelligible chitchat.

Within minutes there was a line of excited foreign tourists queued up, waving their cameras, eager to pay their five dollars to have their photograph taken on Alfie's motorcycle. I looked at Rory and Nigel and shrugged 'why not?', so we also began inviting the tourists to sit astride our bikes, reluctantly accepting their money as we snapped their photos with the Opera House and Harbour Bridge framed by the setting sun in the background. This went on for quite some time until the Opera House security staff turned up and threatened to call the police if we didn't move on. Between the four of us we had collected several hundred in folding money, in addition to our motorcycle escort fees from the wedding party. I should mention that a short time after that experience I found out that Alfie and one of his mates were visiting strategic points around the city, where they'd park their motorcycles and extract camera-cash from tourists. Alfie even had a little folding A-frame sign made up that read 'I will take your photo on my motorbike for five dollars' in Japanese.

Looking back, I think my wife nailed the reason for our success when she confided to her friends that we were adding a touch of genuine romance to the traditional wedding procession. An outstanding example occurred when we were booked to provide four motorcycles for an escort that started at Seven Hills. It was a beautiful spring Saturday afternoon when we pulled up outside the bride's mother's home. We parked the four matching white Gold Wings, two abreast, in front of the white wedding cars that were also parked in the street outside the house. The Wings had white ribbons running from the rear-vision mirrors to the top of the twin aerials, with white rosettes on the windscreens as well as the rear top boxes. As the ribbons gently fluttered in the breeze, with the four riders dressed in their black uniforms, standing at attention next to their machines, the bride opened the front door to walk to her car. She took one look at the motorcade and burst into tears. Alarmed, I hurried over to her and asked what was wrong, dreading that perhaps we had misinterpreted her instructions for her Big Day. With mascara running down her cheeks she blubbered, 'It's just soooo romantic.' They had to take her back inside, clean her face and reapply her mascara before we could get under way.

We occasionally confronted challenges that required innovative solutions, like the time we escorted two bridal cars from a Prospect church to a club at Penrith. The cars were both vintage pink Cadillac convertibles, just like the ones Elvis Presley used to drive in his mid-50s movies. Long, low, burbling V8s with enormous fins and matching pink upholstery, they were the perfect open-top vehicle for a summer afternoon wedding. Flanked by two shiny black Harleys out front, it was an impressive motorcade saturated with rock'n'roll nostalgia.

The first half of the trip passed without incident, all of us holding to a steady 60 kilometres per hour, giving both pedestrians and passing motorists plenty of time to gawk at the bride and toot their horns. Then, as we were travelling along the M4 motorway, I looked in my rear-vision mirrors and noticed that the Cadillacs were slowing up. We kept dropping the Harleys back so we could stay with the Caddies, but they continued to reduce speed until after a couple more kilometres they came to a complete standstill. We pulled over on the side of the M4 and ran back to the cars to see what was happening. It was stinking hot, so hot that it had caused the Caddies' engines to overheat. One of the drivers, who owned both vehicles, said he wasn't prepared to go any further because it could risk major engine damage. The bride was distraught, as were the other five people in her wedding party, all standing there at the side of the M4, being sandblasted by the hot wind gusts generated by passing traffic.

Under the circumstances we were prepared to bend our normal rules against carrying pillions, and offered to pop the bride and groom on the back of our bikes to make sure that they got to the reception on time. The groom was all for taking the ride, but his bride was mortified — there was no way she was going to get blown to bits on the back of a motorcycle. We had to come up with another solution.

I looked down the freeway and noticed a small bus approaching. It appeared empty, so I stuck my finger out in hitchhiking mode. The driver ignored me and went whizzing on by, but to my surprise a van that had been travelling behind the bus screeched to a halt in front of me. The very colourful sign on the side of the van announced the arrival of 'Joe's Water Works'. Out jumped Joe himself, clad in very greasy coveralls, looking and smelling as though he had just climbed out of a sewage pipe. A big grin, a handshake and a few words later, and Joe had assured the bride that he would be only too pleased to give her and her party a lift to Penrith in his plumbing van. With the bride ensconced in the only passenger seat, and the other five crammed in the back, the van took off towards Penrith with our two Harleys riding shotgun out front!

When we arrived at the Penrith club the wedding guests were gathered on the front lawn, waiting to welcome their beautiful bride. They were stunned to see her climb out of a plumber's van, then burst into wild applause as the bride broke into tears of happiness or relief (I'm not sure which). Our job done, we rode away, leaving Joe in his greasy coveralls sipping champagne with the wedding party as though he was one of the family. Come to think of it, I suppose that's what he had become.

Like most businesses, we did occasionally run into a bit of real trouble. When we met with prospective clients, we would always show them our photograph album of weddings that we had done in the past, just to make sure that they knew what to expect. We offered two different types of large motorcycles, Gold Wings and Harleys. Almost always it was the bride's mother who made the final decision because she and the father of the bride were the ones footing the bill. The bride's mother almost invariably chose the Gold Wings, overriding the father who usually opted for the Harleys. Whenever the choice was left to the bride or the groom, they nearly always selected the Harleys and it was only ever at those weddings that we sometimes encountered difficulties.

I'll never forget one particular wedding where the bride booked our Harleys, with the instruction that we were to rev the bikes up and make as much noise as possible when we got to the wedding and reception venues. Also, she didn't want our riders dressed in their normal white tux shirts or white gauntlets, and she didn't want white ribbons on the bikes. Everything had to be black. Black leathers, black shirts, black helmets, black sunnies, black boots and black ribbons on the bikes! It all sounded a bit unusual, but hey, we were there to provide what our customers wanted.

When we arrived at the bride's home to start the escort, we were intrigued to see that the bride had hired two long low hearses as wedding cars — black of course. Even more amusing was the fact that the bride and three bridesmaids were sitting on the front lawn, sipping champagne, all dressed in black. The bridesmaid dresses were constructed of some sort of black fabric, but the bride's wedding gown had been handmade out of soft black leather, including a fairly long train at the back. So far, so good. But as soon as we pulled up and dismounted, the bride came running over and yelled, 'Gawd, I love men in leather!' and started trying to clamber onto the back of one of the Harleys. I thought she just wanted to have her photograph taken, but then it became obvious that she had had a little bit too much to drink already and was intent on riding to the church on the back of the bike, black leather train and all. Although we always bent over backwards to please our customers, we simply couldn't allow a tipsy bride with a long flowing dress to ride on the back of one of the motorcycles. Our insurance didn't cover carrying pillion passengers, plus I could just envisage the dress getting caught in the back wheel of the bike and the bride ending up in a nasty mess on the road. Not a good way to spend her wedding day.

I politely but firmly requested that the bride get off the bike, telling her that we would be unable to start the trip until she was off the bike and in the hearse. She didn't like that at all. She went right off, screaming at me, with some of her neighbours who had gathered to watch her leave the house listening in. Right or wrong, she reckoned that she was paying for our services and that she would ride wherever she bloody well wanted to ride! It was a stalemate. She wouldn't get off, and I refused to start the engine while she was sitting on the pillion seat. I briefly considered pulling her off the bike myself, but then rejected the idea — who knows where that may have ended? We remained glaring at each other for a good few minutes, with her colourful language getting louder and louder.

Meanwhile one of the bridesmaids phoned the bride's soon-to-be husband, who was waiting for her at the church. He asked to speak to his soon-to-be wife. She refused to talk to him so the bridesmaid switched the phone onto loudspeaker, which was great because everybody was then able to enjoy both sides of the entertaining conversation.

'Get off the bike.'

Silence.

'Did you hear me, Kaz? Get off the friggin' bike.'

Silence.

'If you're not off that bloody bike in two seconds flat, that's it, I'm outta here 'n' ya can find some other silly bastard to marry ya.'

Good start to wedded bliss, I thought to myself.

Twenty minutes later the two black hearses with accompanying motorcycles pulled up outside the church. As I held the door of the hearse open, the leather-clad bride struggled out, dragging her bits and pieces behind her. She looked up at me and snorted 'arsehole' as her party of all-blacks tumbled noisily out of their hearse and galloped up the aisle behind their bride. That was it for me. I put the money they had paid for our services back in its envelope and left it with an usher at the door of the church, asking him to give it to the bride after the service. They could find their own way to the reception.

Coincidentally, not long after that 'black wedding' we disbanded Ego Trip Motorcycle Escorts. Why? Well, we were making good pocket money, but the novelty had well and truly worn off. We had all grown tired of being committed virtually every weekend and we had other things we wanted to do. I've heard it once said that when your hobby becomes your business, you no longer have a hobby. That's very true.

Now we just ride for fun.

Except for Alfie. He occasionally sneaks into the city on his Harley to satisfy the photographic demands of the tourist industry. 'Money for jam, mate, money for jam!'

# Arrgh Zed

JD Evans
Sydney, NSW

It was 1987 when I spied the ad in the *Herald* classifieds: '1984 Yamaha RZ250. Slight damage. Easy fix. $700.'

I couldn't believe my luck. It was too good to be true. It must be a misprint.

'Dad ... Dad ... Dad!'

'Your father has a hangover,' my mother said grimly. She spoke as if this was just another episode in a cursed routine, like she'd been married for years to a hopeless drunk.

'Dad? A hangover?' I said.

'I am a bit, yes.' My father spoke with an English accent in a sort of measured, calm voice. His speech gave the impression that he only got drunk because he knew he would get a hangover and he was mildly curious about what a hangover would feel like. If I could remember my father having had three hangovers in his lifetime, I think that would be an exaggeration. He lifted a wet cloth off his face. He looked like I imagined Kermit the Frog might look if he'd lived to about 70, only greener.

'Hell, you look like crap,' I ventured.

'David!' Mum said.

'Dad, we need to drive out and look at a motorbike. It is a bargain. If we don't go now, it'll probably be sold.'

'Where is it?'

'If you buy a motorbike, you'll be living in a tent. Don't even think about coming home with a motorbike,' said Mum, then she turned to my dad. 'Rick, this is your fault. You have encouraged him behind my back. He's like Toad of Toad Hall, he'll kill himself or end up in a wheelchair — you'll be sorry.'

'Where is Glenbrook?' I pondered.

'Oh for heaven's sake, David, it is practically in the Blue Mountains.' Dad winced as he clutched his throbbing temple.

'We have to go, now. Please, Dad. Once I get a bike, you'll never have to drive me anywhere ever again.'

There was silence under the damp cloth as my father processed this attractive incentive.

'Rick promised to make a rockery on the garden terrace today, when he feels better ...' Mum alleged unconvincingly.

Dad sighed under the cloth. He sat up and looked at me. 'Let's go.'

If my dad had had three hangovers in his life, he had defied my mother perhaps twice. She was only five foot two, but formidable. Her blue dressing gown was like a uniform; she wore it all day every day while smoking Sterling extra mild cigarettes. She had curly brown hair to which, as far as I could tell, she had added a few grey streaks. There was also an additional streak at the front which had been tinted yellow by too many Sterlings. Mum wasn't a control freak as such, but she did have a couple of standard quips that she used to try and bring us into line. An early favourite was: 'None of you listen to me because I am only five foot two; but if any of you move a muscle I will explode.' After this had lost its impact, she'd play the sympathy card with: 'I was sent away to boarding school when I was six. I was tiny and petrified and my friend Gay and I tried to run away. But Ms Prayter came and got us in her big black car, and that's why it's so hard for me to trust any of you.'

Once in the car, my father seemed to perk up a bit. He was wearing black Stubbies and thongs, with a tucked-in business shirt, all of which accentuated the length of his long thin white legs. His legs were particularly noticeable in the car because he had a sort of frantic driving style which involved rapid pedal movements. Even a drive to the shops was like competing in the Paris–Dakar rally. My role was not so much to navigate as simply to egg him on: 'Go for the left lane, Dad. Drag off that nitwit in the blue Falcon ...'

Amazingly, my father seemed to think my suggestions were worth following. He agreed that all other road users were idiots ('peanuts' was his expression) and needed to be taught a lesson. The lesson we taught these idiots was that my father's 1976 Triumph Dolomite Sprint was the fastest car on the planet, at least as far as we were concerned. Dad's choice of model, and the particular car itself, is germane to my motorbike experience, because it illustrates that my mechanical aptitude and Zen-like motorcycle qualities replicated my dad's with his car.

'You mongrel, snot-sucking, monkey-flogging pie crust,' my generally mild-mannered dad would howl as he worked on the Dolomite. 'I would like to murder every lint-licking, peanut-chomping bastard who ever worked at British Leyland. It is no wonder they went bankrupt. I am GLAD they went bankrupt.' And then he would beat his toolkit with one of his Franklins spanners like an enraged chimp.

The Triumph Dolomite Sprint was British Leyland's answer to the BMW 2002. It was an evolution from what was a Triumph Toledo 1400. Subsequent models went through a number of engine size increases until the 1850cc Triumph Dolomite, apparently named after the mountain range. The Dolomite Sprint was the crowning glory, with a two-litre, 16-valve 127bhp engine. It had a four-speed gearbox with electric overdrive on third and fourth gears. Unfortunately, this engine had been shoehorned into the same flimsy chassis as the Toledo. While this was a problem in itself, Dad had also managed to find a specimen with a twisted chassis. A good example of the Dolomite Sprint would typically blow a head gasket in the first six months of its life. By then the overdrive function was a button on the end of the gearstick which you could flick for amusement, but which served no other purpose. My father bought his five-year-old Dolomite in 1981 for the discounted sum of $2,700. It had more problems than it had components and was so full of putty it could have driven undetected through the metal detector at an international airport. But we loved that car.

'Standing 400 metres in 16.6 seconds, nought to a ton in 8.8,' I would volunteer from the back seat as bewildered elderly relatives clutched the sides of their seats, or clung to the frayed panic strap which Leyland had thoughtfully added to the Sprint models. '16.5 on a good day ... and on to a top speed of 190 kilometres per hour. Dad'll show you if we can find a clear stretch of road ...'

As we proceeded along the western freeway, Dad's hangover seemed to worsen.

'That turd in the green Sigma needs to be taught a lesson,' I suggested, my head bouncing up and down like a cockatoo. Dad just ignored me.

We had some trouble finding the bike shop because it certainly wasn't a member of a recognised dealer group. 'Lenny's Bike Repairs' operated from a small garage which adjoined a block of red brick flats. Lenny was working on a Kawasaki KR250 when we arrived. He greeted us with enthusiasm, but spoke mostly to Dad.

'He is the one buying the bike,' Dad said to Lenny, nodding at me. I had never seen Dad so unfriendly. 'I know nothing about modern Japanese motorbikes.' I thought I caught a flicker of delight briefly cross Lenny's greasy face as he processed my father's words.

'Well,' Lenny proclaimed, 'RZs are brilliant bikes, go like the clappers, bulletproof motors. The 350 is even better than the 250, but the 250 is still a cracker. I have made a list of the parts this one'll need to bring it back to brand new again. You can get them all at a wrecker's. It'll cost $270, $290 tops.'

I looked at the red and black RZ250. A wave of excitement shot through me. I was suddenly assaulted by some sort of strange mania.

'It looks okay. It doesn't look too bad.' I tried to speak calmly and authoritatively, like I was a regular motorcycle purchaser. 'Can we hear the motor running?'

'Ahh, not right now,' Lenny dodged, 'but I'll have it going so you can check it out if you decide to buy it. It just needs to be set up.' He pushed the kick-starter with his hand. 'Heaps of compression, motor's as fresh as a daisy.'

'Dad,' I said, 'what do you reckon?' I was worried sick that someone else would snap it up before I could buy it.

'Another bloke is coming out from St Marys to check it out,' said Lenny, 'but I'll hold it for a 50-buck deposit.'

'Will you excuse me a second?' My father ran to a patch of weeds just outside Lenny's shed and threw up.

I smiled at Lenny and handed him my $50. 'But on the condition that I see it running before I buy it ...' I was no mug. Dad wandered back over, wiping his mouth.

'Young fella drives quite a hard bargain,' said Lenny, slapping my back.

The following week passed slowly until the Thursday night when we were due to pick up the unregistered RZ on a trailer. I had borrowed my friend Rob's father's trailer and Rob came with us. As we pulled up in my mother's Volvo, which had the towbar, Lenny was outside waiting for us.

'Running beautifully,' Lenny said.

The RZ appeared to be hooked up to a sort of drip and a car battery. The few remaining parts that were not accident damaged had been removed and were scattered around the bike. It looked like it was on an operating table and undergoing emergency bypass surgery.

'Holy dooley,' said Robbie.

Lenny kicked it over half a dozen times before the engine roared into life. Manipulating a maze of wires stretched across the shed, he was somehow controlling the engine's throttle, revving the guts out of it. 'Beautiful!' he shouted above the din. The smell of two-stroke and the sound of the engine made me feel so excited that I broke into an uncontrollable grin.

Dad backed up the Volvo and we loaded the bike and its various appendages onto the trailer. We tied the bike down with windsurfer straps while arguing about the best way to secure it.

Lenny, bank cheque in hand, seemed a lot less friendly now. He slammed the shed's roller door shut, disappearing behind it as it closed. I thought I heard a sort of cannon roll of laughter from behind the door as it bolted from the inside.

'Should the bike be swaying like that?' I asked my father tensely as we barrelled out onto the freeway and my dad dropped the Volvo into third gear. His concentration was elsewhere, anxious not to get overtaken by a Cortina that was being driven by a nun. The windsurfer straps were flapping in the breeze like two loose dog leads and the RZ was bouncing around off the sides of the trailer.

'The RZ has 35 kilowatts,' I boasted to Rob. 'Top speed of 172 kilometres per hour, nought to 100 in about 6.2 seconds, and a quarter-mile in 14.2. Faster than the RG250 ... and it has YPVS, which means Yamaha Power Valve System.' I assumed this could only be a positive.

Rob seemed unimpressed, so I continued: 'Two Wheels reckon that Yamaha two-stroke engines are bulletproof ... and the RZs are no exception ...'

Dad glanced at me in the mirror. 'That will certainly be convenient if you get shot at.' The nun had escaped and he was frowning.

Rob was more diplomatic. 'It's lucky you know so much about bikes — 'cause it sure looks like it needs a lot of work.'

'Yeah ... lucky,' I said. 'It actually isn't that much work. I have a list of the parts I need. Should be right to go in a week.' I felt my face go hot in the gloom of the car. Had I really fooled people into thinking I knew a lot about bikes? I could identify makes and models — 'there goes a GSXR750' — and quote each bike's performance statistics, but I had never actually owned a motorbike in my life, let alone worked on one.

For a couple of years from when I was about 11 I had begged my parents to buy me a Yamaha YZ80. They had no intention of acceding to my pleas, but they'd appease me by remaining vague. 'You can have a motorbike if you buy it yourself,' my mother used to say. 'I'll pay you 25 cents an hour if you work in the garden.' If I'd spent every spare hour of my life in the garden, I may have just about been able to afford a YZ80 by the time I was 40!

The next Saturday morning my dad was lying in bed, hangover long gone. It was 8am. 'Dad. Dad. Dad ... we need to go to Sydney Motorcycle Wreckers. And if they don't have all the parts, we'll have to go to Brison's in Rydalmere too.'

About four hours later, we were back home. I had spent $390 on the various parts required. Dad's toolkit contained a shifter and a set of imperial spanners which he had bought at Franklins. Also included was a reversible Phillips head/ standard screwdriver. For the next two hours I set about stripping or burring every nut, bolt and screw on the RZ.

Dad's long history of the use of colourful profanities soon started to make sense. 'FAAAARK!' I screamed, over and over again. Eventually my elderly Christian neighbour stuck his head into the garage, saying that he and his wife were worried that I may be possessed. They were right. I wanted to ride my RZ to school, on Monday if at all possible. I wanted to pull up nonchalantly outside North Sydney Girls High School, or next to a gaggle of Wenona girls at a bus stop. Sure, I was skinny and ugly. But with the RZ's help, these girls would see that I was a lower North Shore rebel and they'd all urgently want to have sex with me.

Work on the bike progressed slowly, but I was able to make up some time here and there by a process of reverse de-engineering. I worked out that many items on the bike were attached with two, three and sometimes four screws or bolts, when clearly only one was necessary. Indeed, in some instances, even the one was unnecessary. For example, the petrol tank sat on rubber mountings at one end and was held on by the seat at the other, so I worked out that the two retaining bolts at the back were a complete waste of time and space.

Split pins and hose fasteners were other torturous time-wasters that I quickly realised could be discarded to no discernible detriment, at least to an immobile motorbike. By the end of the process, while I had attached many new vital parts purchased from the wreckers, such as handlebars, master cylinder, levers, mirrors, blinkers, mudguard, etc., I had also amassed several large jarfuls of needless small parts. I decided that when I had the chance I would take these parts and sell them to Sydney Motorcycle Wreckers to offset the cost of the bigger components I had purchased.

I also discovered and fixed some weird things on my bike. For example, the washer over the counter shaft sprocket had been mangled and folded over the retaining nut, in a way that almost looked deliberate, so I carefully hammered the washer back to being nice and flat.

I was about three weeks behind schedule when I finally got to fire up the RZ's engine for a pre-registration test ride. Eventually kicking over, it revved beautifully. It sounded very racy, spewing out a haze of blue smoke which smelled fabulous. But it wouldn't idle. I finally had to admit defeat and took it to the local bike shop. I remember explaining the problem to a mechanic while he looked away and smoked a cigarette. 'It has a very good motor,' I said, 'heaps of compression, but it just won't idle.'

Eventually he wandered over to my bike, crouched down, and with cigarette in his mouth said, 'This is the roughest RZ I've ever seen.' Then he shouted to his mate, 'Carl, you gotta come and look at this RZ!'

His mate Carl sauntered over. 'Bloody hell. This yours, mate?' He looked at me with a mixture of amusement and contempt as he pushed down on the kick-starter, just as Lenny had done a few weeks before. 'Bugger me. Hey, Brian, check it out.' Brian then pushed down on the kick-start a couple of times. 'Does it start? That's a miracle.'

'What do ya mean?' My face was hot and my stomach was churning. I was still getting used to feeling stupid around bike mechanics.

'Mate, I seen RZs with worn engines before, but I ain't never seen an RZ like that with no compression at all ... needs a complete engine rebuild, guarantee it.'

'What's an engine rebuild?' I innocently enquired.

I still remember my mother's face as she signed the cheque two months later. Six hundred dollars for a complete engine overhaul. Serious money. She didn't speak to my dad for a week. I also remember the mechanic's face when I brought in the jars full of bolts, screws and fasteners, saying, 'Dad thought you might find these useful.'

Once fixed, at least my rough-as-guts RZ went like the clappers. It still had a twisted steering stem and forks, so it didn't handle all that well, but I guess it matched my dad's Dolomite. With no upper fairing it looked like a Mad Max derivative, so it wasn't the bike's fault that the girls seemed to ignore me more than ever. But I was so happy I didn't care.

The RZ and I had a marvellous fortnight together before I slammed it into the side of an MGB. With the remains of its front wheel now sitting alongside its back wheel, even Lenny would not have been able to sell it.

# Great Balls of Fire

John Bryant
Bilpin, NSW

One of the adventures I look forward to on a regular basis is the aptly named Snowy Ride, an annual motorcycling event that takes place in the alpine region of New South Wales. For me, a Blue Mountains dweller west of Sydney, it usually entails a quick blast down the Hume Highway, jumping off onto one of the scenic high-country roads to Cooma, the exact route determined by how much time I have available. While the event itself is a great opportunity to catch up with mates and get across some of the things that are happening in the motorcycling world, I've always relished the ride itself. Those twisty mountain roads are a motorcyclist's delight, making the journey as much fun as the destination.

The 2005 ride was a particularly memorable experience.

I'd recently returned from an international business trip and was looking forward to the mental relaxation that always accompanied the Snowy Ride. After a couple of weeks overseas in smoky offices and air-conditioned discomfort, I was more than ready for some quality time in the great Aussie outdoors. I've always felt pretty lonely on my business trips, so one of the things I used to do to kill spare time was to troll through foreign retail stores, looking for products that hadn't hit Australian shores. At one end of the scale I'd wander through the monolithic hardware complexes, and at the other I loved checking out the smaller specialty stores, especially the auto and novelty shops.

On my latest trip I had been wandering around an auto accessory outlet when I came across a product that really made me laugh. It was a pair of very large moulded plastic testicles.

They were flesh coloured, quite realistic and designed to hitch onto a motor vehicle's towbar. They were so large that they gave the impression that they had been surgically removed from a gigantic bull. I already had a towbar on my BMW K100 and could just visualise these giant gonads swinging gently in the breeze as I tracked down the Hume Highway, heading off to that year's Snowy Ride.

After landing at Mascot on my way home, I had to go through Australian customs. I copped the usual question as to whether I had anything to declare. I quipped that I had a spare set of balls in my bag, hoping a customs officer would want to have a look and a laugh. To my disappointment, he waved me straight through, ignoring my precious cargo.

When I got home I attached the big balls to the BM's towbar with a cable tie, allowing them enough freedom to swing to and fro with the movement of the bike. I had just finished the installation and was standing back admiring my handiwork when I heard a voice echo out of the garage behind me. 'I'd get rid of them if I were you.' I knew my wife would be unimpressed, but her comment merely served to confirm that my new motorcycle accessory had true novelty value. Muttering a noncommittal 'yes, dear', I ignored her comment, packed the usual minimal amount of gear for the trip, then set off with Jerry Lee Lewis's 'Great Balls of Fire' rattling around inside my helmet.

Heading down the Hume, I had completely forgotten about the Big Ones dangling off the end of my towbar when I became aware of an unusual phenomenon. As I sat on the speed limit, every now and again a car would overtake my motorcycle, but then drop back and fall in behind me. When I looked in my rear-vision mirror I would sometimes have two or three, or sometimes up to half a dozen, motorists following along behind my bike. It then occurred to me that they had spied my towbar appendage and were enjoying a good laugh. Those that did overtake often had a big smile on their face and pointed at the back of my bike with a thumbs up. I must confess I got quite a buzz from their obvious amusement.

But the real fun occurred when I stopped at a servo on the main highway, a bit before the turn-off to Cooma. When I pulled in to refuel the bike I had again forgotten about the novel accessory hanging off my towbar. I walked into the servo office to pay for my fuel and when I came out I noticed that there was a new Volvo parked next to my bike at an adjacent pump. A dapper grey-haired old bloke in a blue Bermuda jacket and cravat was filling his Volvo's tank, staring in the air while whistling tunelessly. I was about to climb back on the bike when I spied a posh old duck with a blue rinse in the front passenger seat of his car. Sitting there motionless, she had her gaze fixed on the rear of my motorcycle.

I was ready to hit the starter to get going when her window slowly descended, the lady still staring intently at the humungous balls hanging off the back of the BM. I nodded to her and said 'g'day'. She looked up at me, but ignored my greeting. She pointed a long painted fingernail at the back of my bike and in a clipped Pommie accent said, 'What on earth are THOSE for?'

'Those,' I said, jabbing my thumb towards the gonads, 'give my bike added grunt!'

She looked somewhat confused and then said, 'Whell ... they are totally disgusting, but very funny.'

With that she closed her window and sat staring straight ahead, but with a wide cheesy grin smeared across her painted mouth. Somehow I couldn't help thinking that it might have been the first good laugh she had had that year. As I gunned the BM out of the servo, I couldn't force the smile off my lips either!

Nearing the completion of my journey, flicking the BM left and right through those delicious mountain curves, I started to conjure up all sorts of humorous ways to deploy those massive gonads. But it was not to be. When I reached my destination I checked into my room, and then went out to the bike to grab my gear. I cast a loving glance at my towbar, expecting to see the object of much future hilarity hanging there after a hard day's work, but they were gone! I couldn't believe it.

Somewhere on the Snowy Highway between Bemboka and the appropriately named Nambugga, the cable tie had worn through and my balls had fallen off. It wasn't so much the $9.99 that I mourned, it was more the lost entertainment value — they were irreplaceable. While I would like to think that some honest person will find my balls and return them to me, I suspect he or she may have far too much fun with them to worry about locating the rightful owner.

What do they say? Finders keepers, losers weepers ...

# 20 Per Cent Man

Thor Lund
Baulkham Hills, NSW

There comes a time in life when most of us men look in the mirror and realise that our bodies have gone south even though we still may be feeling young at heart. It is often at this point in our lives that we discover there are two entities struggling deep within us: '20 Per Cent Man' and '80 Per Cent Man'.

20 Per Cent Man is that part of us that got us into motorcycling in the first place. He's the one who has the extra bourbon, twists the throttle a little harder, does silly dance steps and ogles young girls at the beach. He was largely responsible for all the pain we suffered between about 18 and 30.

80 Per Cent Man is our sensible self. We only got acquainted with him as we matured, but he now controls most of our day-to-day stuff. He puts on a suit for weddings and funerals, observes speed limits some of the time, earns a living, smiles at the mother-in-law and learns how to make small talk with boring relatives. Although he knows 20 Per Cent Man quite well, he realised long ago that it was often in his best interest to suppress him whenever he tried to make an appearance.

Unfortunately, there is also another important influence that complicates the relationship between 20 Per Cent Man and 80 Per Cent Man. Known variously as the Leader of the Opposition, The Boss, Her Indoors and the Little Lady, she is sometimes able to divide and conquer with devastating effect. Her control over 20 Per Cent Man is somewhat tenuous because he is generally deaf to female voices and ignores anything he doesn't want to hear. However, it is very different with 80 Per Cent Man. He is overly sensitive to the dire consequences of ignoring the Little Lady's voice, so he has developed what has become known as the 'yes, dear' response. While not always effective, 80 Per Cent Man can generally steer his way out of trouble by using this response sparingly and with discretion.

Okay, so much for the theory, but what about the real world?

I love attending events with my motorcycle. Show and shine, races, hill climbs, toy runs, fundraisers, club rallies — anything that involves me and my machine. And like most bikers before any major meet, I often stand back and take a long hard look at my Beastie. This is not a critical look. It's more a mix of admiration and aspiration while calculating the perspiration needed to introduce further enhancements. Perhaps a new set of mirrors, maybe a little more chrome, a computer chip, or even a completely new exhaust system could be on the cards? 20 Per Cent Man loves this stuff and could be persuaded by the world's worst salesman to fit the whole lot right now on a 10-year easy-repayment plan! Not so with 80 Per Cent Man; he always ponders the costs versus his priorities versus his budget, secure in the knowledge that he is skilled in the art of delaying gratification.

Still, as I stood there recently staring at my Iron Horse, I realised that it was lights that I needed. Lots more lights! Unknown to 80 Per Cent Man, a whole host of manufacturers, wholesalers, retailers, internet auction sites and bike magazines were all savagely attacking his subconscious, screaming, 'Lights, lights, LIGHTS!' 20 Per Cent Man was totally on board, urging them on, ecstatic at the prospect of lighting up the ol' green machine. 80 Per Cent Man was busy doing his sums and trying to assess whether a 'yes, dear' response to 'You bought what?' would work.

For better or worse, 20 Per Cent Man won the internal battle, so it was off to the favourite bike shop to find some LED-type stuff, under the pretence of returning library books. Not much luck at the bike shop so off to the auto shops — hey, bikes are just cars with a few wheels missing after all. Walking into an auto sports store, I spotted some amazing light displays. I was flat out keeping 20 Per Cent Man and 80 Per Cent Man apart while I wrestled with the Chinese instructions on the back of the pack. Just then a hair-creamed, pimple-faced Kung Fu chick-magnet strolled over and eyed me up and down.

'Putealighey on god fondration wit meal scrus.'

What did he say? It made no sense to an old biker. 'I'll work it out later,' said 20 Per Cent Man. 'Yeah right,' replied 80 Per Cent Man.

'Maayte,' came an exclamation from behind me, 'you want some sick lights for your ride, bro? These are the real deal, man.'

I felt a big mistake coming on as I realised that 20 Per Cent Man had fallen in love with a pack of green things that looked like they had just arrived from the set of *Saturday Night Fever*. 80 Per Cent Man was silent but shaking his head as we headed off to the checkout with our fan club following us, telling us about his cousin's sick car with illuminated door handles and a nodding dog complete with strobe light.

After a short struggle to gain control, 80 Per Cent Man told the salesman he would only consider the deal if he could take the lights home and test-mount them on his motorcycle before making a final commitment to purchase. Parting with a hefty sale-or-return deposit, and with a suitably rated transformer tucked under his arm, 20 Per Cent Man rushed home to start fiddling with the lights.

80 Per Cent Man wanted to take charge of the installation. 20 Per Cent Man refused; he was having too much fun to waste time reading the instructions or double-checking the maze of wiring and connections. Still worried about The Boss's reaction to busting the weekly budget on motorcycle lights, I figured I should invite her into the garage so she could be overwhelmed with the magnificence of my latest acquisition. With a bit of luck she might even sign off on the price. I gave her a yell and waited.

As she entered the garage, I hit the switch. Whoosh. Smoke and an acrid burning smell rapidly filled the garage. The fumes travelled down the hallway where the smoke alarm started screaming, at which point the house lights and power went out. The 'oh shit' factor began to sink in as I made my way through the clouds of smoke to see if there was anything left of the Beastie. An apparition appeared through the haze — it was the Little Lady with a thunderous look on her face. 20 Per Cent Man felt like crying and wanted to run and hide, but 80 Per Cent Man realised he'd have to face the music sooner or later, so he might as well get it over and done with.

After a solid tongue lashing and a no-talkies evening, what was left of the lights went on eBay the next day. The fire brigade was very nice about it all after a couple of them had a ride on the Beastie, who seemed to be no worse for wear after I replaced all the fuses. The neighbours sent me a *MythBusters* video with a rude note on it about the danger of conducting amateur experiments in the family home. 20 Per Cent Man retreated for almost a week before raising his head again the following weekend, which coincidentally just happened to be the first day of summer.

Summer, ah yes, summer! We all love riding in summer, that time of year when 80 Per Cent Man's fancy turns to 20 Per Cent Man's glory days!

As summer arrives, older bikers frequently get the urge to acquire some new riding clobber, often in the mistaken belief that they'll no longer look as worn out as their bodies, even if they can't sit down in the damn stuff. Trouble is, new clobber generally results in conflict because 20 Per Cent Man thinks 'style' while 80 Per Cent Man thinks 'durability'. This is where 80 Per Cent Man makes a common mistake and asks his non-riding Her Indoors what she thinks. 20 Per Cent Man is screaming, 'No, no, leave her out of this, you bloody fool!' But the fateful words have already tumbled out.

'What do you think I should get to replace my old summer riding gear, dear?'

Having recovered a little prestige since the LED light disaster, I still needed to toss in the odd endearment in the forlorn hope of prying open the coffers. 20 Per Cent Man is cringing in a foetal position, dreading the response.

'I'm glad you asked,' said she, with a fashionista gleam in her eyes. 'I'm sick of seeing those tatty old black things you wear, very scruffy. I'm taking you to see Mirrabelle and Blossom, they'll sort you out.'

20 Per Cent Man was banging his fists against the inside of my psyche, seeking revenge for bringing her into it, while it was slowly dawning on 80 Per Cent Man that things were not heading in a healthy direction. But it was too late; we were off to visit the Little Lady's friends. Funny, I've never heard of these friends before or seen any of their riding gear advertised, but I was assured that they knew their stuff and were especially clever with leather. Okay, this couldn't be all bad, some nice leather stuff, and who knows, a couple of chicks measuring my inside leg could be fun. Wifey seemed happy about it so it looked like the money would be non-problemo for a change.

There to greet us at the door of the shop was Mirrabelle, who smothered me in air kisses then herded us into the main fitting area, commenting, 'He's a biggin', ain't he!' We were surrounded by copious quantities of very colourful leather garments, but none that I could recognise as being bike stuff. Still, I think I glimpsed a sign on the way in saying 'Bikes Welcome'. As Mirrabelle called out for Blossom to join us, I was surprised by her voice, which seemed very deep for a lady. When Blossom came prancing forth I couldn't help but notice her facial hair. 20 Per Cent Man was unperturbed and salivating at the smell of all that new leather. 80 Per Cent Man was feeling increasingly alarmed.

'Riding chaps, that's what he needs, with a bolero top and cowboy tassels, finished off with a matching neckerchief,' exclaimed Blossom, looking me up and down like a cat surveying a mouse. Mirrabelle, Blossom and the Little Lady ignored me as they all chattered at the same time. I had no idea what they were talking about and found it impossible to interpret the various hand flourishes and giggles that erupted every few seconds. However, the Little Lady seemed to understand the lingo and was nodding her enthusiastic approval, suddenly announcing that I would love to go and try on the suggested riding outfit. I had envisaged something a little less colourful, such as the latest DriRider gear, or that you-beaut imported Beamer stuff I had seen in a bike magazine recently.

I ended up stuck in a change booth that was hardly bigger than a ferret breeding box, so small there was no room for a second set of clothes. I ended up stripping and passing my clothes to a limp female hand that was disdainfully extended through the curtain, receiving in exchange my new riding gear.

After struggling into the new clobber, I stepped out of the ferret box, surprised to find that the shop was now well populated. Most of them were dressed like they were auditioning for the Village People. They cast glances at me, cooing 'ooohs' and 'aaahs' and 'luvly'. I turned around and faced myself in a full-length mirror. Shock! There is no way to describe it except to say that my extroverted riding mate Stan wouldn't have worn this stuff at the club's Christmas party, even when hammered.

While 20 Per Cent Man was flirting with the idea of buying this ridiculously pathetic outfit, 80 Per Cent Man was fighting off a heart attack and planning his retreat. 'Piss off and get me my clothes,' I muttered as I stripped off the multi-coloured apparel, chucking it in a heap on the floor. 'What the hell, haven't ya seen an old bloke in his undies before?' I asked nobody in particular. It was only then that I realised that I was wearing my workshop grundies, the ones with big holes in strategic places.

As we stormed out the door, I noticed that the Little Lady was scowling. I could sense the bedroom tax was about to be reintroduced, which was a crying shame because it had only just been lifted after the LED light fiasco. It was at this point that I again noticed the sign that I had glimpsed on the way in. It didn't say 'Bikes Welcome'; it said 'Dykes on Bikes Welcome'.

After a silent drive home, 80 Per Cent Man made me slink off into the garage and spray myself with WD40 and old engine oil to mask any lingering aromas. 20 Per Cent Man still hasn't stopped chanting, 'Told you so, I warned you.' The local bike shop had a field day with my credit card the following day despite complaints from the Leader of the Opposition.

# Lost for Words

Paul Saunders
Greenfields, WA

We were on a ride from Sydney to the 1979 Black Duck Rally in Western Australia.

It was quite early in the morning. We had just left Broken Hill on a clear cool day and were riding west at what were probably quite illegal speeds when Jimmy, a mate of mine riding a Suzuki GS850, started weaving all over the road. He was obviously in serious trouble.

He careered over to the side of the road and simply stepped off his bike, letting it and his wife Pauline crash to the ground. This was extremely unusual for Jim as he loved and cherished both his bike and his wife. On top of this, Pauline possessed a fiery temper which a few of us had encountered and which we all feared.

Jimmy proceeded to stagger around, holding his throat. When I rushed up to him I was horrified to see his face was blue and it looked like he was having a fit. He was trying to say something and all I could catch was 'bud'.

I pulled his hand away from his throat to see if I could work out what was wrong and there on his voice box was a very large swollen red lump.

Jim managed to croak out, 'F***ing budgie.'

We all collapsed in fits of laughter, which escalated when Pauline arrived and proceeded to lay into Jim for dropping her and the bike on the ground. It turns out that a budgie had just cleared the instrument panel on Jimmy's bike and hit him right in the throat at around 110 kilometres per hour.

They say that the wildlife in Oz is extremely dangerous and I can see they weren't joking ...

# The Year was 1949

Colin Chambers
Charlestown, NSW

I was one of hundreds of spectators on my way to Bathurst for the legendary Easter Motorcycle Races. There were five solo riders in our group — three were riding 500cc singles, my mate Eddy was on a 150cc LE 'Tin Fish' Velocette and I was on my 125cc BSA two-stroke Bantam.

We set off from various points around Sydney's western suburbs, soon joining a heavy throng of spectator motorcyclists heading for Bathurst. Just as roadkill attracts crows, so the steady stream of motorcycle enthusiasts heading west attracted the NSW police; there were cop cars and bikes everywhere.

Just west of Katoomba there was a long uphill stretch that was followed by a tantalising downhill section that looked like it had been designed for rocket sled racing. Having had a gutful of fighting through the heavy traffic coming up the mountain, this open section of road screamed, 'C'mon!'

As we approached the peak of the hill, the road pointed directly to the west, causing us to be almost blinded by the sun, which by that time was hanging low on the horizon. With visibility severely compromised, and squinting through dirty scratched sunglasses, we suddenly realised we were in the midst of a police operation. There on the crest of the hill was a stack of police cars and bikes, surrounded by about 20 riders that they had pulled over and were in the process of booking. It reminded me of bears catching helpless salmon that jump into their arms as they frantically swim upstream!

Business was brisk and one of my friends on his 500cc was pulled over and booked. Like numerous other riders, he was guilty of exceeding the 30mph speed limit, which was designated on a small roadside sign about four miles back in the Katoomba township. As a bonus, the police were also adding a little extra — booking all riders for crossing double unbroken lines. The fact that the road markings were extremely faint and completely obliterated by the glare of the setting sun raised the hackles of the disgruntled riders.

Luckily my other two mates on the 500cc machines escaped through the police gauntlet unscathed. They headed on west without us; it was every man for himself. The fact that Eddy and I missed out on being booked had nothing to do with being law-abiding citizens. Instead it had everything to do with the fact that the Tin Fish and the Bantam were not powerful enough to exceed the speed limit while travelling uphill. We both kept over to the left-hand side of the road to allow faster traffic, which was every other bike out there, to pass us without obstruction.

The next few miles were uneventful, except for the hundreds of larger capacity bikes that thundered past us at top speed, sometimes almost sucking us off the road into the gravel. Most riders honked or waved or shouted encouragement, with one throwing a pawpaw or banana at me. I didn't notice it at the time, but found it smeared over the side of my helmet when I took it off later in the day.

As we approached Lithgow, we were slowed by another uphill run, made all the more challenging by a slight headwind that we were battling as we neared the summit. We were both lying flat on our tanks in an attempt to minimise wind resistance, but because Eddy's Tin Fish developed slightly more horsepower than my Bantam, he was slightly ahead of me.

Suddenly a rider on a 500cc Triumph Speed Twin, carrying a pillion, slowed down beside me. The girl on the back held out her left hand, motioning that she wanted to give me a tow. The rider was grinning from ear to ear. I immediately kicked the Bantam gear lever into neutral and grabbed the girl's hand. We started to gather momentum as we wobbled up the hill, finally hitting about 60 miles per hour and passing Eddy on the Tin Fish, which was struggling to maintain 25 miles per hour. The Triumph towed me at fairly high speeds for a further three miles; the Bantam had never gone so fast!

Finally, on flat terrain again, I let go the girl and waved the Triumph on. I sat by the side of the road for 15 minutes, watching as yet more bikes rumbled past, until finally Eddy caught up. When I asked, 'What kept you?' he pointed out, 'You had a total of 625cc and I only had 150cc.'

Although we all look back at that weekend as a great chapter in our biking Good Old Days, the most intriguing aspect occurred later the following evening as we were sitting around a campfire at the Bathurst track.

Eddy and I listened in amazement as a bloke recounted something he saw on his travels from Sydney to Bathurst the day before. He reported seeing a Triumph Speed Twin racing a BSA Bantam up a hill just before Lithgow. 'And ya know what? They were locked in mortal combat. The bloody Bantam was going like lightning 'n' the Speed Twin's pillion was fighting with the Bantam rider, trying to slow him down!'

# V-Rod Christmas

Neville Hack
Elanora, QLD

8am Brisbane.

I press the starter and my silver, sleek, sexy Harley-Davidson V-Rod purrs into life. The pack on my back contains a spare set of clothes, but as I fill up the tank at the Goodna Shell Road House I still don't know exactly where I am headed.

West, I think, looking around at the holiday crowds, away from the coast.

My V-Rod is two months new, and although I have taken it for a few runs up and down the coast, I haven't really seen what it can do.

Leaving the city behind, I ride off into the warm summer air, bypassing Ipswich and heading towards the dark blue western ranges. Going up the range leading into Cunninghams Gap, the air becomes cooler and fresher. I climb up the range, passing semi-trailers as if they are sitting still, rounding the 120-degree corners hitting 90k's. The bike is purring and I feel exhilarated! It seems I am the only one moving on the road. I go through the pass of the mountain range, then snake down through the bends and onto the plateau heading towards Warwick, a flat town on the wheat-growing belt. I have to go down through the gears as I enter Warwick, so I pull in and fuel up.

Two dogleg bends later and I'm through town, heading towards Stanthorpe, hitting the throttle as the air warms up again. The bypass around the town of Stanthorpe may be okay for the passing traffic, but I have an urge to cruise around and look at the grapes and apples, to rekindle memories of when I was a kid and living in the area. Stanthorpe is a small town with little wineries dotted here and there along the way.

I head off again down the highway to Tenterfield. The countryside looks fresh and full of colour after recent rain. I ride down the steep hill and into the township of Tenterfield, stopping again to refuel. My bike is a hit everywhere I go, and whenever I stop for fuel there is someone who comes over to ask about the bike. How does it perform? Does it handle well? And so it goes on. And because my bike is so beautiful, people always want to touch it, maybe to see whether it's real or not.

I push on. The air is getting cool again and the clouds are low as I start to climb the ranges, slowing up through Deepwater, then on to Glenn Innes. The bends are getting tighter and more frequent as I go around the mountains, but the bike takes them easily.

Arriving at Glen Innes, I notice the clouds in the distance look very black and heavy. I think I will try for Armidale before fuelling up again, only 94 kilometres away. I am 20 kilometres out of town when the clouds darken over the ranges and I see rain falling to earth just ahead. I hope the rain and road will miss each other as I keep going. I am sitting on 110k's when rain hits me in the face with the force of hailstones. Do I stop or keep going?

I keep up the speed, thinking I will ride through the worst bit, but it just gets heavier. My jeans are wet through and the air is feeling cold. I keep going and 10 minutes later I ride into beautiful sunshine. The countryside is looking green and lush, and I am overwhelmed by the scent of the high mountain air. It is amazing how you take in all the different smells when riding a bike. You don't notice it in a car, with the air-conditioning pumping and the windows wound up tight. This country air is so fresh!

I weave up and down the mountain ranges, passing all types of vehicles, checking the safety ramps at the base of each range that wait to catch the trucks with failed brakes. From the corners of my eyes I see sheep and cattle grazing in the paddocks, and the grass so tall and green, just like a picture postcard.

I ride down a hill and cross a tree-studded creek before entering the main township of Armidale. With its mall in the main street and hotels on the corners, it appears so old-fashioned and peaceful. I decide to stay here for the night and look around for a motel high on the hill. I go to one of the pubs for a big tea and then rest up in the motel room, drying out my wet clothes over the oil heater. It's a cool 12 degrees Celsius outside at night, which is close to freezing for a man from the tropics.

Fed, rested and dried out, I move off at 7am in daylight saving time, now that I am in New South Wales. Not more than 100 metres down the road, at the first intersection, I come across a two-car smash. One had gone through a stop sign and collected someone coming along the other way. Thank goodness no one is hurt.

I ride out into the countryside and the scenery gets even better, with huge, rocky outcrops rising up through lush grasses. I pass through Uralla, the home of Thunderbolt, the famous 19th century outlaw. I used to admire Thunderbolt when I was younger and I can easily imagine him hiding out amongst those huge rocks.

Then on to Tamworth, the 'country and western' music capital of Australia. They are getting ready for the festival, which is held in January each year, and the town is abuzz with activity. Tamworth has a lot going for it: people, layout of the town, coffee shops in the main street and so on. But I have that throttle fever now, and I am starting to love this machine with its contours that hold my body to it as if we were one.

I decide to go further southwest and get onto the Newell Highway, so I fuel up with high octane and head off to Coonabarabran.

This part of the trip is magic — open roads and scenery that is out of this world! Everything looks so lush as the mountain ranges disappear into the horizon. And then, just 10 kilometres from town, the scenery changes: the grasses are sparse, yellow and dry, and the country just looks hard. It seems I have run into one of the huge areas of drought that we're experiencing in Australia at the moment.

I decide to fuel up and get a coffee. The interest in my V-Rod intensifies with every stop and the questions get more complicated. I have one word that covers every question, and that word is 'AWESOME!'

'This bike is just awesome,' I say. That seems to be enough. Everyone understands.

Everything around Coonabarabran looks dry and tired, including the people, and I can't help but feel for those who have to live here through the drought.

I head off to Dubbo and the sweet smell in the air has changed to one of death. The carcasses of dead kangaroos and cattle litter the roadside. I wouldn't want to ride these roads at night, knowing cattle and roos are out there too, looking for food and water.

I pull into Dubbo for something to eat and a look around. It is a nice town with friendly, helpful people. I buy a mouth guard while I'm there because the rutted roads before Dubbo were jarring my teeth. I am back on the road to Parkes before it gets too late and the roos come out.

This bike is a dream!

About 13 kilometres the other side of Dubbo I am cutting the corner about two feet from the edge of the bitumen and doing 100 when, about a quarter the distance through the turn, I notice heavy ripples in the bitumen that follow the edge and feather off to the centre of the road. There are three in a row, about four inches deep. The bike becomes airborne! I hang on for my life, not changing my weight position or line. I come down hard, shocks full down and more. I bottom out, my stomach hits my hip bones and it feels as if my insides are trying to get out my arsehole. Shiiiittt! Well — almost!

Then I notice I am still on the same line as when I started into the corner. Incredible! I am sure that if I was on any other type of bike with a higher centre of gravity I wouldn't have survived, plus I believe my tyres were hot enough to stick to the road when I came back in contact; anyway, that is what I tell everyone.

I pull into Parkes at 3pm and decide to take it easy. I cruise through the main street to a corner pub and park my bike on the footpath right outside the front door. The old pub feels so friendly as I walk through the doors; drinks are put on the table and I am made to feel at home. I eat at the RSL, then that night the boys lock up my bike in the main dining hall of the pub. The bed and secure parking cost me $20 for the night.

Back on the road at 7am to Forbes, which is not far away. I have my morning coffee there and it is a nice place, but still very dry. I hit the road again and head the hundred or so kilometres to West Wyalong. The smells you get! The country is getting dryer and the smell of death is everywhere. What is still alive you come across grazing on the side of the road. Scary when you come around a corner to see sheep or cattle meandering from one side of the road to the other.

I fuel up in West Wyalong and am delayed once more as the people at the service station admire the bike. Again, for some inexplicable reason, people still seem to have the need to touch it. Never mind, I'm in no hurry — I am a free spirit for the week.

On the way to Hay the country is flat and hot. So very hot, and not much grass, and if you do see grass, it's all dead anyway. I am 70 kilometres out of Hay when I see this dark cloud getting closer and closer; I keep my eye on it. The road trains are big around here — three trailers long and flying. I crank it up to 170k's to get past them, then drop back to my 140-kilometre cruising speed. But I'm still keeping an eye on this dark cloud, not sure just what to expect. The cloud grows quickly and blots out the sun.

A dust storm! Before I know it I am in it up to my eyeballs, and with only an open-face helmet and sunnies to protect my head. The dust cuts into my flesh as the wind gusts across the burning plains. Shit! I slow down to 110 and push my feet on the front pegs, forcing all my weight on the seat to allow my hands to relax on the hand grips. I let the front go where it wants, just using my weight to control the bike. This is 100 per cent effective because the solid front wheel is picking up the wind. At times the visibility is down to 50 metres and all passing vehicles have their lights on — not to see, but to be seen.

Pulling into Hay, I clean the visor and clip it over my open-face helmet. The people at the garage and the truck drivers say it is worse ahead and that I should stay in Hay overnight. I want to push on because now I have Mildura in my sights and I have good friends there. I set off again, aiming to arrive by 5pm.

The people at the garage were right! The dust storm gets worse. Cars are pulling up on the side of the road everywhere. No sunlight. The bike is now riding on an angle with the vision down to 20 metres at times. The winds blasting across the plains whip up incredible gusts. I pull into Balranald to fuel up and am invited inside for a drink. It turns out that the garage owner happens to own a Fat Boy. I clean up and take off again, the tree line on the north side of the road helping to cut the dust driving across the bitumen.

I ride through 250 kilometres of dust storm, and just 10 kilometres out of Mildura I drive out of it. As I cross the bridge over the Murray River coming into Mildura, the sky goes dark and dirty again, blocking out the remaining sunlight. I fuel up in Mildura and just as I pull out of the servo the storm hits. It is incredible! A massive storm headed by a huge dust storm — it is literally raining mud!

At that very moment a 4WD pulls up beside me and the guy hanging out of the window yells, 'Follow me to my place! It is close by.'

The wind drives the bike right to the very edge of the bitumen. I am glad this bloke lives so close and it is with relief that I drive into his garage. I see a black Low Rider sitting at the back of the shed.

My new friend makes coffee, a welcome sight, and rings his brother, Smiley, who is a truck driver. Smiley has just come over the same road as I have a few hours before, and he says it is a miracle that I made it. He says he has never driven through such bad conditions and that he could only see 20 metres out front all the time.

The next day I am at my mate Andy's place, just out of Mildura. I remove my air cleaner and blow it out from the inside to remove the dust. It is amazing how little dust there is in there after all. The intake must be at that perfect position. The rest of the bike is covered in spotted rain-mud; however, a shampoo, a Gerni and some elbow grease, and it is as good as new.

For the next three days the Riverside Riders bike club members give me the royal treatment and we get together for a few local rides. I am having a great time until I have to head back home, back to work.

By 6.30am next day I am on my way back to Parkes. The weather is beautiful across the plains — not too hot, not too cold. I am sitting on 145k's. What a dream machine! This is so relaxing and I get to Parkes in no time at all. I decide to stay there the night and do the 900-kilometre run back to Brisbane the next day.

The weather is on my side at last. What a run! The countryside is changing constantly as I head north out of the drought areas, straight up the Newell Highway through Dubbo, Narrabri, Moree and on to Goondiwindi, where the air gets hot. I decide to take a break for an hour before the last leg. I head off through Inglewood and the road gets rough, but the countryside is green and pools of water lie everywhere on the sides of the road. Then on to Warwick and a smooth highway run back to Brisbane, back through Cunninghams Gap for the second time. The high mountain air smells so good!

Then into Brisbane on sunset, having done 900 kilometres in the day, and wanting to do more. I clocked up 3,900 kilometres for the week, the trip there and back being 3,500 kilometres.

What a dream ... and it came true!

V-Rod forever!

# Panniers in Hand

Frank Hildenbeutel
Lammermoor, QLD

The Ulysses Annual General Meeting in Nuriootpa, South Australia, was seven weeks away, my annual leave was approved, and my wife and I were getting excited about the trip. Then the BMW R1OORT decided to play up in the gearbox bearings department, so into the repair shop it went. Ten days later I rang the workshop to find out how things were progressing, only to be told that they hadn't been able to look at it yet. Not a problem as it was still over four weeks before we were due to leave. This scenario continued for another three weeks.

Finally everything seemed in order so we set off from Rockhampton, Queensland, with our Ulysses group on our 5,000-kilometre adventure. At our second fuel stop in Taroom I noticed oil dripping from the engine. After a few choice words, I decided we should struggle on to Orange, New South Wales, where we had family, and get the repairs done there. Thankfully, the bike made it. We left the RT at the local motorcycle shop and, with panniers in hand, trudged to the relative's place, where we bunked down until the repairs were completed. The substantial repair cost was covered by the previous repairer who had installed a seal incorrectly.

We were two days behind schedule by the time we got back on the road again, and then encountered an uncomfortable stretch riding across the Hay Plain in 40-degree heat. With few places to stop and rest, we finally pulled in to refuel just two kilometres short of where we planned to stop overnight at a Mildura campground. My lady didn't want to get back on the bike, but with some coaxing she eventually did.

When the new day dawned, with our bodies rested, our spirits soared as we anticipated a great day of riding. With bike and trailer packed, the BMW wouldn't start. I figured that the battery had carked it, so I replaced it, and off we went. Without further mishap we arrived at the annual Ulysses meeting where we had a wonderful week in Nuriootpa, which was just as well in view of what was about to happen.

With the AGM over we were ready for our homeward journey via Orange, where we intended visiting more friends and relatives before heading home to Rockhampton. But the Bloody Money Waster wouldn't turn over!

The starter motor was diagnosed as the problem, so into the repair shop it went. With panniers in hand we booked into a cabin at the local caravan park, where we planned to wait while the repairs were completed. Then the bad news from the mechanic: 'Sorry, mate, the starter is unrepairable; the glue holding the magnets has melted, destroying the motor.' Apparently a French starter had been fitted to this model and it would take six weeks to get one from Germany. I wasted another few days trying to find a starter in Australia, but my efforts proved unsuccessful.

RACQ Ultra to the rescue.

I bought bus tickets to Orange and arranged for the bike to be trucked to Yeppoon. The trailer was booked to travel too, but at an extra cost of course. So at 6am and at what felt like minus six degrees, with panniers in hand we boarded the bus for the 20-hour trip to Orange. We made it, and after unfolding ourselves things started to look up while we spent a few pleasant days visiting our various friends and relatives. I then bought the bus tickets for our long trip home from Orange to Rockhampton.

So, with panniers in hand, we caught a taxi to the Orange bus station. In the freezing cold the bus arrived, the cheerful bus driver greeting us with, 'Hi, folks, where you going?'

We answered, 'Rocky.'

'Sorry, guys, no seats available,' the bus driver said.

'But we have tickets!'

'Sorry, still can't help.'

With panniers in hand we arrived back at my elderly parents' home well after midnight. In the morning I headed straight to the travel agent who had sold us the bus tickets. 'Sorry, we will get you onto the next bus.' Unfortunately, that wasn't good enough because I needed to be at work on Monday.

'Sir, we have arranged two plane tickets for you. You leave tomorrow morning at 7.45am, via Sydney with connecting flights to Brisbane and Rockhampton.'

THANK YOU!

At sparrows next morning, with panniers in hand, we headed off to the airport.

Waiting, waiting, time 7.50am. 'Passengers on flight 000 are advised that the flight has been delayed due to fog.' When we finally arrived in Sydney, late, we'd missed our connection and the rescheduled flight only guaranteed us passage as far as Brisbane. At least we would be in Queensland and a step closer to home, so off we went. We arrived in Brisbane and marched straight up to the flight desk. 'Would you be able to get us on any remaining flights to Rocky today?'

'Yes, sir, we have two seats available on the next service leaving in 20 minutes.' We raced to the terminal, panniers in hand, and just made it. At last things appeared to be gradually improving. Upon arrival in Rockhampton we were greeted by our Ulysses friends who offered to take us and our panniers home.

Two months then passed without any sign of the BMW showing up.

We figured that someone must have been using the trailer and camping gear before they returned it, but frankly I was past caring; I couldn't give a rats!

Finally the bike and trailer turned up, all intact, on the back of a truck. We placed the loading ramps in position and started to push the bike down when it overbalanced and smashed to the ground.

Thank god the panniers weren't on it!

# Stuntman

Peter Van Saalte
Wilberforce, NSW

I'm one of those blokes who rode motorbikes during my freedom years, starting in my teens. When the wife and kids came along I couldn't afford the rego and insurance so the bike had to go, but I always swore to myself that as soon as I could afford it I would get myself back onto two wheels.

That happy day arrived just before my 50th birthday when I sold my business. For the first time in many years I was about to have some surplus cash, so I decided to indulge myself. My wife reckoned I was having a midlife crisis, but anyone who has ever ridden motorbikes knows that once it gets into your blood, well, the open road never stops shouting your name.

Buying a brand-new motorcycle was a huge challenge simply because there were so many great alternatives to choose from. It's no wonder some blokes have half a dozen of the things sitting in their garages or sheds — better to have too many than to suffer the remorse of having bought the wrong one! After trawling through all the bike mags and motorcycle dealerships, I finally settled on a Harley Road King. Why? Can't really say, except it did something inside me when I laid eyes on it, low, black and mean! Love at first sight? Maybe, or perhaps it just communicated with my midlife crisis.

After riding around by myself for a couple of months, I just happened to be sipping a latte at a local cafe one Saturday afternoon when a bunch of bikes pulled up. I got talking to one of the riders and found out that they were all local blokes who enjoyed sneaking off for a couple of hours on a Saturday afternoon. Mow the lawn, wash the car, and then duck off for a quick ride together. I didn't need much persuasion to get involved, so I became a regular with the group whenever time allowed.

Not long after that, one of my new riding buddies told me about a business associate who was looking to rent a bike and rider for a function. The request was for a Harley, which narrowed the field down quite a bit because most of the blokes rode either European or Japanese machines. As it turned out I was the only one who was available at the time anyway, so the job was mine if I wanted it. The main reason I thought I would follow it up was because I was intrigued by the 'job', plus I just loved riding my bike whenever possible.

Anyway, my mate gave me the phone number of the bloke who needed a bike, so I called him. He was a local fella who explained that he was in the business of staging fashion shows on behalf of clothing retailers, usually at what he called 'ladies' nights'. He suggested that I pop in and have a chat with him, which I did a couple of days later. At our meeting he told me that he was about to put on a swimwear and lingerie parade on the following Friday night. It was to take place in a large local club in their ground-floor dining room. It would all be very professional, with a raised catwalk, spotlights, music and special effects, with about 10 models wearing a range of the new season garments. He said he wanted to end the show with a flourish, which is where the bike and rider came in. He wanted something to cap off what he was planning to be an exciting, high-energy evening. His idea was to end the parade with a model bouncing off the catwalk into the arms of a leather-clad spunk, with the two of them mounting a motorcycle before riding off into the distance. 'Wild and romantic' was the effect he was seeking!

The more I heard about the event the more excited I became. I assured the bloke I had done similar jobs in the past and it would be an absolute breeze. Did I have insurance? 'Of course,' I said, referring mentally to my Green Slip. Okay, so I told a few porkies, but how difficult could this little caper be? The bloke went on to tell me that he had a limited budget, only 50 bucks for the bike and rider, but by that time I would have done it for nothing. It started me thinking that perhaps this could be the beginning of a whole new career — the possibilities were unlimited.

We sealed the deal with a handshake and I couldn't wait for the event to roll around. In hindsight it would have been a very good idea to go and have a look at the venue in broad daylight prior to the event to familiarise myself with the layout, the catwalk, the corridors, the exit and any hazards that could potentially cause grief. But due to my enthusiasm and inexperience none of that crossed my mind at the time.

When the big night arrived I was brimming with confidence and eagerness as I turned up at the venue at 8pm on that fateful Friday. As I switched off my engine, I could hear the thumping of raucous music and wild applause, with the sounds of women shouting, screaming and stamping coming from the building. It sounded more like a heavyweight title bout than a fashion parade — the show was obviously hitting the mark in a big way.

I walked inside and jostled my way around into the staging area at the back of the catwalk where the models were changing outfits and getting their hair and makeup done. The whole place was jumping, people frantically rushing everywhere. The energy was amazing and the atmosphere electric — I figured this was THE business to be in!

I found the bloke who had hired me. He was running around in a lather, sweating profusely, trying to shout his instructions at the models above the din. He told me to stay put while he raced off to grab one of the girls. He came back a few minutes later with a petite blonde in tow, obviously the model I would be working with, and gave us a rushed introduction. Her name was Cherie.

With the music and screaming women making it almost impossible to hear what he was saying, the bloke gave us both some garbled instructions as to what he wanted us to do. We poked our heads around a partition and stared down to the end of the catwalk to where he was pointing. He told me that when I heard 'The Stripper' coming over the PA system, I should edge my bike through the side doors and park it at the end of the catwalk, leaving the engine running. He wanted me to stand there looking like Mad Max, mean and tough, arms folded and no smile. He had timed it so that within two minutes of my arrival Cherie would be coming down the catwalk in her final outfit. She would then slide off the end of the catwalk into my arms. I was to walk a couple of paces holding Cherie, to where the bike was ticking over. I was then to place her gently on the back of the bike, and we were to ride down the aisle and out the door. Sounded simple enough; piece of cake, end of show. I couldn't wait to get started!

I hung around as the show progressed, enjoying the spectacle of all the pretty girls modelling their swimwear and lingerie as they bounced up and down the catwalk. Then the organiser nodded in my direction, indicating that the parade was about to finish. I moved my bike into position just outside the side doors, ready for the big entrance. My heart was thumping a million beats a minute. Finally I heard the distinctive sounds of 'The Stripper', so I started her up then entered the door, riding as slowly as I could to the end of the catwalk. The crowd was going berserk, possibly driven mad by the guy operating the sound system who had ramped the decibels up to a dangerous level. Or then again, maybe it was me! Maybe I looked THAT good!

I arrived at the end of the catwalk, propped the Harley onto the side stand, left it idling, and then stood there with my arms crossed, resplendent in my black leathers, doing my best to look like a sexy version of Mad Max. As 'The Stripper' volume escalated to an almost painful level, I was mesmerised by Cherie bumping and grinding down the catwalk wearing the sexiest see-through lingerie I've ever seen. It was fortunate that it was dark with just a spotlight focused on Cherie, or I am sure the audience would have seen my eyes popping out of their sockets!

The raised catwalk was at about the same height as my chest. When Cherie got to the end, instead of gently sliding down into my waiting arms as instructed, she suddenly did a little jump, launching herself in my direction, legs in the air. She was quite a slender girl, not particularly heavy, and I would have had no trouble at all lifting her off the ground. However, with the force of gravity accelerating her mass it was like trying to catch a one-tonne block of concrete. Cherie came crashing down; I was unable to hold her. She landed on top of me and we both ended up sprawling in a tangled heap on the floor. Fortunately, neither of us was hurt so we scrambled to our feet amidst deafening cheers and catcalls from the women in the crowd; they loved it and probably assumed it was all part of the act.

We both clambered onto the bike. I had the presence of mind to retract the side stand before we threaded our way slowly down the aisle towards the door. 'The Stripper' was playing so loudly and the crowd screaming so piercingly that I couldn't hear anything else. Then without warning I was hit in the face by a spotlight that someone turned on in front of the bike, training it directly into my eyes. I was totally blinded. I'm sure the crowd had a perfect view of us, but I found it impossible to see where I was going. To add to the mayhem, a smoke machine was spewing out a billowing cloud, and just as the spotlight hit me I entered the cloud, which completely enveloped me and the bike. I started to panic as I wondered how I was going to navigate to the doorway. I couldn't hear, I couldn't see, and only had a vague idea of where the door was located. I remember thinking that this may not end well.

Driving almost blind, all I could do was simply follow the strip of carpet that ran down the aisle, trusting that it led out the door. Suddenly the door loomed up in front of me, but I was going a little too fast, so I slammed on the rear brake. I heard a slithering noise that resulted in a long black skid mark on the light-coloured carpet, followed by a shudder as the carpet ripped up under the locked rear wheel.

In what must have been one of the greatest flukes of the 20th century, we somehow made it through the narrow doorway without hitting anything and without falling off the bike. We were now out of the building, but my troubles weren't over yet. One moment my eyes had been caught in the full glare of the spotlight, the next moment I was in almost complete darkness. I suddenly appreciated how roos must feel under the spotties just before the bullet arrives!

With absolutely zero vision I chose my only option and hit the brakes again, hard — well, the back brake anyway. Not realising I was on the edge of the car park, my back wheel locked up in the deep gravel, slewing the bike sideways and pitching both of us into the shrubbery. Once again we both scrambled to our feet, and once again I was relieved to find Cherie shaken but unharmed, only her lingerie a little worse for wear. The bike was lying on its side, still idling, the back wheel spitting the occasional tulip or whatever onto the pavement. I hit the kill switch then hurriedly helped Cherie to the door of the parade room and waved her goodbye.

Dazed and disappointed, I didn't wait around to collect my 50 bucks — I figured that he could keep it as a contribution towards the cost of carpet repairs. The Road King started first go, so I jumped on and gave it a handful of stick. On the ride home the muscle in my left leg started hurting. I later found I had sustained an ugly wound which must have been caused by something in the garden when we fell off the bike. Although it healed quite rapidly, it has left a star-shaped scar on the side of my leg, a permanent reminder of my one and only stunt-riding experience.

Word of my adventure and injury rapidly filtered back to my Saturday afternoon riding buddies, who thought the whole affair was one hell of a hoot. They now call me 'Stuntman', a nickname I carry with pride, especially since it was earned during my midlife crisis. And not only that, but I have the scar to prove it ...

# Fault

John Scholz
Willunga, SA

Neil looked out over the service station forecourt, its six bowsers standing to attention in the fluorescent light. He had to admit the early morning shift was damn good. For the first time in years he was starting to feel his shame and guilt lift for a few hours. From his console he felt in control again, useful and honest. It was therapeutic to look out through the big windows and watch the sprawling town awaken; to see life creeping into the world, a country sunrise washing the wide tree-lined streets in clear orange light, the new day burning the past further away. In an hour or so the highway traffic would build — mine vehicles were common these days, along with the usual farmers, grey nomads and truckers, and later people off to do the shopping or whatever, all with a purpose, money in their pockets. And out here none of these people knew what he'd done.

A motorbike pulled up outside the front windows by the gas bottles. He peered at the grainy grey image on the CCTV monitor, his heart leaping as he recognised the bike. It looked like an original CB750, just like the one he'd lost oh so many years ago. The rider had already dismounted and was walking slowly towards the doors of the servo. They slid open and the rider hesitated as if unfamiliar with automatic doors, then came in, his boots shuffling on the lino floor.

Neil smiled across the counter at the dusty full-face helmet and scuffed leather jacket. 'G'day, mate. Um, might get you to take that helmet off if you don't mind. Sorry, company policy, you know ...'

A gloved hand thumbed up the helmet's tinted visor. Aviator sunglasses looked out. How the heck could this bloke actually see anything at this time of the day? Some people ... Then the other glove shakily unfolded a note on the counter and a leather finger pointed at typewritten words on it: 'I GOT A GUN GIVE ME ALL TEH MONEY.'

Neil gasped and looked up. He didn't think it was a good time to point out the typo on the note. 'Cripes! You serious?'

A pistol appeared and pointed at Neil's nose. The helmet cleared its throat and said, 'Um, sorry, please hurry.' It was a mature voice, perhaps around Neil's own era, gritty, gloomy and trembling.

Neil hit the till. The drawer slid open. They'd never had a hold-up and didn't expect one out here. Security consisted of the ring of keys Neil had been given to open up at 5am and the pathetic CCTV monitor.

Despite entertaining suicidal thoughts in recent times, Neil did not want to be shot in the face by a nervous old biker who may not even be able to see him clearly. He'd have to appease him with the float in the till. It wasn't much, with most customers these days paying by card. Neil slid out the crisp notes and pushed them along the counter. Gloved fingers flicked clumsily through them, and they disappeared into a pocket of the leather jacket. The pistol wobbled at Neil's chin. The gloomy voice trembled again. 'Um, the safe? Could you open it please?'

Neil shrugged his shoulders. 'Look, I don't know the combination. The owner will be in soon.' Neither of these things were true, but maybe it would make the bloke clear out.

'Oh.' The helmet twisted around anxiously, scanning the deserted forecourt and the servo doors, the pistol waving at the ceiling, the drinks fridge, the pie warmer, racks of almost-out-of-date chips. Neil noticed that the chamber of the pistol above the trigger was missing and pocks of corrosion marked the remaining metal. The sunglasses were looking at him again, the pistol hovering around his neck region. 'Well, I, I expected a bit more. It's not enough to pay our ...' There was resignation in the voice, defeat, feelings Neil was very familiar with.

'Look, maybe take a few chockies or something?' Neil offered. The helmet looked along the row of confectionery, the pistol barrel sagging downwards. If the thing could actually fire, it would blow a hole in the counter and probably Neil's balls.

A Cherry Ripe was selected and brought up to the sunglasses with a shaking hand. 'I love these things but, er, nearly a thousand kilojoules. What's that in calories? I've gotta be careful with my diet, the doc says.' He put the Cherry Ripe back and picked up a Crunchie, again peering at the wrapper, before putting it quickly back as if he'd read cyanide in the list of ingredients. 'No, thanks.'

'Well, what about a chocolate frog? They're only 60 calories and if you buy four you'll get two cents a litre off your fuel, if you want to fill up? Er, not that you'd be paying I s'pose.'

The hand holding the gun was now resting on the counter, as if the weapon had become too heavy. It was aimed at a bowl of overpriced fruit. 'Could I have one of these bananas here? They're healthy.'

'Help yourself.'

'Thanks.' The voice seemed to brighten a little at this small win. 'I need to get my money's worth, so to speak. It's been so hard since we lost everything two years ago.'

'Really? Me too.'

'Yeah, look, mate, I'm not a bad person. I lost everything to a bunch of pricks called Paramount Investments. You may have heard of them? The returns were so good in the early years I talked my wife into borrowing against our house and investing more, to set us up for a good retirement, and something to leave our grandchildren. Well, when the GFC hit they went bust and it all vanished. The bank took our house, everything. Can hardly keep up the rent on our little unit now with this so-called mining boom taking over the district. You?'

'I lost ...' It was Neil's turn to have the shaky voice. He was in shock at the man's revelation. 'Well, er, something similar.'

'At least you've got a job to go to.'

'I was lucky, I'm related to the owner,' said Neil. After two years of trying, he'd been unable to get a job anywhere except out here where a second cousin owned this service station. Neil's former boss, the CEO of Paramount Investments, had only recently gotten out of jail, a fate Neil narrowly avoided by not actually having broken any laws that they could find, though he had been banned from the finance industry for life. 'Before this I was out of work for ages. It's hard to get a job at our, er, my age.'

The helmet nodded. 'Of course nothing is said. But it's age discrimination for sure. Our state manager always said I was one of her best people, but they laid her off too. An American hedge fund or something bought the firm, management moved offshore and they employed a few young people on new contracts.'

'Our experience, our work ethic, all mean nothing,' said Neil. 'And we're not that old.'

'Not old, just mature. And everything's so expensive now. It's a two-speed economy alright, but some of us are stuck in blimmin' neutral. They're threatening to shut off our electricity if I don't pay something off the bill soon, and my wife's cancer has come back. I reckon it's from stress, and it's all my fault. I got greedy.'

Neil knew about greed and about fault. He didn't remember this bloke, understandably with the sunglasses and helmet hiding his face, but he'd talked people just like him into borrowing against their house to invest in Paramount's high-risk, high-return setup. He'd genuinely believed that the good times would go on forever, even invested all his own savings and then watched helplessly as it all disappeared.

'Look, I hope this won't get you into any trouble?' said the helmet.

'I'll be alright. You've got a gun. What could I do?'

'Oh, this old thing?' He lifted the pistol off the counter and turned it to show Neil. 'It's not loaded. And it's stuffed anyway. It was my grandfather's. He was an officer in World War I. Killed by an artillery shell on the Western Front. His best mate somehow smuggled it back, gave it to the family. Anyhow, I better get going.' He picked up the banana.

Neil nodded towards the Honda gleaming on the forecourt. 'Nice bike you've got there. Used to have one just like it meself. Candy Red.'

'Yeah? The Candy Red, eh? God, she woulda been beautiful.'

Neil noticed the tremble in the voice had been replaced by a spark. The shoulders were suddenly set more square in the leather jacket, the back straighter.

'Yeah, bought it new,' Neil explained. 'Had it until 1983 when it got burned to bits in the Ash Wednesday fires.'

'Geez, destroyed totally?'

'Yeah. We were renting an old farmhouse on a few acres in the Adelaide Hills. I'd just been moved to head office at the bank and my wife was home with our two-year-old son and the bike was in the shed. I'd taken the train into the city. Lost everything.'

'Everything? What do you mean? Your family, they got out okay?'

'No. When I say everything I mean *everything* but the clothes on my back and a few photos I kept at work. When they let me back onto the property all that was left was twisted iron, crumbling walls and the skeleton of the bike sitting like a ghost frozen white in the ashes. But I was beyond caring about the bike by then.'

'Bloody hell, I'm so sorry, mate ... I don't know what to ...' The helmet bowed towards the ancient pistol. It turned guiltily in the gloved hand, as if he wanted it to disappear.

'Don't worry about it. It was a long time ago. I've had a few bikes since then and a few girlfriends too, but there's nothing like that first love.' Neil realised he was talking about both his wife and the Candy Red Honda. Back then he had everything a bloke could want, including his integrity. It had been the best time of his life. And strangely he also realised that with a young family and a mortgage they'd been relatively poor in financial terms, just like he was now.

The bloke went silent, the sunglasses staring at Neil. Then he jerked a gloved thumb back towards the forecourt. 'Er, would you like to have a look at her?'

'I'd bloody well love to,' said Neil.

'What about your boss?'

'The boss? Oh, he doesn't come in till after lunch.'

Under the glaring white fluoros in the servo forecourt, they marvelled at the gleaming machine in silence. A Candy Gold CB750. Unmarked. Neil was reminded of the day he'd walked into the showroom and laid eyes on his own Candy Red. It was his 18th birthday and he'd just been made permanent as a teller at the local bank branch. He'd been in a mood to celebrate and immediately fell in love with the distinctive louvred side covers and hump in the seat, the lustrous powerful-looking engine, the way the thing started almost before the salesman hit the button. Then the perfectly balanced hum of those four cylinders singing of the open road, calling him to twist the throttle. He'd paid a deposit on the spot, knowing he'd be able to organise a cheap loan through the bank. One of his favourite photos was of the Candy Red backgrounded by the ivy-laced white wall of their little Adelaide Hills cottage. It was the last photo he'd taken of the bike.

His reverie of memories was interrupted by the owner of the Candy Gold. 'Bought her brand new in Sydney in 1969, before we were married. Knew I had to get her then or I never would. Hung onto her through all those temptations and pressures to sell. Mortgages, kids, you know ... er, sorry.' The bloke's voice throttled down to a murmur, and he changed gear quickly. 'Have to sell her now though, got no choice. Went into the library and put her on the internet a coupla weeks ago. Had quite a few calls but no one has been prepared to do the drive out here. I'm kinda relieved every time that happens, as if the distance is protecting me, giving me an out from selling, even though we're desperate. When she's gone, well, it'll break my heart, but we're on the bones of our arse at the moment, as you can tell. Can't even afford to put petrol in her these days. This is the first time she's been out of the shed in a year.'

'Well, the bike's an absolute credit to you. Isn't there any way you can keep it?'

'I've tried everything, mate, believe me. But I can't seem to get a job at my age, and my wife's cancer, well ...'

Neil suddenly remembered something. 'Hang on, my cousin told me he's planning to extend our opening times. With the mining boom around here there'll be vehicles coming and going at all hours. As soon as he can find good staff, he said. And that's not as easy as you'd think given the wages the mines are paying. There'll be a part-time job opening, if you don't mind working a few hours at night? He's actually a bloody good boss and he pays well. I could have a word with him?'

'Really? That's ... well, I, geez, after me sticking a gun in your face you'd do that for me?'

'Some things are not our fault. Drop off your details later and I'll put in a good word. The owner likes us *mature* types, reckons we know how to work, that they don't make 'em like they used to.' Neil and the bloke looked at each other and the Honda, and they both understood.

'I don't know how to thank you. A few hours' work at nights would be perfect. It'll take the pressure off; keep our heads above water and the bike with me where she belongs. Here, take this money back, and the banana. Er, I suppose the job will be safe? Don't servos sometimes get held up at night?'

'Out here? Nah. We've never had a hold-up, ever.'

# Hag with a Fag

Steve Drury
Mosman, NSW

It was late Friday afternoon when the impact rocked my office. Before I could race down to the warehouse, a voice yelled up the stairwell that Ahmed had smashed the forklift into the roller doors. Again! This time an entire wall had collapsed. It was only the forklift's excessive speed that had carried Ahmed through the wall and out the other side, saving him from being trapped under the debris. I sat at my desk with my head in my hands; I didn't even have the strength to go fire him. It had been one hell of a week when nothing had gone right and I was just about stuffed. As I wallowed in self-pity, I automatically reached for the ringing phone, about to tell Betty to hold my calls because I was going home early for a change. When she said it was Clem I stabbed Line 1.

Clem and I were riding buddies who had enjoyed some serious adventures together. Like most bikers, we'd owned a heap of different bikes over the years. We were both currently on Harleys — him a Sportster and me a Softail Custom. Clem came straight to the point; he'd rung to find out if I was in the market for a ride. He was organising a group of Sydney blokes to ride down to his Jindabyne cabin the following weekend and figured I'd be a cert to tag along. I thought about it for a few moments, realising that I desperately needed to climb onto two wheels and get my brain into neutral for a while, but somehow, sitting there in my office listening to the mayhem downstairs, Jindabyne just didn't seem far enough away. 'Well, come up with a better idea,' challenged Clem.

Somewhere in that secret place in the back of my head where impossible dreams are stored, I had long harboured a desire to ride a motorcycle across America. Yes, clear across the US of A! At that moment, on that Friday afternoon, with shouts echoing up from the warehouse, a voice whispered in my head that if I didn't fulfil my dream now I probably never would. 'What say we go ride the USA? That's what I would call a real ride.'

About four weeks later Clem and I boarded a Delta flight to Denver, Colorado, via Los Angeles. Apart from our motorcycle helmets and leathers, we had only one bag between the two of us; we were travelling light. It was to be a classic blokes' trip where we'd buy 30 pairs of cheap underdaks and socks each, then throw them away each day after we wore them. Clem ended up buying only 10 pairs because he's a cheapskate and figured he wouldn't smell too bad after three days, especially sitting on a motorcycle, out in the open air, with the wind whistling up his trouser legs. True to his pathetic plan, he extracted three days' wear out of each pair, sometimes turning them inside out to extend their usage. He also made the mistake of buying a cheap brand that had quite bulky seams which cut into his bum after long hours in the saddle, so he got into the habit of chopping off the seams before wearing them. After three days of non-stop abuse, each pair of mutilated underpants looked like the wearer had been the victim of a suicide bomb. I hate to think what the housekeeping maids might have thought when they pulled them out of the motel rubbish bins!

We had considered hiring motorcycles in America but had talked ourselves into a more exotic plan. This was back in 1991 when the Honda Gold Wing was sold in a number of overseas markets but for whatever reason was not available in Australia. We had read a lot about these giant touring bikes in American magazines and managed to convince ourselves that we both desperately needed one. After chatting to Honda Australia's marketing guru, he agreed to supply us with compliance plates if we bought two Honda Gold Wings in the USA and brought them back with us when we came home. All we would have to do in return was give him some feedback on our impressions of the bikes. Easy. So a week before we left Australia we transferred the cost of two brand-new Gold Wings to Aurora Honda in Denver, arranging for them to have the bikes registered and ready to roll when we walked through their showroom door.

We figured Denver was a good jumping-off point for our trip for a couple of reasons. One was that I had a brother living in that city who could look after any hiccups or warranty issues with the bikes, plus Denver was almost smack bang in the middle of the USA, allowing us to take off in whatever direction took our fancy on the spur of the moment.

When we walked through the entrance of Aurora Honda, there were two gleaming new Wings sitting there, winking at us. The emotional impact was similar to when I saw my lovely bride walk down the aisle towards me on our wedding day. Only a beautiful woman or a majestic pile of metal, chrome and paint can send a man weak at the knees like that. We sipped on apple cider while the Aurora boys completed the paperwork, installed the microphones and speakers in our helmets, and offered conflicting advice about possible itineraries. I didn't hear most of it because my attention was captured by the dealership's pet ferret, Son of a Gun, who ran around our feet, sniffing our Johnny Rebs.

Finally we were ready to roll. Significantly jetlagged yet full of confidence, we waved goodbye to the ferret, pulled out into Denver's afternoon traffic, somehow found our way onto an interstate and took off. In front of us lay four deliciously empty weeks. No fixed itinerary, no commitments, no plans, no agenda other than to eat steaks, drink beer and RIDE!

After having ridden Harleys for the last couple of years, we were both immediately impressed with the smooth power of the Gold Wings and their ease of handling due to the low centre of gravity. Both bikes were equipped with CB radios, which meant we could communicate while riding. This was something we hadn't experienced before and it added a whole new dimension to our riding experience. When I got sick of hearing Clem's advice about which road we should go down next, I could turn off the CB and hit the stereo tape deck. As we said to each other many times: 'It doesn't get any better than this.'

After clearing Denver on the interstate, we jumped off onto secondary roads and established a pattern that we followed for the rest of the trip. We weren't interested in simply chalking up long distances on major highways; instead we wanted to see small-town America by travelling the back roads. It was summertime and the days were long, so we would usually get a reasonably early start, hit the road and put down a few miles before breakfast, thereby avoiding at least some of the heat of the day. We would keep an eye open for some interesting little town or tourist spot where we'd pull in for a long lunch, often followed by a snooze in a park or next to a river. Like most tourists in that country, we were amazed at the cheap food and low-cost accommodation.

Back home we had a mate who had ridden America a few months before our trip, and he hadn't stopped boasting about how he had stayed in a motel in Nebraska for a night for only $22.95 a double. 'It wasn't real flash, mate, but it was bloody good value for money.' When we told him that we were going to do a similar trip he challenged us to find a cheaper motel. He promised that if we could prove that we had stayed somewhere for less than $22.95 a double, he would shout us the accommodation out of his own pocket. His idle boast and silly offer were responsible for provoking an experience that turned out to be one of the craziest events of our entire trip. To our mate's surprise, when we returned home we were able to present him with an invoice that proved that we had indeed stayed in a motel at less than his $22.95 hovel in Nebraska.

Motivated by the challenge, we regularly bypassed classier motels while searching for cheapies, hoping to claim a free night's accommodation from Old Mate when we got back home. Well, we struck the jackpot when we were riding across Texas one afternoon and started seeing billboards advertising the 'cheapest motel in the USA'. The billboards must've started 200 miles before we arrived at the motel and since the advertised tariff was only $19.95 a double we were driven to spend the night there. We almost didn't make it to the motel because riding across Texas in the middle of summer is a little bit like tackling the Nullarbor at a similar time of year. It was so hot that we were forced to stop at nearly every gas station we passed and literally pour water over our heads and soak our clothes, but even so we would be bone dry after being back on the road for 10 minutes. The extreme heat almost caused us to stop before reaching our $19.95 target, but the promise of a free night at our mate's expense kept us going.

When we finally pulled into the Snyder Sunset Motel we were delighted to see a rusty 44-gallon drum at the entrance with a hand-scrawled notice on the side that screamed 'free breakfast'. We had been drawn to the place by the promise of their $19.95 room rate, but never in our wildest dreams had we anticipated that a free breakfast would be included in the price. We were about to make history!

The place may have been given a coat of paint when it had been built some time back in the 1940s, but a combination of a half-century of sunstroke and the sandpapering effect of grit whipped up by the surrounding desert winds had denuded the place of any aesthetic charm. A giant half-dead cactus next to what looked like an old outdoor dunny appeared to be the only attempt to beautify the exterior of the building. Even the sign at the entrance had been peppered with shotgun pellets, almost obliterating the Snyder Sunset Motel's identity.

Parking the Gold Wings on the gravel drive, we saw no sign of life. Clem noticed the misspelt word 'Reseption' scrawled on the wall next to a doorway, so we walked in. The place reeked of cigarette smoke and there sitting at a counter was a very old lady with her faded grey hair in curlers, a burning fag hanging between dark brown nicotine-stained fingers and a mangled toothpick dangling out of one side of her lipsticked mouth. A dog somewhere under the counter barked frantically as we approached, but promptly shut up when the old duck gave it a swift kick without moving off her chair. We stood there, still sweating from the day's exertions, trying to comprehend the reality of a $19.95 motel. The old lady sat there looking at us blankly, not saying a word, the blue smoke lazily wafting up and adding to the dark brown layer of crud already stuck to the ceiling.

Clem finally broke the silence by asking if there was any chance of a room for the night, which was a pretty stupid question because there wasn't one vehicle, not even a horse and cart, in the gravel parking lot. The hag grunted, which could have meant yes or no, but which obviously meant yes because she put her hand out, indicating she needed our $19.95 room rate. Clem handed her a $20 bill whereupon she threw him a hand-scribbled invoice and a key, which was attached to a chain, which was attached to a battered tin cup. She then went back to reading her paper, still not having said a word. Clem started for the door, but I stood there looking at the hag with the fag and said, 'Where's our change? You owe us five cents.' I was stuffed if I was going to have our room rate escalate to $20 just when we were about to set an international cheap-as-chips motel spending-spree record.

Well, stuff me; she just sat there ignoring me, reading the paper! Clem said, 'C'mon, mate, forget the five cents, it's not worth the hassle.' He said something else, but I didn't hear it because the hag with the fag kicked the dog again, which then went berserk, barking and tearing at the underneath of the counter like an enraged bull. I consoled myself as I remembered that the inflated $20 room rate now included free breakfast, which sort of justified being cheated out of five cents. I gave up on the old lady and followed Clem to our room.

I've stayed in a lot of low-cost accommodation in my time, but the Snyder Sunset Motel really scraped the bottom of the barrel. No pillow slips, no sheets, no soap, one towel to share between the two of us, cigarette butts in the ashtray next to the No Smoking card sticky-taped to the wall, and the stink of cigarette smoke and sweat. The pillows were disgusting; each exhibited a large stain that looked like previous guests had dipped their heads in a vat of sump oil before retiring for the evening. The door appeared as though it had been opened each morning by a SWAT team with a battering ram, with both the lock and the chain broken. 'Pathetic,' muttered Clem, wrinkling up his nose, 'bloody pathetic. The only things lacking are the second-hand condoms.'

If it hadn't been just on dusk, and if it hadn't been over 40 degrees Celsius outside, and if we weren't already completely stuffed, and if there had been another motel within 100 miles, we never would have spent the night at the Snyder Sunset. But stay at the salubrious Snyder Sunset we did. I didn't suffer too much because I was mostly asleep, but when Clem got up to have his middle-of-the-night pee, he claimed he got bitten on both bare feet by 'sumfink'. I don't think he was exaggerating either, because in the morning there were half a dozen squashed cockies on the floor which I couldn't remember seeing before we went to bed.

We were both awake well before dawn due to the racket caused by the dog barking on the other side of our door, doing its best to rip its way through the already badly damaged bottom panel. We both had another shower without soap in an attempt to remove the bacteria that we were sure had migrated to our bodies from the beds where we had just slept. Our one threadbare towel had now been used a total of four times. As he chucked his old disposable underpants into the corner of the room, Clem was all for getting out of the place as quickly as possible and finding somewhere else for breakfast. I reminded him that our room rate included free breakfast, and if we were really serious about claiming bragging rights to the cheaper-than-chips motel record, we needed to avail ourselves of the complimentary cuisine.

We wandered back into the 'reseption' area where the hag with the fag still sat, not appearing to have moved since we saw her the evening before. The dog snarled as we approached. When we asked where breakfast was being served she grunted something unintelligible and pointed her yellow-stained finger down an adjacent hallway. At the end we found a small dark room decked out with several tattered tables and chairs, no tablecloths or cutlery, with a peeling picture of the Marlboro Man on his horse wallpapered onto the ceiling. In pride of place, under a bare light bulb swinging from a chain, stood a greasy bain-marie. Peering through the steam and condensation, we saw what appeared to be the mouldy leftovers from previous meals bubbling in an unknown juice. 'No way I'm eatin' that,' said Clem, almost puking on the spot. 'Let's get out of this dump.'

We grabbed our gear and headed out to where the bikes were parked, pulled the covers off them, stuffed our gear into the panniers, and were about to take off when I had this feeling that justice needed to be served. 'Wait a minute, mate. You stay here; I'm going back inside to get compensation out of that old con artist for no free breakfast. I'm going to ask for a refund.'

Ignoring Clem's protestations, I tramped back into 'reseption'. There she was sitting with her hair in curlers, fag dangling through her fingers, toothpick drooping out of her mouth, reading her paper to the cacophony of the unseen hound frothing its head off under the counter. I stood looking at her for a moment, but she simply ignored me. To be honest, I felt a twinge of compassion. I thought to myself that it must be tough being an old lady trying to run a motel way out here in the sticks, with only a dog for company. I felt the best approach was probably to appeal to the old lady's sense of justice.

'Look, let's not play games. You know and I know that there is no free breakfast available at this motel this morning. Those bits of bubbling burnt crap that are sitting in the bain-marie are probably only good for use as rat poison; human beings just don't eat that sort of stuff. Now when we rode in here we were enticed by the proposition that you were offering a free breakfast, which I see now is clearly not the truth. Where we come from we call that a con and we don't like being conned one bit. Now I don't want to get nasty about this and I'm sure you don't want any trouble, so I suggest you give me a two-dollar refund to compensate for no breakfast, and we'll call it quits. We will ride away happy and you can rest easy knowing that you have two more satisfied customers. What do you say?'

The hag with the fag slowly raised her head and stared blankly at me, leisurely chewing on her toothpick. I thought for a moment that she was seriously considering my proposition. I stood there staring eye to eye for what seemed like a full minute. She didn't blink her watery bloodshot eyes. She just stared in blank defiance, making it patently obvious that she had no intention of acceding to my demand.

I have never punched an old lady and I didn't want to start now. But something deep inside rebelled against the injustice that sat there staring me in the face, stinking of cigarette smoke.

'Okay. Here's the deal. If you don't refund our two dollars, me and my mate are going to climb on our motorbikes and ride out of here. We've got CB radios on both bikes and we're heading northwest. For the next 200 miles we will be passing literally thousands of cars and trucks, and for the whole 200 miles we're going to be sitting on our CBs telling everybody we come across that the Snyder Sunset Motel is the worst, I repeat, THE WORST, motel in the whole of Texas.'

Finally the hag with the fag spat out the only words that I ever heard her speak. 'Good luck, buddy. Everyone already knows the Snyder is the worst motel in Texas!'

# Riding Down Memory Lane

Phillip Lawton
Blewitt Springs, SA

My riding career began in 1962 in the Sydney suburb of Arncliffe when my younger brother and I pooled our hard-won pocket money and, for the princely sum of six pounds, bought a mid-50s James Cadet powered by a 150cc two-stroke Villiers engine. I use the term 'powered' loosely because the engine was a non-goer.

After pushing the little bike home one Friday afternoon after school, we hid it down the end of the backyard in between the wooden caravan and Dad's old Dodge truck, so he wouldn't see it until my brother and I had explained how good a deal it was. Our father, being on afternoon shift that week, would have no chance to spot it in the dark when he arrived home at midnight.

Next morning at breakfast, while containing our excitement and waiting for the right moment to break the good news, Dad asked in a conversational tone, 'What's that down between the van and the truck?' The moment had arrived to blurt out the news about our excellent two-wheeled, motorised (though not running) acquisition.

Now that my grandson is the same age as my younger brother was back then, I reflect and think how silly, dumb, or maybe even a bit stupid we were, thinking that Dad wouldn't see the little James 'hidden' between those two vehicles. After all, they were parked with the front of each of them facing the kitchen windows through which our father, sitting at the breakfast table, could survey his vast property, all quarter-acre of it. Not only that, but being a father myself I have come to the conclusion that fathers and mothers do talk to each other.

Mum just sat at her place at the breakfast table, tending to her third and youngest son, knowing full well the outcome of the ensuing conversation.

Dad was a retired motorcyclist, having put his old 1936 BSA in the shed back in 1956. It stayed there until one sunny morning in 1972 when the battered and well-worn old bike once again was brought out to face the world; but more on that later.

In the weeks to come I was riding the James in circles around Mum's clothesline, wearing a furrow in the lawn. Mum was none too happy about this, and as mothers and fathers do, they talked. They must have discussed the groove in the lawn and the dust problem under her feet on washing days, and that it could not continue. It was at this juncture in our budding motorcycling careers that our father, who must have been instructed by our mother, spoke to my brother and me. He told us that it was about time we either got rid of the bike for family peace, or more than likely for his peace, or pushed it the mile or so to a disused stock car track that ran alongside the river. Heaven! It was on this track that we learned to actually change gears.

Before we could push our bike to our very own track, 'down the track' as we all called it, sharing the venue with other hopefuls, we were mindful that we needed to do something about the engine. Dad's second question to us at the breakfast table that fateful morning was 'Does it go?' The answer of course was no. 'Well then, we had better have a look and see what can be done to start it' was his rejoinder. Leaving our poor mother to do the dishes, three young boys and one young father traipsed out of the house, down to where the bike was 'hidden' to see what could be done to bring it to life. That was the day I learned what a piston is, what a carburettor is for and why there is need for an electric spark. With not a little fiddling and a surprisingly small amount of time, the engine was humming away nicely, blowing a considerable amount of white smoke.

Over the next several years many more motorcycles came and went. My younger brother gave up on bikes when he discovered girls, swapping bikes for a black, lowered FJ Holden and an Elvis-style hairdo. But our youngest brother, to this day, has continued with motorcycling, as have I.

There were Matchless, Triumph, an Ariel, BSAs in all sizes, an Indian, a couple of antiquated Harley-Davidsons, one with a wooden sidebox attached, even a Panther plus a scooter or two in later years, and then various dilapidated second-hand machines from the Orient, all of which graced our family's backyard for a time. Most of these bikes were stripped of any unnecessary parts that weren't needed to make them go, or sometimes stop, when ridden around that dusty track down by the river.

Many times I said to my father that I was going to get his old BSA out of the shed, to which his answer to that high-blown statement was 'No you're not!' I suppose, looking back to those days, all I ever did was get an old bike from somewhere, usually for nothing or near nothing, dismantle it, thrash it, wreck it and dispose of it. Not wanting his old BSA to suffer the same fate, no matter how worn it was, his answer was always the same: 'No you're not!' Now that I am older than he was back then, and the father of two girls, I can understand his response!

In 1965 I obtained my permit to ride a motorcycle legally on the Queen's highway. My mode of transport then was a 1949 250cc BSA, a small bike that normally didn't lead to too much trouble. At home in the shed I had also parked a similar-aged Vespa motor scooter that I had bought. The BSA cost 12 pounds; the cost of the Vespa, two pounds. At least the BSA was registered, but no one looks cool on a Vespa, do they, especially a 16-year-old man, er, boy.

No, one shouldn't get into much trouble with a small bike, although 11 days before my 17th birthday I ran headlong into the side of a Vanguard ute, breaking my right arm. Two weeks later my younger brother took off for a ride on the Vespa, although it wasn't registered and he didn't have a licence. The young — I don't know! Now, the scooters of that era had very small wheels, the front very capable of disappearing into a reasonable-sized pothole. And that is what happened. The young rider was pitched head first over the front of the scooter, landing on his left arm, breaking his fall and his arm. There we were, two brothers, feeling very sorry for ourselves, one with a broken left arm, the other with a broken right arm. As Dad put it, we were both now 'armless'! That scooter ride was the end of that brother's riding days. Dad insisted I stop. I didn't, I still ride.

The arm healed, and with Dad's help the little Beeza was repaired. Many other bikes came and went over the years, not least of all bigger Beezas with 650cc engines, which were absolutely lovely to ride. In 1967 a red Triumph Bonneville appeared. Now that Bonny had one other rider while in my ownership, none other than Dad himself.

On the Saturday I bought it I just had to take it for a spin, and where better than to show Dad who was at work at the time. I rolled to a stop in front of the little office where he was employed as a security officer at the oil refinery. I killed the engine and sat there on the bike looking through the window, wondering what his next move would be. He just sat there looking back at me with what one may consider a blank look. Then his lips parted into a smile. He came out to inspect the Bonny, walked around it, and as I got off he promptly got on. I could see the memories flooding back as his hands fell readily in place on the bars. He didn't say much, just swung the kick-start lever downwards with the result that the engine ticked over at idle nicely. Next, he slipped it into first gear, rode out the gate and out of sight down the road. I wasn't at all surprised that he took it for a test ride, but I didn't expect him to stay away for the best part of half an hour, leaving me in charge of security at the oil refinery. Thankfully, no trucks came in or out and the phone didn't ring.

Two years later the Triumph had long gone and I was commuting on a 175cc Honda twin. At this time in my eventful life — well, I thought it was eventful — I decided to have a go at short circuit racing, and so I bought a new Kawasaki 250 trail bike and joined the Annandale-Leichhardt Motorcycle Club. That exercise lasted for a couple of years until I got engaged to the girl of my dreams and ran out of money. So racing ceased, the bike was sold and I continued to commute on the little Honda. But ... I did gain a third place in the Senior 'C' at Arcadia short circuit track on Sunday 17th May 1970. I was presented with a white sash that says so, which I still have. How cool am I now, brother?

During those years, motorcycling was my whole life. I was employed by a major bike importer based in the then home of motorcycling, Wentworth Avenue in Sydney. I was commuting by bike, restoring bikes, racing bikes and meeting all sorts of personalities to do with the sport. It was the best time.

February 1972 rolled around: 'Hey, Dad, how about we get your old BSA out of the shed?' It was a question, not a statement. His answer almost blew me away! I should mention here that the previous year I had bought a tired-looking 1962 BMW twin and set about restoring it to its former glory. This had perhaps proved to Dad that my days of wrecking bikes were over and that I had grown up at last. So his answer to my question about getting his old BSA out of the shed brought forth these very words, words I shall never forget: 'What a great idea!' The grass had grown back under the clothesline by this time, so that may have been in my favour too.

His BSA was not a tiddler, not even a mid-weight, but the granddaddy of them all — a V-twin of monstrous 986cc capacity! The controls consisted of a foot-operated clutch, with a hand gear change on the side of the petrol tank. On the handlebars there was a lever for decompressing the engine, which lifted the exhaust valves, so it could be stopped, with another small lever to advance or retard the spark so that the engine could be started. How about that? A lever to cause the engine to go and another lever to cause it to stop.

I remember, as a preschooler, Dad riding this bike to work each morning. The day we dragged the old girl out of his shed he sat on it for the first time in 16 years and I could see his memories come flooding back once again, just as they had on my Bonny. Over the next few years I restored his old BSA to as near-to-new condition as I could. Before he too went the way of older people and joined my mother, he had the satisfaction of seeing it wearing new tyres, a freshly painted black frame, new chrome, and green paint on the petrol tank resplendent with gold pinstripes. I still have that bike in my possession to this day along with the BMW that I preferred for daily transport for many, many years.

The first of a long line of Gold Wings from Honda started in 1975. I bought one of these with sidecar attached in 1980. Our two baby daughters were the first excited passengers to travel in the steel-bodied Australian-made sidecar. I assume they were excited; they never complained. The youngest was two years old, er, young, the oldest was six. I fitted a detachable roof in case of inclement weather, which I'm sure they appreciated; neither said otherwise. As a family we had a lot of fun on that Gold Wing. Sometimes I would ride it to work, sometimes I would ride my old faithful BMW and sometimes I would ride my other BMW, a 1972 R75/5 750cc model. At the time it was an exceptional bike: good handling, plenty of power and aftermarket exhaust pipes that sounded spot on.

The Gold Wing had four into one extractor-type pipes and sounded great. I was a Cool Dude when riding that bike. I had 15-inch wire spoke wheels specially made, fitted with steel belted car tyres, which helped the handling enormously. Several camping trips saw the outfit carry children, tents, cooking utensils and sleeping bags, one of which was called a 'cuddle pouch' for the littlest kid.

It was on one of those trips in 1981, up the NSW coast then over the mountains to Dubbo, Orange, Bathurst and home, that two big people got talking, as mothers and fathers do. We discussed moving interstate, way out of suburbia, somewhere with a bit of space.

The Gold Wing was sold. The 750cc BMW was sold. The house was sold. The household furniture along with the older BMW and Dad's precious BSA were packed into a removalist's semi-trailer and shipped off to South Australia. Go west, young man, go west.

That was in 1982 when we acquired 10 acres of land with a house and not much else. We put in the hard yakka developing the property; we built stables with yards and fenced the paddocks to contain a couple of horses. You see, mothers talk and fathers have a habit of listening. We even built sheds to house the bikes.

Meanwhile the BSA and BMW both waited their turn to be let loose on the Queen's highway once more. Don't get me wrong here; the Bee Em was pressed into service occasionally, but only occasionally. When a man's busy building, there isn't a lot of time to spare for pleasure riding.

My next machine was memorable for all the wrong reasons!

There I was, minding my own business, riding my latest acquisition. It was a cloudless day, not a breeze in the air, and I can even remember the exact time: it was 1.20pm the day before Australia Day, 25th January 2000.

My acquisition was, and I emphasise *was*, a 1982 Honda Gold Wing Interstate, black in colour with all the bells and whistles for which Gold Wings are famous, right down to the twin AM-FM radio and CB radio aerials fixed to the rear top box. As fate would have it, I never got to figure out how to operate the radio and CB.

I was riding along that beautifully winding tree-lined two-lane road in the hills above Willunga, south of Adelaide, just cruising, listening to the muted burble of the flat-four engine and enjoying the day, snatching an occasional glimpse to my right, down through the trees to the coast far below. The gold-pinstriped deep glossy black paint on the 'pretend' petrol tank glistened in the dappled sunshine as it filtered through the leaves of the overhanging gum trees. Absolutely idyllic!

I was suddenly snapped out of my euphoria when a tight right-hand bend presented itself just ahead. I am not afraid of corners, but this one was approaching way too rapidly; not idyllic, not even good! I swiftly changed down two gear ratios in quick succession. As I leaned into that tight right-hander, I felt both tyres of the big Wing start to give way. Why was I losing traction? What was causing the slide? I wasn't travelling that fast. To this day, more than 14 years later, I can still vividly recall thinking that if I touched the brakes I'd be off. I also realised that if I didn't hit the brakes, then the big tree dead ahead would arrest my headlong rush, potentially leading to oblivion. What sort of a choice was that to have to make in a hurry? A really big hurry!

Crunch!

I found myself lying on the ground at the side of the road. I don't recall it happening, but there I was in the dirt amidst pine needles and fallen eucalypt leaves. I have no memory from the time the Wing began its slide until my open-face helmet hit the ground, my head still firmly ensconced. I can recall thinking about whether or not to hit the brakes, but that's about it.

After I regained my somewhat shocked senses, I inspected the scene of the crime and noticed a very clear telltale trail behind the Gold Wing, which was now much the worse for wear. There were dark marks in the dirt at the side of the road. I must have applied both brakes simultaneously, which is what every decent rider learns to do when braking rapidly. But what caused the slide? Was there something invisible on the road, shaded by the trees, something that shouldn't have been there?

I staggered out onto the shaded road to have a closer look, and there I found the answer — it was painfully obvious. Pink circles had been painted on the road surface where a number of potholes had been repaired. In their enthusiasm the road repairers had left behind what seemed like multiple barrow loads of fine gravel. It was scattered around the potholes and also along the edge where the blacktop met the dirt. There it was inches thick for several yards and almost invisible. So THAT's what caused the big Wing to take its fatal slide.

As the bike fell, it slid on its side before hitting the big tree, the headlight taking the full impact. Upon collision the headlight was crushed, abruptly stopping the front of the bike. But the rear of the bike kept going! It left the ground, flipped upwards and became stuck in a vertical position, wedged between the gum and the adjacent tree. The front wheel was still on the ground, leaving the bike standing up in the air with the rear wheel at head height. My Wing is still the only bike I have ever seen standing vertical, upside down, impaled on gum trees, looking as though it had been parked by aliens!

The windscreen survived with only a few scratches, the front guard had none, but the headlight was in small bits. Those twin aerials? Not broken, not bent, not as much as a scratch, and I was grateful that at least I still had my head.

There was my Gold Wing, upside down, leaving me to wonder how I was going to get out of this mess. I had no option but to sit patiently, waiting for someone to come along that lonely road to lend a hand and extract the bike from its undignified position. It was so strange, or funny, or sad an end for such a wonderful machine, depending on how you look at it.

I was finally rescued and the Wing was carted off to a repair shop. Upon close inspection it was determined that the frame was damaged around the steering head area. According to the experts, the Wing is a pig of a bike to repair, so the insurance company simply wrote it off. I wondered at that!

Ouch!

Ten days of ownership ...

Double ouch!

Only my sixth ride ...

Bugger!

It was early 2003 that ushered in my modern era of riding. I was still taking the old BMW out on the occasional run just to keep my hand in, until I got the bug to move into the realms of modern motorcycling. At that stage in my life I didn't have the need or reason to ride every day. Riding was more a pleasure activity — I must have been getting older.

It was a momentous day, that Saturday morning when I mentioned my latest motorcycle acquisition thoughts to my darling wife. Her response was: 'Let's go shopping.' I kid you not, shopping we did go. The arrival of the 1998 1100cc Yamaha Virago was exciting. Not new, but looking like it, all credit to its previous owner. A beautiful bike to ride, light to manoeuvre, powerful, and I looked oh so cool on it, even if I was the only one to think so. She was such a joy that I ditched the car and went back to being a daily rider commuting to work. Fortunately, the journey between my place of employment and my residence was all on rural country roads. What better way to start and end a day, swinging the leg over the seat of a bike and going for a ride. Maybe I wasn't that old after all?

Then without warning bike fever struck again in December 2003. I was perusing the 'motorcycles for sale' section of the Saturday morning paper when I happened to notice a Kawasaki with sidecar attached. Now that sounded interesting. Having had sidecars before, not only on the Gold Wing but also on a couple of older British bikes way back in antiquity, plus two different types in two different eras on the old Bee Em, I made the call to get a little more information. Well, what can I say? The information led to the bike, a 1996 Kawasaki Vulcan Classic with double sidecar, being transferred from there to here.

Several months later, May 2004, I was perusing the weekend paper once again when I spotted a bike advertised that I had secretly desired. I had only ever seen one, but that was enough to whet my appetite and generate my ambition to own it, if only I could ever find one. Here was my chance. Would my darling agree? 'Call the number,' she said. I did. Following is the conversation with the owner of my next bike, a 2001 1500cc Kawasaki Vulcan Drifter, the model that is a copy of a late 1940s Indian Chief.

'Hello, you have a Drifter for sale?'

'Yes.'

More talk, as fathers do; more banter, as motorcyclists do.

'Why are you selling it?'

'Because I'm too short for a big bike,' he confessed.

As quick as a flash I said, 'I have the opposite problem — I'm too tall for the bike I have.'

'What do you have?' he asked.

'Yamaha Virago,' I answered.

'How about a swap?' he ventured.

'Okay,' said I.

That was around 10 years ago; I love it. Not as much as my old BMW, but I love it just the same. Is the BSA jealous? I dunno, she has never said anything about her latest stablemate. Maybe it's because the Vulcan looks to be of a similar vintage.

Then, the icing on the cake!

Upon my retirement from the workforce my lovely wife bought a Harley-Davidson Ultra Classic Electra Glide for me to enjoy.

With a shed full of bikes and a head full of two-wheeled memories, a bloke just has to be happy, don't you think?

# Tex and Bundy

As told to John Bryant by Tex O'Grady
Coffs Harbour, NSW

They've motorcycled all over outback Australia, raised over half a million bucks for charity, and brought smiles to the faces of millions of Australians; not bad when you consider that one of them is a motorcycle-mounted stumpy-tailed cattle dog!

Once you've seen Tex and Bundy you'll never forget them. They've been turning heads for years on their blue Suzuki Hayabusa motorcycle, and now attract even more attention after moving on to a magnificent NTX Stelvio 1200, fully sponsored by the Australian Moto Guzzi distributor. Over the years they have become an inseparable team, Tex O'Grady in his colourful motorcycle gear, with his Blue Heeler Bundy decked out in 'doggles', bandana, custom-made coat covered in patches and badges, with a safety harness under her jacket which is secured to Tex.

Like many older motorcycling enthusiasts, Tex traces the beginning of his passion for biking back to his younger days. He got involved in road racing motorcycles in the 70s and in late 1978 decided to jump on his Honda F2 750 to have a shot at the 'Around Australia Motorcycle Endurance Record'. To his credit, Tex catapulted himself into *The Guinness Book of Records* by shaving a whopping 24 hours off the previous record held by the NSW Highway Patrol. His time for the 15,500-kilometre circumnavigation of our great country was an incredible eight days, 23 hours and 57 minutes. This included the time taken to rebuild his bike's motor on the side of the road after an engine blow-up!

In 1985 Tex tackled the Wynns Safari on two wheels: a Suzuki DR 600. Swapping over to four wheels, he again competed in the Wynns in '86, '87 and 1990. However, his motorcycling adventures, particularly road racing, were hampered by his commitment to his career in the Australian Navy.

In 1992, after serving 20 years in most of the RAN Oberon Class submarines and being awarded the Australian Service Medal, he retired from the navy and settled on the Coffs Coast in New South Wales. He returned to his passion for motorcycle road racing in the late 1990s, winning two national BEARS titles as well as a number of other races. He also competed successfully in dirt track racing with solo motorcycles and sidecars.

Like many ex-servicemen seeking new horizons, Tex tried a few different money-making ventures. He qualified as a commercial pilot, then got involved in organising and leading outback adventure tours. Gifted with mechanical ability, he ran his own mobile workshop before taking on the job of Workshop Manager in a large Sydney-based firm. This opened up new opportunities which saw Tex managing and then owning a number of automotive and motorcycle businesses around New South Wales.

Although not realising it at the time, a significant turning point occurred in Tex's life in 1999 while he was managing a 1,000-acre rural property on the outskirts of Cooma, New South Wales. He owned a Rottweiler called Tango and a friend, who figured that Tango should have a companion, gave Tex a Blue Heeler pup which he promptly named 'Cash'. The new pup quickly developed into a mate that went on to have an incredible impact on Tex's life, as well as provide inspiration and entertainment for literally hundreds of thousands of Australians.

Almost from the word go, Cash insisted on accompanying Tex no matter where he went around the farm. He relished hitching a ride on all Tex's vehicles, not just on the ute and quad bike like some of the other dogs in the neighbourhood, and developed a passion for riding on two-wheeled motorcycles, particularly road bikes. Whenever Tex fired up an engine, Cash would be sitting there with his tongue hanging out panting, wanting to go for a ride!

Tex quickly decided that if Cash was going to become a regular passenger on the front of his motorcycle, he needed to be protected from the elements; after all, he didn't want a wayward bug taking out one of Cash's eyes! And so little by little Cash's riding ensemble developed to the point where he had his own set of goggles specially adapted to his canine head, a tailor-made jacket that fitted like a glove and a bandana to reflect the larrikin flair of this lovable thrill-seeking pooch.

Almost instantly Cash, decked out in his flamboyant riding apparel, became a big hit with the public, and not just in motorcycling circles. Tex and Cash pulled a crowd no matter where they went. As soon as they stopped at a servo or milk bar, the bike would be surrounded by spectators wanting to pat Cash, take a photo, and find out all they could about the amazing pup and his laid-back chauffeur. Soon the pair was being asked to participate in charity rides to help raise funds for a wide variety of good causes. This developed into visits to hospitals and nursing homes where they so readily brought joy to the sick and the elderly. Their visits expanded to include people in palliative care as well as kids in children's hospital wards where they were able to minister to the terminally ill. It soon became evident to Tex that they could make a unique contribution to the wider community, so he decided to toss in his other activities to enable him and Cash to concentrate on becoming full-time self-funded philanthropists. Looking back, Tex credits Cash for teaching him about the valuable contribution that animals can make to helping people and funding charitable activities.

By 2005 Tex and sidekick Cash had become a familiar sight in outback areas and country towns, having travelled more than 400,000 kilometres on Australia's highways and byways.

Tex, a big-hearted true-blue Aussie larrikin, always wearing a cheeky smile and ready to lend a helping hand, along with his faithful motorcycling companion, seemed to be destined for 'happily ever after'. But then, disaster struck!

When crossing the road one day, Cash was struck by a vehicle and killed. Tex was devastated, as were many thousands of Australians who had warmed to this lovable animal, a pup that had contributed so much joy to so many people. This tragedy could easily have been the end of the road for Tex too, but with the help and support of his friends, he embarked upon a search for a replacement for Cash.

Tex reasoned that while his beloved mate was gone he was not forgotten, and that by finding another unique Blue Heeler Cash's legacy would live on. The search for a new 'bluey' was a monumental task because not just any dog would do. Tex was looking for an undefinable special quality, something that would make the pup stand apart from the crowd. He had big shoes to fill! Tex travelled all over New South Wales and checked out well over 250 working dogs. Finally his travels took him to Mudgee, where he identified a six-week-old stumpy-tailed Smithfield Blue Heeler bitch. She was the one! He bought her and gave her the new name of Bundy. Tex was back in business, with his new mate Bundy about to bring joy and hope to a whole new generation of Aussies.

In 2010 the pair moved back to Tex's old stamping grounds on the Coffs Coast, a place they now call home between their philanthropic engagements. Bundy has her own goggles, bandana and harness, just like Cash before her. Her coat is covered in patches and pins, and she shares the same passion and commitment to riding on Tex's motorcycle as her predecessor.

Perhaps one of her most intriguing attributes is that Bundy is the only dog in New South Wales to carry a 'ministerial declaration' specifically granted by the state government, permitting her to ride on the front of a motorcycle. This came about after the NSW government changed the law, making it an offence for dogs to travel on motorcycles (Rule ARR 297-3), which threatened to terminate Tex and Bundy's two-wheeled charity work. The motorcycle community rallied around them, circulating a number of petitions aimed at getting the law changed. The media climbed on the bandwagon and added its voice to the outcry, with Tex and Bundy appearing on a number of TV programs where they explained their predicament. The appropriate government minister of the day reviewed their unique circumstances and decided to create a special exemption that permitted the famous duo to continue their charitable activities. Today Tex and Bundy are waiting for similar responses from Australia's other states and territories from whom they have requested the same exemption that has been granted by New South Wales, Victoria and Western Australia.

It hasn't all been plain sailing though, as Bundy has faced her own serious health challenges. In 2009 she broke her back in an accident — and no, it wasn't in relation to motorcycling. She was running on the family property when her leg disappeared down a concrete culvert, causing her to flip over and break her back. Bundy fractured a couple of discs, which resulted in her rear legs becoming paralysed. Surgery was going to cost around $15,000 and it carried an 80 per cent risk of mortality, so the vet recommended that Bundy be put down. Tex couldn't afford the operation, but he steadfastly refused to give up on his best mate.

When news of Bundy's predicament circulated within the motorcycling community, donations started to pour in. Tex was able to beg, borrow and not quite steal the shortfall, which ensured that Bundy was given the 24/7 care that was needed, instead of a lethal needle. Six months of intensive rehabilitation resulted in her being able to walk again and eventually she was well enough to return to her position on Tex's motorcycle once more. Since her recovery, Tex has put

Bundy on a strict diet and exercise regime so that she can continue doing what she loves best — making a difference to people's lives while perched on the big Guzzi's petrol tank, strapped into her safety harness.

Watching Bundy in action is an absolute hoot. As soon as she realises that bike riding is on the agenda, she sits next to the bike, just itching to go. When Tex mounts and taps the tank she leaps up in a single bound, ready to take her position on the front of the bike behind the bikini windscreen. She readily submits to having her leather vest, bandana and 'doggles' fitted, and then waits somewhat impatiently while Tex fits her with her safety harness, which he then attaches to himself. As the machine fires up and moves off, Bundy will stand on the tank for a short distance, and then settle down in a crouching position as speed and wind force increase, tucking in behind the fairing where she avoids the worst of the turbulence. Sometimes on a long ride she'll fall asleep in that position, secure in the knowledge that her trusty master will pilot his two-wheeled rocket safely to their next appointment. When she senses that the bike is about to reach its destination, as indicated by the downshifting of gears and a reduction in speed, she will again raise herself to a standing position on the tank to get a better view of the welcoming crowd. She is a real performer at heart!

Bundy, being the accomplished rider that she is, absolutely loves twisty roads at high speed, the faster the better. When she senses an increase in the angle of lean on the bike she gets quite excited. She immediately stands up on the tank and looks through the corners! There are quite a few sport bike riders out there who have thought they were doing pretty well as they cranked their machines through a tight twisty, only to sense another bike coming around them on the outside. It's a wonder none have fallen off with the shock of seeing Bundy flash past staring at them as Tex, sometimes even with a pillion on the back too, puts the hammer down.

At Christmas time Tex has developed a habit of dressing up Bundy in her own little Santa Claus suit, a tradition that has never failed to bring smiles to the faces of people of all ages. At the end of 2013 the duo was travelling through Orange, New South Wales, just two days before Christmas when Tex spotted an approaching police roadblock where they were operating a Random Breath Testing unit. The police officers were preoccupied with several drivers that they had pulled over into their cone-marked siding, all under the watchful eye of a crusty old sergeant who was leaning against an adjacent fence. The sergeant had obviously noticed Tex coming down the road, but initially the Guzzi was too far away for him to identify the object on the front.

As Tex drew nearer, the sergeant's casual glance became a stare, then he unfolded his arms, shook his head and dropped his jaw as Tex rode past, giving him a friendly wave. Remember, it is illegal for a dog to ride on the front of a registered motorcycle, unless it carries a special certificate of authorisation. As Tex sailed off into the distance, he couldn't stop laughing, thinking that the sergeant would probably scramble a highway patrol car and send one of his boys after him. Just when Tex thought the police had forgotten about him he heard the unmistakeable sound of a siren and, checking his rear-vision mirrors, saw the all-too-familiar sight of flashing blue and red lights. Tex pulled over, unclipped Bundy from her safety strap, flipped up his helmet and smiled a greeting to the officer with, 'The boss send you after me?'

Grinning from ear to ear, the officer replied, 'You nearly gave him a coronary — he said he must've been seeing things — that a bike just went zipping past with a Blue Heeler perched on top of the tank — and the dog was dressed in a bloody Santa Claus suit!' They enjoyed a good laugh, wished each other a Merry Christmas and went their separate ways.

Bundy has that effect on just about everyone. Even frustrated motorists sitting in their cars in peak-hour M2 gridlock, tempers frayed and potential road rage approaching boiling point, will melt and smile. Their typical reaction is to forget their woes and reach for their phone to grab a snapshot as the duo glides past. Bundy has easily become the most photographed dog in Australia, which means that whatever bike she is riding also becomes the most photographed motorcycle in the country.

Riding on Tex's motorcycle aside, Bundy's other great passion is sausages — she can never get enough of them. During the course of a typical year she will cover around 80,000 kilometres on Tex's bike attending charity events, quite a few of which involve a barbecue or some other opportunity for getting stuck into the tucker. It's not a problem when one of her admirers slips her the odd snag, but when 30 people all do the same thing at the same event, Bundy is suddenly threatened with an obesity issue. Add to that the inactivity of sitting on a motorcycle for long stretches between engagements and it's easy for her to add a couple of kilos without even trying. Like all stumpy-tailed Smithfield Blue Heelers, Bundy doesn't appear to have a tail, so when she puts on weight she tends to look a bit like a cuddly fat wombat!

Since Tex first trained Bundy to ride back in 2006, the duo has travelled over 700,000 kilometres on Australian roads, all without incident. Apart from her impressive charity work, Bundy also boasts some credentials that are the envy of most other dogs. She proudly carries the title of 'fastest dog in the world', having been clocked riding on a motorcycle at a speed of 283 kilometres per hour. But even though she already holds the fastest dog title, Tex has plans to take her on a run across the salt flats at Lake Gairdner, South Australia, with the aim of making her the first dog on the planet to join the 200mph club. Yes, that's a whopping 322 kilometres per hour!

Bundy's amazing achievements aren't just limited to motorcycling on dry land. In 2009 she and Tex rode a jet ski from Phillip Island in Victoria to Cairns in far north Queensland!

Bundy also enjoys special privileges in quite a number of outback pubs that are off-limits to other canines. Signs that say 'No Dogs Allowed' do not apply to her! Bundy was specially trained by a behavioural specialist to be an accredited 'assistance dog' to Tex, who has post-traumatic stress disorder as a result of several submarine patrols during the Cold War. Not only that, but Bundy is also an accredited 'therapy dog' for her hospital work.

The organisations that benefit from Tex and Bundy's fundraising activities include Project KidSafe, Prostate Cancer Foundation of Australia, Breast Cancer Research, Tarangoa Blue (Marine Debris Initiative), Lifeline/Black Dog Ride and others. They also assist government-funded tourism initiatives such as 'The Legendary Pacific Coast', which promotes a variety of holiday attractions between Sydney and Brisbane where motorcycle- and pet-friendly establishments are given special emphasis.

So, if you happen to come across a stumpy-tailed Blue Heeler riding a motorcycle bearing the number plate 'DOGGY', think about putting your hand in your pocket to support one of the duo's many worthwhile charities — and you'll end up with a smile on your face too!

*Keep up to date with Tex and Bundy's charity fundraising adventures on their website (www.texandbundy.com.au) or Facebook ('Tex O'Grady' or 'Tex & Bundy Charity Fundraisers').*

# The Old Bullock Road

Sean Greenhill
Kirrawee, NSW

A man in his late 30s, dressed casually with neat black hair, entered the pub and looked around slowly as he made his way to the bar, pausing to take in the 10 or so men drinking and playing pool, noting their ages, their clothes. The bartender, a short man with a red face and shirtsleeves rolled up to his elbows, broke away from the small group of men gathered at the end of the bar.

'What can I get you, son?' the bartender asked.

'Do you have a Corona?' the man replied.

The bartender nodded, grunted as he bent low to get the Corona, opened it with a deft flick of his wrist and put it down on the bar. He took the man's $20, rang up the sale without looking and slapped the change down beside the beer. 'So,' he enquired, 'are you just passing through or up here on holidays?'

'Neither actually,' the man replied before taking a long swig of his beer. 'I've come up here for work. My name's Nickolas, Nickolas Marker. My friends call me Nick. I'm a journalist.'

The bartender's face hardened slightly, but he shook the hand Nick offered. 'Brian,' he said, 'Brian Potter, I'm the owner of the Commercial. You've come about the ghost, right?'

Nick, sensing the change in the bartender's mood, smiled and chuckled. 'You got me,' he admitted, 'guilty as charged. I was hoping to speak to some of the locals, get their opinions and see how they feel about all this publicity. You don't mind, do you?'

Brian shrugged. 'I'm not going to stop you, but I don't want any of my customers upset either. You can ask around, but don't push it, or I'll have to ask you to leave.'

'Sure,' Nick agreed, 'no problem.' He'd dealt with small-town people before and knew if they didn't want to talk then no amount of cajoling would change their minds. 'Is there anyone in particular that I should speak to? Maybe someone who has been living here since before these stories started.'

'Maybe,' Brian replied. He glanced at one of the men in the group at the end of the bar then back to Nick. 'I'll see.' He walked down to the group and said something Nick couldn't hear. The four men listened closely to the bartender, and then turned as one to stare at Nick. Eventually a small thin frail-looking man with grey hair nodded and stepped down off his stool. He picked up his glass, drank the little that remained in one gulp, then put it down and walked up to where Nick sat.

'My name's Charlie,' he said, taking the stool beside Nick. 'Charlie Wakelin. You want to know about the ghost?'

'Yes,' Nick replied. 'You know I'm a journalist, right?'

Charlie nodded.

'Good,' Nick said as he pulled a pen out of his jacket and flipped to a new page of his notepad. 'You don't mind if I take a few notes?'

'So long as you don't use my name or quote me,' Charlie stated in a soft tone that told Nick it wasn't a point he was willing to negotiate. 'I'll answer your questions and I'll tell you what I know, but you'll have to confirm it for yourself.'

'Sure.' Nick smiled, humouring the old man. 'Of course; anything you tell me will be confidential, off the record. I just need the notes to remind me, that's all.' He gave another reassuring smile. 'How long have you lived in the area, Charlie?'

'All my life,' Charlie told him, '67 years, boy and man. Still live in the same house I was born in.'

Perfect, Nick thought. Born and bred. If I play this right, I can get everything I need from him then I'll be back in Sydney in a few hours and sleeping in my own bed tonight. 'So,' he said, deciding to dive straight in to see how the old man would react, 'are the stories about the ghost true?'

Charlie didn't answer immediately. He looked down to his hands as if gathering his thoughts, and then back up again. 'That all depends on what stories you've been listening to. Some of you journalists down in Sydney will print just about anything to sell your papers.'

'True, Charlie, true,' Nick conceded. 'I'm not going to deny it.' He picked up his Corona, took a sip and then looked over the bottle at the old man. 'But if you disregard the UFO theory, it comes back to the same story. Supposedly, about 20 years ago, some kids were speeding along The Old Bullock Road with their lights off when they hit and killed a young local guy on a motorbike. Ever since then, late at night when there are no other cars on the road, a speeding driver will suddenly see a strange bright light in his rear window. The light seems to be following him, or chasing him. People say it's the ghost of the deceased kid on his motorbike. That's the basic story, isn't it?'

'Yes,' Charlie agreed. 'That's what they say.'

'Okay,' Nick smiled, 'so we may as well start with the guy on the motorbike who got killed. I did a quick check on the records before I came up, but I couldn't find anything in the archives going back about 20 years. Do you know if there really was a motorcyclist killed on The Old Bullock Road?'

Charlie looked down into his hands again, but when he looked back up he didn't look at Nick directly. 'Yes,' he replied, his voice soft, 'yes, there was. His name was Charles Michael Wakelin Junior. He was my son.'

'Your son?' Nick said slowly, his tone neutral, trying to keep the surprise and doubt from his voice. 'Your son was the young motorcyclist who was killed?'

Charlie nodded. 'He loved that bike.' He smiled at the memory. 'Started saving up for it when he was 14. Don't know how many times Mary begged him not to buy it, and then begged him to sell it, but he never listened to her, or to me. Just used to repeat the same thing all the time: "Got to ride,

Dad. Live to ride, ride to live." Even had the slogan air-brushed on his tank.'

Both Nick and Charlie sat in silence as they harboured private thoughts. Nick didn't believe there was a ghost, and if there was one, he doubted it could be coerced into performing tricks for speeding drivers. More than likely it was just the old man's way of keeping his son's memory alive. But if nothing else came of this trip, at least he would have a good puff piece that would pull at his readers' heartstrings. He felt for old Charlie though. He decided the least he could do was show him and his 20-year-old grief the respect they were due.

'You really believe in the ghost out on The Old Bullock Road, don't you, Charlie?' he eventually asked quietly. 'You truly believe it's the ghost of your son, don't you?'

Charlie took a deep, slow breath, then turned his head and looked Nick eye to eye. 'And I suppose that you don't believe there's a ghost at all, do you, Nick?' he asked in a friendly tone. 'You're from the big city where people are too smart, and too educated, to believe in things like ghosts and UFOs and black panthers roaming the Blue Mountains. No, those sorts of things are for gullible country hicks like us, aren't they?'

'Not at all,' Nick protested, although the truth was that he had lived all his life in the big smoke, and tended to think that people in the country had a simpler way of looking at life. 'I don't think like that at all, Charlie. I just think that if this light that people have claimed to see is real, well it can be explained logically, scientifically, that's all. I mean, it could be as simple as the cars' tail-lights shining back off the reflectors in the middle of the road. You'd probably only notice it late at night when it's dark and there are no other cars around. It would explain why the light jumps around and flickers.'

Charlie nodded. 'Yes,' he said, 'I've heard that theory, but it doesn't explain why it's only seen by young people who are speeding.'

Nick waved one hand dismissively. 'I've been thinking about that. Maybe it's a strobe effect that only becomes visible at high speed; we know teenagers are more apt to drive dangerously than older people. Or maybe everyone can see it, but older people are just too embarrassed to admit they've been speeding. Or maybe older people slow down when they think they've seen it, and so the effect stops.' He shrugged his shoulders. 'Or maybe teenagers are just more observant, or more impressionable, than we are.'

'So that's it then, eh?' Charlie asked. 'You'll take a few photos and write a story about how "quaint" we all are up here and forget about it tomorrow.'

'I'm not going to lie to you, Charlie,' Nick admitted. 'I don't believe in ghosts, but my opinion doesn't really matter. I'm a journalist. My editor has given me one day to get up here, check it out and get back. I'll write what I find out. I'll report any alternative theories or explanations I come across, and I'll let the readers decide for themselves. That's the best I can do with the limited time and resources available to me. You have to understand that.'

Charlie didn't speak, but put one hand in his pants pocket and pulled out a black leather wallet worn smooth by years of use. He opened the wallet, thumbed through the assortment of folded papers until he found the one he was looking for. He unfolded the paper, smoothed it out and studied it for a moment, then slid it across the bar to Nick.

'What's this?' Nick asked as he picked up the paper.

'Rego papers,' Charlie told him.

Nick ran his eye over the registration document, noting the date and printed receipt number. 'This is current,' he said. '1985 Ducati 900. Number plate CMW 001.' He raised one eyebrow. 'CMW? I presume that stands for Charles Michael Wakelin?'

Charlie nodded.

'You've kept his bike registered this whole time? For 20 years?' Nick asked incredulously.

Charlie shook his head. 'His bike was destroyed in the accident,' he explained, 'a total write-off. And the number plates were returned to the Roads Department. I know they were, I took them in myself. And yet every year we get the rego sticker for a bike that doesn't exist any more.'

Charlie allowed himself a faint smile as he gazed at the registration document. 'You'll probably explain it away as being some sort of computer error or other, but I know the truth.' He looked up at Nick, his expression intense. 'My son's still out there. He's out there for sure, and he's racing anyone silly enough to challenge him, just like he did when he was alive.'

'Have you ever been out there yourself, Charlie?' Nick asked. 'Have you ever tried to contact him since the accident?'

Charlie shook his head again. 'Mary never wanted us to when she was alive,' he admitted. 'Charles was our only son, and she loved him as much as I did, but she couldn't bring herself to go out there. She thought it was wrong.' He held out his wrinkled hands, showing Nick how they were shaking gently. 'And now I'm too old.'

Poor bastard, Nick thought. His kid's an urban legend, his wife is dead, and he can't even get around by himself. Those guys at the end of the bar are probably all he's got.

'Look, Charlie,' he said, 'I'm intrigued. I've decided to stay over and check this out. I'm going to go out on The Old Bullock Road late tonight and do a few runs up and down to see if I can see this light. I don't want you to get your hopes up, but if you'd like to come along, I'll take you with me.'

'Yes,' Charlie smiled, 'yes, I'd like that.'

### Journalist Nickolas Marker killed in car accident

*Colleagues and friends have been shocked by the death of journalist Nickolas Marker while driving in the Hunter Valley region yesterday.*

*Mr Marker, 38, was investigating the recent spate of reports of paranormal activity in the Newcastle area when* his car hit a tree on *The Old Bullock Road* at approximately 1am. Mr Marker and his passenger, Charles Wakelin, 67, both suffered severe head injuries and were transferred to Newcastle Private Hospital, where they were pronounced dead on arrival. Police believe that excessive speed may have contributed to the accident and have once again issued a warning to drivers who speed in an attempt to summon the 'Old Bullock Road ghost'.

This latest accident follows reports from several locals who claim to have seen the ghost while driving in the vicinity of the accident. Folklore suggests that a vehicle travelling at a dangerous speed will summon a motorcycle-mounted ghost, which suddenly appears as a bright white light behind the speeding vehicle. A police spokeswoman said, 'We want irresponsible drivers to know that the only bright light they'll see in their rear-vision mirror will be the red and blue lights of a police car.'

A full accident report is being prepared for the coroner.

# Granny Annie's Postie

Anne Appleby
Bermagui, NSW

In 2007 my husband, an avid motorbike man, purchased a postie bike and announced with puffed-out chest that this was a gift for me. I was 58 at the time and had never had the opportunity to ride solo; pillion had always been my place.

It was an awesome gift. With great trepidation I accepted his beautiful postie with tact, diplomacy and grace, thinking to myself, oh god, I hope he is a patient teacher. My darling also gave me the link to the RTA website so I could study for a learner's permit. I booked in then sat for the exam. Oh my, it became my turn to puff out my chest and boast, because I scored 100 per cent! Maybe a middle-aged grandmother on a postie bike could do this after all — I must have had some nous to gain a perfect score!

The day of reckoning arrived. We were going to a town 30 kilometres away on a test run. The road from Bermagui to Tathra was fraught with hairpin bends and sheer drops to gullies below. I could do this. With determination we both set out.

Our driveway was gravelled and decidedly steep. My husband went first on his bike. Very slowly I followed him, managing to get to the top without incident. We made it to town and stopped awhile for coffee and talked about my first ride. He said he was very proud of me. We jumped back on the bikes for our return journey.

Alas, on the way home I quite inexplicably mounted a rock wall and came down the other side with the bike half atop of me. SPLAT! What a horror, and all I could think was did anyone catch a glimpse of Granny Annie hurtling over the rocks with legs splayed and a look of pure horror upon her wrinkled brow? My pride hurt far more than the bruises I sustained. Sympathetically, hubby gave me a much needed breather to compose myself for the rest of the ride. I felt sick, but with an air of false bravado that shouted 'I can do this', we set off again for home. I did do it too, without any further problems. I even managed to ride down the very steep, slippery gravel driveway when we reached our house. My head was growing bigger along with my rising confidence. I had a renewed sense of self-worth, having overcome the big challenge with dignity.

The very next day I took the postie out on my own and rode into town. All went well, and on the return trip I again managed to negotiate our horrific gravel driveway unscathed. I hoped that ungainly rock-climbing incidents were now behind me.

The following week I wanted to show off to a friend how clever I was in conquering this new bike. It had been raining and the entry to my friend's property was blocked by a deep puddle of water that I thought was far too deep to traverse. With a sense of determination I proceeded to try and ride around the puddle, but could not understand why the bike shivered, shook, slid and then hurled me off, cracking my scone on a tree root. Thank goodness for my helmet!

Shaken and uttering several oaths and expletives, I righted the bike. Holding my winded tummy and gasping rhythmically for breath, I tried to kick-start that blasted postie. Try as I may, the bloody thing would not kick over. I walked the 500 metres to the property and asked my friend's husband if he would try to start it for me. He was a big strong chap and on the third attempt he had it going. I pushed the postie past the puddle and hopped on. I rode it into town and stopped at the wharf. I was really quite shaken and in retrospect somewhat concussed. I couldn't find my beloved and thought, what the heck, I'll just ride home again, it's only 10 kilometres.

Well, that infernal bike would not kick over. I had probably damaged something in the fall. I reluctantly rang my husband's mobile and he gallantly came to my assistance. At that stage I didn't tell him that I had come another cropper. Why worry him, and besides, I couldn't bear his piteous 'what a loser' look.

I rode home feeling terribly unworthy of my postie gift, only to find that yet another challenge lay before me. After the recent rains our driveway was a disgusting mess. How could anyone conquer it on skinny postie tyres? But ha-HA! I got down that dastardly excuse for a driveway with my sense of achievement soaring.

I didn't ride again for a while because I didn't trust those skinny tyres in the inclement weather conditions. Well, that was what I told myself. Then I awoke one morning to glorious sunshine and my beloved said, 'Great day for a bike ride.' He set off on his bike and I agreed that I would meet him a little later at the wharf, which I did, and thoroughly enjoyed the experience.

Riding back home again along the country roads was glorious. Dry roads and sunshine, which meant our dreaded entrance should have been okay. I proceeded down the steep drive. Then my skinny front tyre hit a loose rock and I fell off. The bike slithered along beside me as we both travelled down the gravel. We took forever to come to a halt.

The next day my beloved parked the postie at the wharf with a huge 'For Sale' sign on it. It sold in 10 minutes.

I felt somewhat betrayed, but knew in my heart of hearts that pillion riding or bicycling would prove to be the safer option for Granny Annie.

# Metaphysics and Motorcycles

Simon Beatty
Hawthorne, QLD

The Committee is meeting in a distant galaxy many light years in the future.

The Members, the ultimate expression of power at the very peak of evolution, discarded their stumbling physical bodies long ago. Their amorphous energy is eternal, but they face a problem because something has gone seriously wrong with the development of the human race. 'It is beyond logic,' they murmur. 'These humans are the only beings capable of solving Schrödinger's theorem in their heads, but they have ceased responding to stimuli. The digital age has caused them to grow lethargic, demotivated and lazy. It appears very few humans have retained the will to win; the boy Aaron and his brother Izzy, they are our only hope.' The Committee puzzles over this enigmatic problem and a consensus takes shape. 'Let's pay our protégés a visit,' they resolve. 'Let's travel back in time and drop in on Earth 2024.'

And the world turns.

The Committee Members are secretly thrilled at the prospect of visiting Earth again. Not just because it's Earth, but because it's Phillip Island, Australia, where brothers Aaron and Izzy are about to enter an epic motorcycle battle that will transport them beyond the limits of physical endurance; they will be attempting to transcend the laws of physics in breathtaking feats of racetrack lunacy. The Committee Members, having had human bodies some 20 billion years previously, empathise with the brothers and their mammoth challenge. However, there is no room for paternalistic benevolence in their collective psyche because running the

Universe must meet Hubble's paradigm. Failure is unheard of; it couldn't be more serious.

The Members nod in agreement, one to another. 'Izzy's the one. He may only be 14, but look at his aura — it exhibits the same iridescence as ours. Oh yes, he's the da Vinci of 2024, we'll invest in him.' When the Committee speaks or makes a pronouncement, everybody listens, because they're the ultimate voice, the supreme power in the Universe. Their form is pure energy, coherent, dynamic, omnipresent megaflux.

The race has started as Aaron nestles beside the Phillip Island racetrack, holding Izzy's lap board. He is unaware that the Committee is hovering far overhead at the edge of space, spectating. Aaron is also unaware that if Izzy loses the race and drifts into obscurity, then the human race is doomed. Of all the humans on planet Earth, Aaron and Izzy alone carry genes infused with intact survival markers, otherwise known as 'the will to win'. Can the brothers topple the forces assembled against them on both the physical and metaphysical levels?

Aaron speaks to no one, mainly because he is totally focused on the screaming dots which are blurring into view as tortured tyres tramp for traction when the leading bunch of bikes blind into Doohan's.

'Come on, Izzy,' Aaron grits out through clenched teeth, willing his brother to dominate the pack. 'Mate, come on, you can do it!'

There's an immense collective 'ooh' from the Phillip Island crowd as they spot the blood-red missile hurtling towards the first right-hander at over 250k's. Izzy is skimming fairings with Poggy, Lochi and Casey when, as though in a high-speed ballet, their right knees act as air-brakes in one orchestrated movement. Not one of these gladiators give a single millimetre as their eyes lock onto turn two and they shift their weight through a central fulcrum for the gut-wrenching left-hander.

Aaron's competitive mind processes information at the speed of light. His role is to use any means to empower Izzy, the current world champion, to speak with the voice of a prophet to his fan base worldwide. The Committee expects yet another win, but in order to dominate, the brothers have to walk where no human has ever been before.

Izzy's little plastic cockpit is a cacophony of sound which shreds his senses as he blasts through the envelope of gladiatorial combat, willing his screaming engine to give him more. He's the trail-blazer punching through the atmosphere as the other two riders tuck into the relatively still air of his slipstream. Man, it's extreme.

Aaron squints and clenches his fists as he glimpses Izzy riding at an impossible angle around the Southern Loop ... then Izzy gets crossed up and another 'ooh' vents out of the crowd. A spectator in a brown Driza-Bone mutters, 'C'mon, Izzy, what d'ya expect on cold tyres?' Even this seasoned spectator gives out an 'aah' along with everybody else as a puff of amber dust hangs in the air. Aaron grins, knowing his brother has rescued the bike by controlling it with his left knee and elbow as his titanium sliders spit sparks. The wagging headstock is reminiscent of a brumby's snorting bid for freedom as Izzy takes the bike beyond any mechanical law that governs adhesion or centrifugal force.

In the upper amorphous reaches of the Phillip Island ether, the Committee studies the rictus of effort reflected on Izzy's face, indicating his sheer determination to rise above any adversary. That these brothers appear to be the right choice is noted with satisfaction, but even so, to relax at this juncture would be premature. The Members' energies fuse as a quantum nod signals their unanimous resolve, but a shadow of doubt swirls around them like a rising vapour. Will the boy win? They concede that Izzy is pushing the envelope, but then again crossing metaphysical boundaries is the norm for these Aussie lads.

On board, Izzy's got enough on his mind as he takes the ram-air effect on his torso, using his body as a 'chute to slow the howling missile when Honda Curve fills his screen. He downshifts four gears and the engine wails, gnashing its teeth in protest, the chain vibrating with nine tonnes of tension. The carbon-fibre brakes glow cherry red as they bite — and they bite deep. He explodes out of the corner and it's all about streamlining as he tucks in and lines up his helmet with the Perspex cut-out in the screen. He then hauls the bike into position ready for Siberia. For a millisecond his cold blue eyes meet those of Aaron.

And time stops!

It never stops, but like a spoked wheel when it's on the point of revolving the other way, there is a point of hesitation. It's called the 'zenith area' (physicists call it the 'neutral zone' or the 'neutral dimension') and this is when the world holds its breath. At this precise moment Izzy, the planet's most respected world champion, leaves his human shell and joins forces with his brother's psyche. For sure, his body is still racing in a 27-lap Grand Prix, but energy-wise the brothers are psychologically united, constituting the most formidable force ever unleashed in the cosmos.

'We'll show 'em,' mutters Aaron, thinking of all those jerks in white coats with stethoscopes around their necks, poking at him and trying to make him respond to their infantile psychometric tests. His quantum mind, one that can beat literally anyone at three-dimensional chess, sniggers at the memory of their vapid attempts while he engages on another plane; his thought processes are glacial.

Meanwhile the Committee is becoming unsettled, off balance. They are unused to not having total control. Not only could Izzy lose the race, but they have reason to worry about Aaron's occasional lapses of logic. Foremost in their collective mind is the knowledge that he has at times been unable to make decisions that accord with the way they run the Universe. Doubts arise. Are they about to lose control? Their energies probe every corner of creation and the response is irrevocably the same: the absence of logic in the brothers' brains represents a level of risk that could threaten the future of mankind. In a nutshell, these boys are about to either save the world — or destroy it!

Aaron is conversing with his alter-ego about race tactics when the phrase 'absence of logic' plummets from the ether and zips into his brain. Faster than a bullet he responds, 'No logic? Bullshit! Of course you can't detect any logic because you haven't the moral framework through which to assess logic. We're not a game to amuse you guys. You are old, your thoughts are old. Izzy and I are your future, the planet's future, so don't you dare play games with us. Leave us alone and we'll re-jig the destiny of our galaxy.'

A sinister neural path threads through his mind as his brain massages the appalling implications of a future saturated with the stinking thinking of an all-powerful, tired, worn-out amoral Committee. He remembers energy cannot be created or destroyed, and the Committee is the epitome of energy. Can he and Izzy emerge victorious? Only a nanosecond has elapsed while Aaron fuses with his brother's vibrant plasmic energy, causing shock waves to rattle between them faster than the speed of light. They are in the place where thoughts that make thoughts emanate.

If a casual observer was to stand behind Aaron, he would appear just like any other kid at the racetrack, with his back-to-front red baseball cap squashed firmly on his head. Except for one thing. He's the only person in shorts and T-shirt with the track temperature at a mere 14.5 degrees. But the little fella is beyond the reach of the chill wind that's blowing in from Bass Strait because he's identifying with his brother's anxiety: a concern that a wet track could derail Izzy's epic ride. Aaron whispers, 'I'm gonna leave my skin now, Izzy,' as he braces himself for a trans-dimensional jolt. 'I've got a big job to do, mate. Stay safe and keep her nailed to the stops. Oh yeah, don't worry about the tyres because I'm not gonna let it rain ... okay?'

Izzy nods. He tears off a clear-vision strip as the front wheel paws the air on the blind summit of Siberia. 'Thanks, mate. Get back before the end of the race, will ya? I need you with me all the way. Good luck, buddy.'

The little form at the fence doesn't move, but he's gone.

The Committee Members snigger as they consider the ease with which they are attempting to manipulate the human race, but their jubilation is short lived as they see their protégé Aaron assume and then discard several physical shapes, shapes which are deeply embedded in the primitive areas of the human brain, some mythical and others based on the most ubiquitous forms of reptilian crocs and cockroaches. The Members have become complacent due to their unquestionable power over every aspect of the Universe's development, and they, in their cocoon of amorphous energy, scorn Aaron's perceived simplicity.

'Aah, I'm getting there,' mutters Aaron with a shudder as he wriggles out of a unicorn guise. 'I know what to do. I'm going back to the start of creation and I'll work forward; that way something must fit. I've just gotta get it right ... for the sake of Izzy and the future of the world. I know if I allow thoughts to transfer through my auditory loop I will be able to filter out the rot and make the right choice.'

As Izzy guns through the Haystack and fights the g's of Lukey Heights, heading for the fifth gear turns of laps 11 and 12, he whips off a telekinetic message to Aaron: 'Mate, look after your tail and toes, okay?' Aaron's mind receives a vision of an imperial dragon in all its karmic glory. In an instant he transforms, stretching to his full scaly height, checking out hands and feet that indicate the ultimate in preternatural power.

'Yeah, five fingers and five toes on each ... wow! That means I've got both Confucian and Zionic powers. Whew, how good is that?' He scans Bass Strait with yellow glinting eyes as the cruel wind probes his soft belly and, with a lazy flap of his metamorphic 10-metre wings, he approaches the black, menacing cloud formation that is threatening to bucket rain down on the island's racetrack far below. Icy shards of hail and spiky snow envelop his galactic armour and angry smoke pours from his distended nostrils as he hisses, 'You bastards, take on someone your own size ... not a kid motorcyclist.' With one sweep of his fleur-de-lis tail he splits the cumulus hammer-head into smithereens and peers into its murky depths.

It's lap 20 and Izzy's fighting his own battle down there on the dry track, and he's only holding onto the lead by going into unknown territory. He knows his tyres are being mercilessly punished as he hurtles down the 800-metre straight. He glances at the pit board and catches the vibes of frenetic frenzy from his mechanics. There's a strange buzzing sound in the cockpit, so he glances at the water temperature gauge and the rev counter. The blood drains from his lips. The buzzing is coming from the rev counter, which is vibrating against the stops, as far into the red zone as it can go, and he knows the shrieking engine could seize at any time. There's only one option, one he rarely exercises ... to back off. He can feel the satisfaction on Poggy's face as he slips in behind him, tailgating at over 240k's.

Having eliminated the chance of rain and hail, Aaron folds his leathery wings and spears into the black heart of the cloud. He sucks in nature's kinetic energy and like a ram jet he breaks into the ionosphere. It is this respite that gives him time to think matters through, and the dawn of realisation is stupefying because he has seen the effect, he knows the cause, and now he knows the reason. The Committee wants Izzy to self-destruct because he represents the threatening metaphor of the future!

'Huh,' he concludes, 'the only thing standing between us and the future is the Committee ... it's time for a showdown.' But before his treasonous thoughts can echo around his skull, he observes that the Committee has vacated its vantage point above Phillip Island. Gone. Faster than thought he surveys the cosmos, finding them in an instant, tucked away in a corner of the Milky Way.

A syrupy voice welcomes him, unperturbed that he is manifesting as an imperial dragon. 'Welcome, Aaron. We knew you'd come home eventually. Mankind is doomed, you know.'

'That's the devil in you talking! Okay, so you're having your fun, moving my planet on its axis and changing the seasons, but in your arrogance you have made a big mistake ... and you're looking at it right now. Me and Izzy are creations of your collective intelligence, but you have forgotten that we have your intelligence as well as our own. C'mon, I'll prove it; let's have a game of 11-dimensional chess. If I win the chess, and if Izzy wins on the island, you'll vacate our galaxy. Deal?'

History confirms that Aaron beat the Committee, but he had little time to bask in the glory.

'Aaron ... Aaron, are you there, mate? We've gotta do something quick, buddy. The last lap board's out, pal, and I'm balls out. Honest — I need ya, mate.'

Aaron turns himself into anti-matter and blazes from the Milky Way to Phillip Island, where 50,000 Aussies are yelling their hearts out, urging Izzy to finish riding the impossible race. Nobody except the Committee notices the body of a little boy at the fence shudder violently as his psyche joins his human shell. No one, that is, except for Izzy, who grinds out the words, 'Thanks, mate, I feel all joined up now. My tyres are burning up. This is goin' to be one hell of a final lap.'

Even the super-hot sticky slicks skip around as Izzy winds on the power again down Gardner Straight — surely nothing mechanical can withstand this abuse. The exhaust howls its devilish challenge as Izzy slick-shifts into top at the commentary box. Five riders, a congealing mass of bright colours, bullet down the straight. The shock waves buffet the soft tissue of the spectators as they switch their attention to the Southern Loop, where the cheering crowd is hearing a sound no human ear has heard before. Tortured metal, howling exhausts and squealing brakes set the scene as Izzy quarters down the leader. He's flat out in fourth, shifts to fifth and peels into the left-hander drifting wider, and wider, in a 10g drift thrusting Izzy closer and closer to the rumble strip. With one accord the spectators are pulled to their feet as he blurs past them and their collective will for him to succeed tips the balance.

He bombs into turns four and five a fraction of a second behind Poggy as each of the spectators turns to his neighbour and sneers wanly. They are drained. The acrid smell of fibre against sintered steel drifts across the stands. The brakes vainly try to dissipate the colossal forces of dynamic energy created by supreme braking. Little Aaron watches in horror as Izzy defies science and the laws of gravity. Izzy pins the red machine onto the stops, but it's not enough.

'Kill, kill!' Aaron screams telepathically. Izzy acknowledges him with a psychic nod and starts to use the kill button to zip the gears into place. The vital thousandths of a second are telling on Poggy's lead as the pack disappears in a haze of blue smoke and burnt rubber, screaming towards Lukey and MG.

The high-speed game of outmanoeuvring an opponent is a huge adrenaline rush. As they swoop into MG, Izzy knows his exit speed has to be much greater than his opponent's, but Poggy's got the crucial outside line. Izzy swallows and glances across. The decision is made; really there's no choice. He leans on Poggy, hearing the fairings scrape, and then feels Poggy's front wheel biting into his leathers as the Italian mouths insults inside his helmet, then gets hopelessly crossed up. The crowd erupts as Izzy stands triumphantly on his foot pegs during his cooling-down lap, acknowledging their huge support, but his joy is short lived as an Italian machine goes out of control and they both land in a heap in the kitty litter. Who else but the fiery Poggy!

Izzy gets his crown which consummates the inter-galactic deal between Aaron and the Committee. It's sad, but no one gives the little boy wearing a red baseball cap a second glance as they walk past him. A very tired little boy at that; one who has just saved the world.

# Meeting by Accident

Steve Edmonds
Palm Cove, QLD

A lot of people meet the love of their life at a party or bar, or, if they're lucky, they score an introduction through a mutual friend. Failing that, some poor sods have to run the gauntlet of the online dating services. Not me though. I met the love of my life by accident, motorcycle accident. I'll never forget that day because the bittersweet memories have been permanently etched into my brain by the finger of fate. But before I get into the juicy details of how I met Brenda, I need to jump back a few years.

My parents reckon that I was born a highly independent extrovert and the first words I uttered were not 'mum' or 'dad', but rather 'I do it'. For my third birthday my dad bought me a little ride-on plastic motorcycle with trainer wheels which I loved to bits. By the time I was four I had somehow managed to remove the trainer wheels and learned how to scoot around on two wheels without losing my balance. As far as I can remember, it was at about this time that I developed a crazy bike routine that still causes people to crack up to this very day. I stumbled upon my trick by chance during the course of a family get-together when everyone was gathered around the outdoor barbecue.

I don't remember it all that clearly, but my dad says that I came coasting down the pathway into the midst of the crowd balanced on my plastic two-wheeler. When the little bike came to a standstill, instead of putting my feet out to steady myself, I kept my feet on the pegs and let the bike fall over sideways with me still crouching on the seat in a riding position. Apparently I just lay there, motionless on the ground, straddling the bike, while friends and rellies roared with laughter. Word got around about my party trick so I was encouraged to repeat the performance whenever there was a gathering. It sort of became my childhood specialty and I enjoyed the laughter and attention immensely. It seemed only natural when I was old enough to have my own real motorcycle that I would repeat the same stunt, especially after a few drinks. It looks really stupid but still gets a good laugh whenever I do it! By the time I hit my late teens I had a whole repertoire of stupid tricks and practical jokes, all of which tended to make me the life of the many parties to which I was regularly invited.

I was 22 when I met Brenda. By that time I had already had several other girlfriends and had developed a distinct preference for quiet, mysterious, introverted types of girls. I think the old maxim 'opposites attract' carries some truth because I tended to be repelled by extroverted females with personalities similar to mine.

Brenda came along smack bang in the middle of that golden era of Japanese motorcycles, 1982 to be precise. Back then the Japanese seemed to be getting their act together by producing fantastic motorcycles with engines, styling and prices that just happened to be what we, their customers, wanted. At the time I was riding a magnificent Yamaha XJ650RJ Seca, which I had bought brand new a few months earlier. After having owned a mishmash of other brands, mostly British and all second-hand clunkers, the Seca was heaven on two wheels. I loved the way it handled — it weighed only 230 kilograms with 20 litres in the tank — coupled with an amazing engine that delivered bucket loads of power through a very slick gearbox. The Japanese had stolen the Seca name from the Laguna Seca raceway in California, which gave the bike a bit of a racy image, designed to attract extroverted rev-heads like My Good Self.

Anyway, on the momentous day I met the love of my life I was out joyriding on my precious Seca. Winter had just passed the baton to spring, so there I was revelling in the warm sunshine, relishing perfect biking conditions. I had no particular destination in mind, simply enjoying the wind whistling up my nostrils. Riding along Pittwater Road at Collaroy, I was keeping up with the traffic when I spotted a wedding car coming towards me from the opposite direction. As it got closer, I recognised it as a 1920s Rolls-Royce Silver Ghost, festooned in ribbons with a bride sitting in the back. I still have a bit of a thing for exotic old cars, so as the Rolls went past my eyes followed it instead of watching the road ahead.

As the Rolls disappeared behind me, I turned my attention back to the road in front and was horrified to find that the traffic was stationary, everything had stopped for a red light. Everything, that is, except me! I was going way too fast to stop and didn't have enough time or space to manoeuvre around the car directly in front of me, which was a VW Beetle. I hit the anchors aggressively, locking up both wheels, but still smacked into the back of the VW hard enough to be thrown over the handlebars. Fortunately, the old Beetle had a pretty rounded profile, so after I landed on the roof I slid down the bonnet onto the road in front of the vehicle, taking one of the windscreen wipers with me.

On the spur of the moment I felt extremely angry that any car should stop so abruptly without warning, wrongly assuming that the car driver was at fault. Feeling shaken but with nothing broken, I rushed to the driver's side and wrenched the door open. Who was sitting there? No, it wasn't Brenda. The VW contained four nuns dressed in black and white habits, looking rather like traumatised penguins. My sanity returned so I respectfully closed the door and walked around to the back of the car to inspect the Seca. The bike was standing upright with the front wheel collapsed, wedged tight in the rear bumper of the Vee Dub.

As I stood there surveying the damage, one of the nuns, who by this time had all scrambled out of the vehicle, said, 'You're hurt.' I felt the back of my pants, which were wet — with blood.

I then realised that as I had tumbled over the roof of the car and slithered down the windscreen, the wiper mount had cut a deep gash through one buttock and partway down the back of my left leg. The next thing I knew I was in an ambulance heading for Emergency at Mona Vale Hospital. When we arrived an attendant wheeled me into an emergency room and told me that a doctor would be with me in a few moments.

In sauntered Brenda!

To this day I can still clearly recall the visual feast that triggered my emotional overload. My heart felt like the silver ball in a pinball machine as it raced around inside my chest, flashing the lights and ringing the bells. She filled out her nurse's uniform like a shrink-wrapped ripe peach, but that was only the beginning of the intrigue. Underneath the white nurse's cap her jet-black hair cascaded down her face, resembling the curtains in a movie theatre, with a pair of thick glasses penetrating the opening. The only facial feature I could see clearly was a pair of slightly parted rosebud lips revealing mildly bucked teeth. Buck teeth have always turned me on!

'Let-th have a look at your injurie-th,' lisped Brenda, whose name I didn't know at that stage, as she gently rolled me over onto my stomach and started cutting off my bloodied jeans. I almost forgot my bum was hurting as I tried to twist my head around to get a better look at her.

'What's ya name?' I asked, now totally oblivious to the pain.

'Th-tay th-till or I'll cut ya.'

I tried several times to strike up a conversation, but the only response was a soft giggle. Who was this mysterious woman? What did she really look like? Why wouldn't she engage in any conversation?

'Thi-th i-th gonna need th-ome th-titche-th,' her ruby-red lips lisped, followed by yet another giggle.

As if on cue an intern suddenly materialised and the two of them cleaned me up and inserted 38 stitches. But I still hadn't been able to get a decent look at Brenda.

'I bet ya feel thi-th,' she warned, followed by a giggle, as she plunged a large tetanus shot into my undamaged buttock. She was bloody right!

As soon as the procedure was finished, she and the intern disappeared without saying another word. Gone. I contemplated the possibility of limping off down the corridors trying to find her again, but my plan came to naught as an officious admin lady hustled me down to the emergency desk to sign forms.

'Who was the nurse that treated me?' I asked the penpusher.

'Oh, that's Brenda. Isn't she a sweetie?'

For the next few days all I could think about was Brenda and the Seca, almost in that order. After getting the bike into the repair shop, I plucked up my courage and phoned the main hospital switchboard, asking for Nurse Brenda. I was told she was on duty and couldn't come to the phone. I waited eight hours and phoned again, only to be told the same thing. I got really cranky and phoned a third time, this time asking for the person in charge, who turned out to be a really sweet Sister. She said it was not policy for nurses to take personal phone calls while on duty, but anyway, Brenda had just gone off on three weeks' leave. She told me that if I wanted to leave my number and a short message, she would ensure that Brenda received it when she returned.

It was nearly three weeks later, after my stitches had been removed and I could sit down without too much discomfort, that I got the Seca back from the repair shop. They had done a good job and the bike looked and rode like new. I had been uninsured so I had to stump up the $700 repair bill out of my own pocket before they would give me the bike back. But that wasn't the worst of it. In the meantime I had also received a letter from the nuns' insurance company demanding $2829.14 for repairs to their Beetle. I didn't have that sort of money so I stuffed the Letter of Demand in the rubbish bin, praying that God would somehow sort the nuns out; after all, they were really His responsibility, not mine. Added to that, He had far more money than I did, He could afford it. So instead of stressing out about my pitiful financial circumstances, I decided to concentrate on something even more exciting than being back on two wheels again: Brenda!

She was still very much on my mind so I was hoping like crazy that I would get a phone call from her during the week after she returned from holiday. Ten days later I had still heard nothing and was agonising over whether to phone her or maybe even pop in at the hospital on the off-chance of seeing her. I was about to dial the hospital when the phone rang. I nearly jumped out of my skin with excitement when I heard Brenda's voice lisp, 'I-th that you, Th-tevie?' I tried to come across as cool, calm and collected, but my chest felt very tight, causing my voice to escalate an octave.

She didn't know who I was until I mentioned 'sliced buttock' and '38 stitches', then she confessed that she remembered me clearly. She readily consented to our first date, which ended up a barefoot stroll along Mona Vale beach at dusk, sucking banana Paddle Pops while the Seca sat idly by, jealously watching from the car park. She wore a baseball cap and hung her hair across her face, so I still wasn't too sure exactly what she looked like, but what I could see I liked a lot. This just added to her intrigue and sort of confirmed my impression that she could be the girl of my dreams: quiet, mysterious and introverted.

'Have you ever ridden a motorcycle?'

'Can't th-ay that I have, but I'd love to give it a go.'

I borrowed a mate's helmet for her and the next Saturday evening saw us weaving in and out the centre line along Mona Vale Road. After a tentative few kilometres clutching me like I was a gold brick, she started to relax and really enjoy the excitement of two wheels. She was the perfect pillion. She didn't try to counterbalance against the angle of the bike in corners like some novices, she just sat there like a rock. After the first few k's, she actually started squealing with excitement when I put the hammer down.

We started dating regularly and as she got to know my riding buddies she really got into the biking thing. She jumped at the chance of riding pillion at every opportunity. She started talking about learning to ride herself, maybe even buying her own bike. I was so wrapped up in Brenda that I immediately dirt-binned the second Letter of Demand from the insurance company, unconcerned that they were threatening legal action if I didn't pay up within 30 days. Bring it on! With Brenda sitting on the back of the Seca, clinging to me in a bear hug that got progressively more passionate as time went on, I couldn't give a stuff about the insurance company.

After the first few dates I got to see all of Brenda's face, which was prettier than I had imagined: large round brown eyes and dimples everywhere. She was very short-sighted, so much so that without her Coke-bottle-bottom glasses she was as blind as a bat. She was really easy-going and fitted in well with the crowd, but hated being the centre of attention. She loved practical jokes as long as she was a spectator and not a participant. It was this aspect of her personality that almost caused us to break up.

It happened after I had been invited to a friend's 21st birthday party, which was being held at a house in Burwood. Brenda was working that night, leaving me to head off to the party solo. It had been raining so I tossed up whether to ride the Seca or get a lift with a mate, but the bike won as I hadn't done much riding in the previous week, and I missed it. Threading my way along Parramatta Road in light traffic, I was taking it pretty easy because the road was greasy and my visor was misted with road grime, affecting visibility. Just as I turned off Parramatta Road into a side street, I got a brief glimpse of a pedestrian standing on the kerb in the dark. Without warning he stepped out in front of me and I hit him. I was probably only doing about 10k's, just a little above walking speed, but we both went down. The bloke was dead drunk and pretty well unhurt by the collision. I was unhurt, but the bike sustained minor scratches on the front guard and rear-vision mirror housing. A witness called the police and ambulance, so while I was waiting I took off my leather jacket and spread it over the drunk, who was by then fast asleep in the gutter. The police arrived and were surprisingly sympathetic. After writing up a report and taking my details, they told me to take off and enjoy my evening. The whole thing was such a minor incident that I hardly thought any more about it, until a week later when Brenda and I were at a Sunday afternoon barbecue with friends.

We were all seated at an outdoor table and I was in the middle of telling one of my many jokes when Brenda tugged my sleeve and asked for my cigarette lighter. Somewhat distracted by my comedy act, I reached into my leather jacket pocket and handed her what I thought was my lighter. I was startled by her squeal. I glanced down and instead of holding my lighter, I had given her a set of filthy nicotine-stained false teeth! The crowd roared with laughter as she screamed again, dropped the filthy teeth and rushed into the house sobbing. I was stunned. I had never seen the teeth before. I rushed in to comfort her, but she was angry, embarrassed and inconsolable. She wouldn't believe my protestations of innocence, accusing me of playing a practical joke at her expense in front of all our friends. She wouldn't speak to me and asked someone else to drive her home. I was bereft.

As I lay in bed that night, I had two big issues on my mind. Number one was Brenda and the grotty teeth. The other was a further summons that had arrived in the mail that week from the insurance company's solicitors, launching legal action to recoup $6116.28 for repairs and legal costs associated with my Beetle prang. I must admit the legal letter worried me, but not as much as my falling-out with Brenda. I kept massaging the 'teeth issue' over and over in my mind, until suddenly the penny dropped. Of course! When I hit the drunk at Burwood I had covered him with my leather jacket to keep him warm until the ambulance arrived. Either the impact with the bike had knocked his false teeth out, or else the ambos had removed them when they were checking him over. Whichever the case, someone must have assumed the jacket spread over the drunk belonged to him, so they popped his false teeth in the pocket so he wouldn't lose them! I refrained from the urge to phone Brenda straight away, as it was 2.20am, and I doubted that she would be in the right frame of mind to consider my explanation. I waited until morning, called and asked her simply to listen to my story. Fortunately, I had told her about knocking into the drunk shortly after it happened, so she believed me when I offered my explanation about the teeth. Our relationship survived and then continued to flourish, to the extent that we have now been married for nearly 30 years.

As luck would have it, the cost of the Beetle repairs was sorted out almost as easily.

Scared witless at the thought of being sued by an insurance company, I decided to try phoning the nun who had been driving the Vee Dub when I hit it. Maybe I could extract some compassion, get some sympathy, beg for mercy, have a go at sweet-talking the little old lady, or perhaps even get the repair costs taken care of on the Papal Budget.

When I got on to Sister Theresa I found her to be a very nice lady indeed, and she was quite upset to hear that I was about to be sued. Then she told me something that blew me away. She said that the same day I had run into the VW with my Seca, the NRMA had got the car running again, and she had then continued her trip to Asquith to visit friends. But before she got there, as she was sitting at a set of lights waiting to make a right-hand turn, a concrete truck had failed to stop and ploughed into the back of the Beetle. None of the occupants were hurt, but the insurance company had written off the VW. She had already received a full payout and was driving a new car.

I jumped on my Seca and shot down to Barry's place, where I found him out in his shed working on another of his Norton restorations. Barry was the baby-boomer equivalent of Wikipedia; he had a small smattering of knowledge about everything. Everyone who knew him trusted him, so any advice proffered in Barry's shed was considered gospel. After listening to my rundown on the Vee Dub saga and details of the pending legal action threatened by the insurance company, Barry spat a goolie into his sump oil bucket and licked his lips. 'They're bluffing, mate. Tell 'em to get stuffed.' It turned out Barry was right. Since the insurance company wasn't able to produce a repair quote before the Beetle was written off, they couldn't prove the extent of my damage, so they had no case against me. Not only was I free, but I had Brenda and the Seca.

I kept that bike for nearly a decade and always got a thrill when I heard Brenda say, 'Th-tevie, let-th go for a ride on the Th-eca.'

# My Man

Corinne MacKenzie
Carlton, VIC

It's Saturday night and my Man, as usual, is replaying the day's 'legend' moments after cruising with the boys at their off-road dirt bikers' nirvana in Gembrook, Victoria.

I am watching the scene from a camera mounted in my Man's goggles. The world suddenly spins and then comes to an abrupt halt, wet dirt and pebbles completely filling the screen. His sideways glance reveals the bike lying on its side half submerged in water, the treetops and sky below. The view switches back to the ground as two gloved hands appear, pawing and crawling towards the bike, accompanied by loud panting, puffing and the occasional expletive rasping through the microphone. The heavy breathing gets louder as gloved hands grasp the bike. In close-up the bike rocks back and forth, shrouded in a mist of blue smoke, engine revving madly. Then the world flips upside down, the camera coming to rest at ground level yet again. I hear the sounds of other bikes approaching, then voices. One of my Man's mates has arrived to help drag him and his bike out of the sucking mud.

What a wonderful invention, these high-definition digital goggle cams! They allow the Man, and me, to relive his incredible legend moments over and over, and over. Play, rewind, replay, and let's see that spectacular fall in slow motion. Brilliant! Yes, modern technology is such a treasure, permitting me to share his remarkable exploits.

Fresh video footage is gathered most weekends, when my Man and his mates suit up and head to the hills. They spend their days pitting their skills and endurance against the adrenaline-pumping ascents and descents of steep winding mountain trails. These two-wheeled warriors also revel in long straight stretches, accelerating hard with trees whipping past in a blur whenever they can get a clear run. During their adventures my Man and his co-legends constantly strive to conquer ever-greater challenges, seeking out deeply furrowed trails, fallen logs and, if it has been raining, slippery surfaces, thick layers of mud and water crossings galore.

As each weekend approaches, the volume of phone calls increases. The animated debates about their bikes and biking gear and destinations are not unlike me and my girlfriends preparing for a night out, comparing lipstick colours and outfits — something that the men would never concede.

My Man's bike is a 2001 Suzuki DRZ 400 — a much heavier bike than the latest Yamaha WR 450 his mate rides. In the right hands the Yammy is a lightweight Australian championship race bike. However, my Man claims the Suzuki is capable of greater things, legendary things even. He claims that it allows him to chug up hills as if on a tractor. He says that the young bucks can only watch him in awe after red-lining and pinging on their latest Euro Enduro two-stroke KTM and Gas Gas bikes.

Zzzzz … sorry, I must have dozed off for a second — truly, this is thrilling stuff!

My Man's mates are always telling him that he needs to update his bike, but why should he when he kicks their arses regularly? I happen to know that my Man's bike is yellow, so it's pretty fast, the fastest colour, apart from red, naturally. But each man is convinced nothing compares to his own awesome mechanical beast. Each one tells his lady that *he* is the real legend of the group, that the others eat his dust all day, and jealously aspire to acquire his prodigious skills and emulate his amazing feats.

My Man admits that even a legendary rider like himself can occasionally be found sprawled across the track on a steeply curved hill ascent. Blocking the track with no way past, the following riders are forced to stop. They are then in deep distress, faced with executing a standing start on an almost vertical greasy dirt track. Only the lead rider is guaranteed unimpeded progress up the slow narrow path. What a test of rider and machine — impressive stuff! An annoying non-motorcycling mate, a lounge-chair critic and self-proclaimed authority on all things, later explained that a heavier rider puts extra weight on the bike's back wheel, making the vertical standing start no big deal. But this wimp has never toughed it out with sliding tyres spitting mud all the way up those near vertical tracks.

Having nudged his way past 40 years of age, my Man is the old bloke in the group. He says the young bucks always jump off hard and set a cracking pace, which requires superhuman stamina to sustain. On the other hand, my Man relies on mature wisdom and cunning. He takes it easy early on, allowing his elderly bike to warm up gently. It's all about who is King by the end of the day, he says, and riding too hard too fast too soon has its consequences.

My Man and his mates have had their share of bad falls and injuries. A split-second lapse of concentration on the path ahead is all it takes to become one with the landscape, bouncing off a tree, slipping and thrashing about in a puddle of sludge, or lying dazed in the dirt. Sometimes they need only a few minutes to recover and catch their breath, other times will see them crashed out in the back of a car, moaning and exhausted, or if they've really stacked hard, visiting an emergency ward to patch up that broken collar bone. Once, after failing an attempted log crossing, my Man ended up prostrate on the ground with a torn groin. The multi-coloured purple, black and green bruising that developed shortly afterwards testified that this was indeed a cringe-worthy injury.

The days following each ride I listen to my Man's gripes about how sore and tired he is, how he needs to be pampered in a hot bath. But when his mates call he's casual, undefeated: 'No, I'm fine, pulled up great. Next Saturday? Bring it on!'

My Man also, of course, owns a road bike. It's a Kawasaki ZRX 1200, or 'mean black muscle machine'! When he rides my Man wears only the latest and greatest in designer black: leather jacket, pants, gloves, boots and helmet. His gear is not only the best available in protective gear, he fills it out looking pretty darn hot!

I guess that's why he's my Man ...

# Show-off!

Mick Browne
Narrawallee, NSW

One weekend a few years ago, me and a mate rode to watch the Moto GP races at the Phillip Island racetrack.

On the Sunday afternoon, after the event was finished, we headed off the island with everybody else in a mass procession of noisy machinery. There were three bike lanes with two car lanes in between, all heading slowly in the same direction.

In accordance with tradition the locals were lined up along the road, complete with tables, chairs, drinks and nibbles, with friendly waves and smiles, to farewell the spectators as they departed the island.

I was riding my '83 Electra Glide Classic, which is a heavy machine, especially at low speed. In front of me was a high-powered Japanese bike, crawling along at a slow pace but at high revs. To my right was a LandCruiser with two young ladies in the back seat. Up ahead there was a group of young blokes seated by the roadside, farewelling the departing motorists with the aid of a few beers.

As we approached the blokes, they held up a large white sign that read 'CHUCK A MONO'. The rider in front of me did just that, standing his high-revving machine up on the back wheel, much to the delight of the locals. I slowed up a bit to give him more room to perform. This brought me in line with the girls in the LandCruiser.

Just then the young blokes flipped their sign over so that it read 'SHOW US YOUR TITS'.

One of the lovely buxom young ladies in the LandCruiser directly beside me thrust herself out the open window and obliged their request! My eyes left the road and fastened instead onto a most incredibly beautiful spectacle, something I had not witnessed in many years.

Mayhem followed.

A middle-aged bloke on an old Harley was so distracted by the unexpected bonanza of flesh that he suddenly veered off the road and headed straight for Ma and Pa Kettle who were picnicking on the verge, forcing them to dive for safety. I also only just missed them, sending their tea and scones airborne. Somehow we all avoided disaster and regained our positions in the procession, much to the cheers and laughter of all who witnessed the show.

I still cannot remember who won the last race at Phillip Island that year!

# Wheeling and Dealing

Max Zalakos
Nowra, NSW

'When are we going riding?' asked the voice the moment I picked up the phone, not even a 'hello' first. The question didn't throw me though, because apart from when he rang to announce 'it's a boy', Lionel always started our conversations with the same familiar words. He was my best mate, forever eager to crank up his ST1100 for a run to anywhere, the further the better. The only problem was that he never seemed to be able to suggest a destination — he always left that to me.

We had ridden our bikes over 800 kilometres to Gulargambone and back the previous weekend to watch a mate in a Camp Draft competition, and here it was, only Wednesday, and he was itching for more! One of the reasons I liked Lionel was that he was the perfect motorcycling companion. Once a trip was under way he would agree to almost anything. He didn't care about the destination, the route, the accommodation or even the drinks; as long as he could chalk up plenty of kilometres on his beloved machine, he was as happy as a pig in mud.

'What about a run down to Canberra this weekend?' I suggested. I had an old aunt living there on her own and had been promising to replace a leaking tap washer in her shower for quite a while.

'Good, good, see ya same time, same place,' and the line went dead.

When I pulled into the Liverpool Maccas that Saturday, Lionel was already there sitting on his bike, clutching a coffee, looking somewhat impatient. I was about to go in for a quick brekkie when Lionel said, 'Can't you do that later? Let's get on the road and put some miles behind us.'

As we headed south on our fabulous white ST1100s, we chatted away on the CB about motorcycles, motorcycles and motorcycles. Lionel mentioned that he'd read that a new Honda Valkyrie had gone on sale recently, but after visiting two local dealers he'd found that they'd both sold out, with no more stock due for a month or so! He felt there should be a law against companies tantalising their customers with products they couldn't supply — jail the lot of them, he reckoned! I could sense the topic turning into a major rant as Lionel started to unravel his favourite conspiracy theory, which involved big business taking advantage of motorcyclists. I'd heard it all before and couldn't be bothered listening to it again, so I simply switched off my CB and left him delivering his diatribe into the ether. After listening to both sides of a Linda Ronstadt cassette, I switched back to the CB and sure enough Lionel was still at it, waffling on about the injustices suffered by innocents on two wheels.

As I thought about it, it occurred to me that we'd be passing pretty close to a Honda dealership on our way through Canberra and there was a possibility they may have a Valkyrie on their showroom floor. I hesitated to convey my thoughts to Lionel because disappointment might lead to another tirade of CB twaddle and I didn't think my eardrums could stand a further battering on the way home if he got let down. But then again, he was my mate.

'Okay, Lionel, if you stop ranting we'll drop off at the Honda dealer up ahead and see if they can show us a Valkyrie.' Silence. Lionel's CB shut down as his one-track brain processed the probabilities. I just prayed that even if the dealer didn't have a live Valkyrie on the floor, at least they might divert his attention with a glossy brochure for bedtime reading. He'd be unbearable if he didn't get his fix!

It was getting close to lunchtime and I was starving, still not having had breakfast due to Lionel's impatience to get started.

We weren't all that far from the bike shop when I pushed the transmit button on the CB, suggesting that we stop for a hamburger before checking out the bikes. But Lionel was a man on a mission and wouldn't be diverted; I could starve for all he cared! A few minutes more and we were there.

Lionel slid his bike to a halt, kicked it onto its side stand, and ripped off his helmet and gloves in one fluid motion. Then before I had even switched off my engine he had disappeared through the front entrance. I followed him in and there he was, sitting astride a huge yellow, black and chrome bumblebee! Yes, they had a real live Valkyrie just sitting there, on the floor, in stock, brand new, available for purchase.

'Mate, I've just got to have this,' he repeated quietly to himself as he clung to the handlebars and wriggled his bum around on the seat. He looked like one of those contortionists as he twisted his head from side to side, trying to check out all the features of the machine without dismounting. I stood back and said nothing, but I must admit it was a pretty amazing-looking piece of gear. It boasted the legendary Gold Wing flat six-cylinder 1500cc engine, wrapped in a visual package that could only be described as hugely impressive. It had big doses of what every decent motorcycle should have — 'presence'!

A salesman wandered over and started giving Lionel a thorough workout. I stayed out of earshot, trying to look disinterested, not wanting to get caught up in the crossfire of his sales pitch. By this time my stomach was rumbling audibly — I just had to have something to eat. Just then the salesman walked back to his office to get some brochures, so I seized Lionel by the arm and insisted that we go grab some lunch. 'We'll be right back after lunch,' Lionel promised the salesman. 'Don't you dare sell that sucker in the meantime.' Clutching the handful of brochures, we headed for a cafe not far down the street.

As I sank my teeth into a toasted chicken and avocado sandwich, I had to shield my food from Lionel's spittle while he raved about the absolute necessity of buying that Valkyrie. He was far too excited to eat; he was suffering from a severe case of new bike lust. 'It's the last bike of its kind available in Australia,' Lionel stated emphatically with a worried look on his face. 'If we don't act now, and act fast, there's no guarantee that we'll ever be able to get hold of one. They're like hen's teeth, mate — great investment — destined to become a collector's item overnight.'

I was too busy munching my sambo to say anything, so Lionel decided to fill the void by reading me his sales brochures. Unfortunately, he had barely got past primary school as a kid and was a terrible reader. 'What does t-o-r-q-u-e spell, mate?'

I suddenly realised that not only was I not listening to what he was saying, but in my mind I was massaging the possibility of purchasing a Valkyrie! I could just imagine myself on one, mentally enjoying the surge of acceleration as the awesome engine propelled it in and out of corners. I was shocked. Had I caught Lionel's new bike lust?

I was forced to turn my attention back to Lionel, who had given up trying to read the brochure and now had it thrust under my nose, exhorting me to look at the pictures. Although I hadn't confessed it to him yet, in the last few minutes I had come to the conclusion that maybe buying a Valkyrie was a very good idea indeed. The only real question was 'How?' I was pretty sure neither of us had enough cash in the bank for a new bike, and I knew from past history that we both had an aversion to getting into debt. Then the idea hit me!

'Lionel, how would you feel about us being joint owners in a new Valkyrie?'

'Whadyamean?' he asked, his bunch of brochures suspended in midair.

'Consider this. If we're really honest, neither of us can afford to buy a new motorcycle without selling our STs. I'm not prepared to do that, and I suggest you wouldn't want to do that either. But, I could scratch up half the price of the new bike, and maybe you could too. So here's what we do. We buy the new one in joint names, share the ownership, share all the running costs and work out a way to share the riding. What do you think?'

Within 15 minutes we had scribbled out the 'Rules for Joint Ownership' on a paper serviette, convincing ourselves that we could both enjoy all the benefits of new bike ownership, but at only half the cost. The most important rule was 'he who prangs repairs', followed by 'if one wants to sell, the other has the right of first refusal to buy'. Apart from that it was pretty cut and dried; we would go 50-50 on everything.

It all seemed so simple. Why hadn't we thought of doing this before? As Lionel rightly pointed out, we could take the new bike on all our future runs and swap bikes halfway through so that we both got a ride. On top of that, most motorcycles spent 90 per cent of their time doing nothing, sitting in a garage, so it wouldn't be too hard for us both to enjoy some good solo riding time on the new machine whenever we wanted. The longer we discussed the idea the more enthusiastic we both became. Without warning Lionel suddenly leapt to his feet, causing his chair to make a horrible screeching sound across the terrazzo floor, alarming the other cafe patrons.

'Let's go buy the bugger!' And with that he slapped me on the back then disappeared out the door while I lingered just long enough to chat to the waitress and pay the bill. As I walked leisurely back up the street towards the bike shop, I suddenly remembered that Lionel was the world's worst negotiator. I broke into a trot, hoping to get there before he had had a chance to do any damage. The showroom was empty so I headed for the salesman's office. As I walked through the door, there were Lionel and the salesman both grinning from ear to ear, shaking hands on the deal!

'Good one, fellas! Old Mate here tells me you are going to share ownership. What an excellent idea, wish everybody was that smart. Now let's get some personal particulars so we can fill out the paperwork. Got your driver's licences?'

I think I had tears in my eyes as the salesman pumped my hand. They were tears of joy mingled with tears of regret — I hardly dared imagine what agreement Lionel had reached with the salesman in terms of price. I tossed up whether to broach the subject on the spot, or whether to save it until later when we were alone. I'm one of those people who considers a 'deal is a deal' based on a handshake, so what was the point of embarrassing Lionel in front of the salesman?

Thirty minutes later the salesman was pumping both our hands yet again, telling us how much he looked forward to seeing us the following weekend when we had arranged to call back to pick up the Valkyrie after it had been pre-delivered and registered.

'Yeah, now don't forget to give me a call any time if I can be of assistance, boys. Day or night, public holidays, Christmas, birthdays, we're here for yous 24/7. Nothing is ever too much trouble. 'N' don't forget to remember me to your wives — you are married, aren't you?' I felt deeply concerned as I had never seen a new motorcycle salesman this happy.

As the dealership disappeared in my rear-vision mirror and we pointed the STs towards my aunt's place, I dreaded asking Lionel the big question. But I figured that it was probably better to get it over and then just look forward to the joy of taking delivery of our new baby. I flicked on the CB and pressed transmit.

'By the way, Lionel, what sort of deal were you able to arrange on the bike?'

'Mate, it's an absolute pearler! As you know, that Valkyrie was probably the last one available in Australia, if not the world. If they'd advertised it, they'd probably have gotten well over their asking price. I mean, at auction who knows how high it would have gone? But, get this, mate, not only was I able to hold him down to the sticker price, but I also forced him to throw in a new helmet for absolutely free.'

I almost vomited into my slipstream as I realised that Lionel had committed us to the full recommended retail price plus anything the salesman might have been quick enough to add on. And a free helmet? He took a size M while I wore an XL, so there was a zero chance of me squeezing my bloated cranium into his tiny new helmet even if I did want to share, which I didn't.

Again, the thought of trying to reopen negotiations to save a few dollars flashed briefly through my mind, but since I was only going to have to pay half the money that Lionel had wasted, I thought, what the heck, better to retain my mate's friendship than make him look like some sort of turkey. I decided to say nothing.

By mid-afternoon my aunt's tap washer had been replaced and we were back on the road, heading for home. We sat on our CBs, eulogising the virtues of six-cylinder motorcycles and raving about the huge financial benefits of shared ownership of an expensive machine. We weren't sure whether we could wait another week before picking her up. Our plan was for the two of us to return to the dealership on one of our existing bikes, and then the pillion would ride the new bike home. We both secretly yearned to be the first to ride her on her maiden voyage, but to be completely fair we decided we'd flip a coin.

We pulled in for fuel near Goulburn then wandered into the adjacent shop for a coffee. Lionel suggested we toss the coin then and there, which we did and I won. Apparently I hadn't understood that it was the best of three, so Lionel was lucky enough to call the next two in a row. He was so excited he almost had an orgasm.

When he calmed down a bit he surprised me with an announcement: 'Mate, I've got a real treat for you, the icing on the cake so to speak.' A sudden pang of hope sprang up in my heart. Maybe he had only been kidding about paying full bottle for the Valkyrie; maybe he had been having me on and was now about to tell me that he had struck a really fantastic deal.

I looked at him expectantly. He slid his hand into the front of his leather jacket and pulled out a packet, which he slapped down on the counter in front of me.

'There you go, mate, your very own set of Valkyrie brochures, and they didn't cost either of us one cent extra!'

It's dangerous riding with a mate like Lionel!

# Making an Axe

Neil Collier
Blaxlands Ridge, NSW

I have enjoyed two special hobby interests during my life. The first is a love of the freedom that I got from riding motorcycles over the past 38 years, and the other is a passion for working with wood that I have had for about the same period.

We were given our first motorbike, shared amongst myself and four brothers and two sisters, when I was about 15. It was an ex-postie bike that was a great introduction to the thrill of riding. We could never get it to wheel-stand, but it helped me learn how to manoeuvre these two-wheeled contraptions around obstacles on the open terrain near home. I still have a scar on my right arm that measures 100mm long by 8mm wide, testifying to the importance of not getting too close to an eight-gauge wire fence!

I have held a motorcycle licence for more than 35 years and have had numerous bikes during that period, the last being a Vulcan 1500 cruiser that was written off by a driver who just didn't see me. I was fortunate that I only sustained a broken big toe and some bruising. The car driver's phone call from my mobile phone to the first three people on my contact list was answered by my daughter. The driver asked, 'I don't know whose phone this is?' to which my daughter replied, 'It's my dad's.' The driver said, 'Well, I've just hit him — he's on the road but still breathing,' which of course sent my baby into a panic. Between her and her mother I was persuaded not to go straight out and buy another bike. I even got comments from the ambulance attendees and the tow-truck driver as to how lucky they thought I was to survive, considering the carnage they witnessed.

About three months prior to the accident I had started a woodworking project where my bike had come in very handy. I had decided to make a life-sized timber motorcycle, using my own bike for reference. I would go to the shed and check the size of links in the chain, the size of tyre valves or the way in which a cable ran from the brake to the brake lever. Now I have never been all that mechanically orientated, with only a general appreciation of basic repairs, so I had to rely on other sources of information to construct some of the parts needed to finish my project. Fortunately, two members of the Hawkesbury Woodcraft Co-operative, of which I am a member, were also Harley-Davidson owners. I had previously been on rides with both these men and they were very helpful in assisting me to achieve the end result. They were kind enough to allow me to measure their bikes and discuss the items that I was trying to fabricate. As with many things in life, the devil was in the detail. For example, I learned that different brands of motorbikes have different angles for their V-twin engines.

I was pleased that I had settled on a chopper-style of bike for my timber model because custom choppers don't all comply with the same manufacturing standards. The chopper owner usually builds his machine to express his individual aesthetic taste, so every one is different. This suited me completely, because if I had built a standard mass-produced model motorcycle, the die-hards would have had a field day pointing out any mistakes that I may have made. My custom chopper design meant that I didn't have to worry about having the wrong style of headlight or the wrong angle of engine for any particular brand of bike.

Having said all that, I still have to admit that I did make a couple of mistakes. One was that I was completely unaware that a motorcycle battery has a cell for each two volts, resulting in the standard 12-volt battery having six filler caps. Quite a few people have gleefully pointed out that I have seven caps on the top of my timber battery, which would make it a 14 volt!

At the time I calculated the size of my timber battery, I just divided it into equal sections governed by the fit of the caps, ending up with a result that I felt looked good. Unfortunately, I had space for seven caps, not six, so mistakes happened. I also relied on the internet for a lot of information, but overall I followed the plan in my head of what I expected the bike to look like when it was completed.

I christened the bike 'The Axe' because it was a 'wood chopper', but I also considered calling it 'Chainsaw'. The Axe is constructed 100 per cent of timber, with over 80 custom-made dowels used to join the various parts. There are 660 individual pieces with 408 used for the chain alone. It took over 300 hours to complete the project, only working on it when time was available and I was in the mood.

It took a lot of time and effort to complete this venture, but the thing I enjoyed the most was the fact that the final result was as envisaged at the outset. I can now look at my finished artwork with pride, while the sense of achievement has encouraged me to further pursue my hobby. The Axe has evoked great responses from members of my woodworking group. I have also displayed it twice at public events with very complimentary feedback from the spectators. I entered the Axe in a Show and Shine at Forster last year in the hope of receiving a trophy to use as a prop for future public displays. I was fortunate enough to win the Encouragement Award in the motorbike section, but the prize of a first-aid kit in a plastic bag does not have quite the effect I anticipated; maybe next time.

When people look at photographs of the Axe they assume that it is a small-scale model; however, it actually measures 2.4 metres long and stands 1.2 metres high. The majority of timber used in its construction is camphor laurel, but the piece of timber I used to fabricate the seat had been stored under my father's house for 47 years. Dad had assumed that it was a large wedge of Australian red cedar and had given it to me five years previously on the assumption that I could use it in one of my woodworking projects. When I finally got around to using it I discovered it was white cedar, but it suited the purpose and holds special significance to me.

# Sickie

Murray Eccles
Purnim, VIC

Waking before the alarm, as the sunlight squeezes around the edge of the blind, I immediately realise that I am far too sick to go to work today. I self-diagnose a protein deficiency and prescribe myself a good dose of breakfast: steak and eggs.

Time to fire up the Beast.

At last the lush western district farmland is behind me. The smells of cow shit and silage are replaced by salt and tea tree as I turn the little XBR towards Peterborough. Mentally I switch on my radar because the Great Ocean Road is the favoured hunting ground of the Hyundai Getz and lumbering Winnebago, piloted by unpredictable tourists. You always need to be aware down this way that a vehicle may stop suddenly in front of you or throw an unindicated U-turn to take a photo of a stick that looks like a snake. Further up the road towards Lavers Hill it is not uncommon to hook into a 30kph corner, perhaps at just a little over 30, to suddenly confront a stationary hire car and a group of tourists on the road taking photos of a bit of foliage that looks like a koala.

The mighty Honda XBR500 is an undiscovered gem, a single 500cc pot pumping out 40 wild ponies in a lightweight package. It makes me smile every time I look at it because it takes me back 30 years to when I first started riding gutless, noisy, anti-social machines. It's even more anti-social now with the open pipes, which have added a few extra, possibly imagined, ponies.

Burbling through Peterborough off the throttle so as not to attract unwanted attention, it sounds like Mick Fleetwood is behind me, knocking out something mellow. I know from experience that as I head up past Moonlight Head, Mick will disappear and John Bonham will take his place. Further on when I cut across Turtons Track to dodge the tourists and wind the revs up past 6,000, it will feel like the sound is coming from inside my head and not from the pipes. When it gets to this stage there is nothing else in the world except for the sound of the little engine roaring in my head and echoing off the bush and cliff faces. This is when I stop thinking about riding and just ride; I no longer have to plan the entry to the next corner or the best exit to set up for the following one, it just happens.

I make a quick visit to the newsagent at Port Campbell, remembering to remove my helmet so as not to get a face full of mace if mistaken for an armed robber, to grab a copy of the local rag for perusal later over a coffee. As I stuff the paper down my jacket, I have a flashback to 20-year-old me, midwinter on Hoddle Street in Melbourne, getting ready for another Friday night run to Warrnambool. Filling the CB250T, not an undiscovered gem, more of a slug, and purchasing two copies of the evening *Herald* to stuff down the front of my jacket in what I knew from experience would be a forlorn attempt to keep the winter cold at bay over the next 300 kilometres. Close to four hours later, I'd pull up at the little farmhouse, smiling and prising my creaky hands from the bars, while trying to get my knees to work again. The thought of the beautiful young art student waiting inside for me with an open fire, a bottle of Stones and a single bed made it all worthwhile. Even now I wonder how she has managed to put up with me for all these years.

Back on the road I pass through Princetown and head along the ridge. The eternal question here is whether to wring its neck on the relatively open stretch or kick back and cruise. Deciding to be sensible, I sit around 100k's and admire the scenery. Most people know that the Great Ocean Road was constructed by returned diggers after World War II; parts of this stretch appear not to have been touched since.

Crossing the raging torrent that is the Gellibrand River, I hunker down over the bars. The second best stretch of road in the area is from the river here up to Moonlight Head. Some days when time is on my side and the bike is on song, I can spend a blissful couple of hours running up and down this stretch until I scare myself. Not today though, so I keep moving forward.

I cruise through Lavers and Beech Forest on my way to the best bit of road; it's free of both tourists and the accepted conventions of road engineering. Turtons Track is another one of those undiscovered gems — a single lane with a sign at each end advising a 25kph speed limit, with another sign instructing caravans not to enter. Actually, I think there should be a law that prevents all caravans travelling on the road in daylight hours. Worryingly, there's a further sign warning that the road is frequented by logging trucks. I have yet to have the pleasure of meeting a logging truck coming the other way on this track and hope that I never do. The road twists up and across the ridge where it has a liberal sprinkling of gravel and in wintertime unwary riders can be introduced to the joys of traversing moss and damp leaf litter. It's not the place to confuse ambition and ability; if you go over the edge here, your bleached and broken bones won't turn up until after the next ice age.

Making it to the end of the track unscathed, I continue down to Skenes Creek. Coming around a tight right-hander, I encounter Sven in his Swedish death machine. He has decided that the reception on his brains-free mobile phone handset would be better on my side of the road than on his. I get the bike up straight and make use of the last couple of centimetres of bitumen. Sven is unblinking as he checks the latest value of his share portfolio.

The Volvo is the natural predator of the motorcycle. In the early days, once you had a modicum of experience you could identify Volvos from a distance as they stalked towards you, giving you time to take evasive action and remain relatively safe. God bless those Swedish engineers though, they were quick to catch on and now disguise Volvos as Commodores so that you can't recognise them until they are right on top of you, sometimes literally. I regularly hear the proposition that it would make for safer roads if all drivers were required to spend some time on a motorcycle prior to getting a car licence. I would like to see them spend some time UNDER a motorcycle, sliding on their arse across the bitumen; I'm sure that would provide a more memorable learning experience.

Apollo Bay was once a bucolic hamlet populated by Southern Ocean fishermen, taciturn farmers and the odd, sometimes very odd, ahem, organic herb grower up in the hills. Now everyone is named Tristram or Myfanwy and drives a black BMW or Porsche. I join the latte-sippers from Melbourne for a brew and a stretch while I watch the parade of Ducatis and shiny new Harleys trundle by. It looks like the riding gear on some of these guys is worth more than my whole bike. When I started out our motorcycling gear was sourced from the local army disposal shop. WWII greatcoats, fur-lined flying boots and the very best Chinese PVC gloves that money could buy. As another hog rumbles past, I ask myself: if a Harley rides in the forest and there is no one there to admire it, does it really exist? After ridding myself of such existential nonsense, it's on the Beast again for a civilised cruise back to Lavers Hill. This is a great bit of road, not too twisty, not too straight. As always I wave to every bike I see, as always 90 per cent of them don't wave back ...

Steps up onto soapbox ...

Back when I was a lad, living in a cardboard box, cold gravel for tea, etc., you waved to all oncoming riders and most waved back. The exceptions were the Harley riders, who really were outlaws back then, and chookies, who for some reason didn't seem to feel they were part of the gang. There was a sense of community that seems to have since been lost. These days it appears to be more about what you possess rather than enjoying the shared biking experience. Every spotty-faced 19-year-old on a 30-grand Ducati provided by mummy and daddy, and every redundant accountant who spent his package on a Harley and a skull bandana, think they are too cool to acknowledge a fellow traveller. In the words of the Dalai Lama, 'Sod the lot of 'em.'

Steps down from soapbox ...

From Lavers all the way back to Peterborough, it's more of the same with every corner a joy to attack. Ten kilometres west of Peterborough and the road loses its sense of adventure. There is a push by the local tourist bodies and councils to 'extend' the Great Ocean Road through to Warrnambool. Obviously they are not going to re-construct it along the coast, but rather rename the existing route in an effort to capture more tourist dollars. It seems a bit problematic to me because after Peterborough the road ceases to be great, is no longer near the ocean and in some places turns from being a road into a goat track.

Almost home and once again I am confronted by a huge slick of fresh cow shit spread across the road. If I am walking my dog on the beach and he drops a turd the size of a banana, I have to pick it up and 'dispose of it thoughtfully', or else cop a fine. If I let 600 dairy cows roam and empty their bowels in the middle of a public road, then apparently it's quite okay to leave it there to spray up and coat passing motorcyclists. How does that work?

Arriving back home after my big day out, I can hear the bike ticking as I take off my helmet. It's been pretty much a perfect day. I can only hope I am too sick to go to work again in the not-too-distant future.

# When Two Wheels aren't Enough

Anthony Rogers
Kilsyth, VIC

My most memorable motorbike adventure takes me back a few years to a trip to a friend's property in Manns Beach, Victoria. It promised to be a great weekend, riding our dirt bikes and dune buggies along some fantastic sandy trails.

We arrived on a Saturday afternoon and were keen to get out amongst it before it got dark, so we unloaded the bikes and buggies straight away and prepared to get going. As I was the first one ready to ride, my friend, who owned the property, gave me directions. He told me to follow the track along the side of the paddocks and just keep going straight, so off I went alone. It was a great feeling to be on the bike again after a month or so without a ride, and I was thoroughly enjoying the unpredictable contours of the sandy track. After about five minutes I came to a point where there was an option to turn 90 degrees to the right, or continue going straight ahead. As my friend had said 'just keep going straight', that was the direction I chose. After riding a further 200 metres or so, I noticed that the ground was becoming very slippery and a bit boggy, so the fun factor really kicked in.

I was just getting into some cool power slides when I came across a small water crossing about three metres wide. I braced myself, gave it a handful of throttle and gleefully roared into the water. Everything suddenly changed. As soon as I hit the water, the bike stopped dead, flipping me over the handlebars and splat, into the water! A bit stunned and in disbelief, I looked around and saw that the bike was still standing up, on its own, in the middle of the crossing. I scrambled to my feet and sloshed my way over to the bike to push it out. Then

I realised that my feet were beginning to sink into the mud beneath the water. I was finding it very difficult to keep my footing and my balance; I was really struggling to even move the bike. I tried for several minutes, but was just getting more and more stuck as I tried pushing harder and harder. Then, as I gave it one huge desperate push, disaster! The bike overbalanced, falling towards me. With my legs nearly knee-deep in the muddy base of the waterway, I fell backwards with the bike on top of me.

I was very fortunate that the water where I fell was only about six inches deep, but I was now stuck fast, struggling vainly to get out. I wondered where everyone else was and how long it would be until they arrived to help extract me. With the power of a desperately panicking man, I managed to slide and wriggle my way out from under the bike, and within a few minutes I was on my feet and had the bike standing back on two wheels once more. I clambered out of the water to the relative safety of the bank, sitting down to catch my breath while I reflected on the gravity of my situation. I still couldn't believe that no one had come to my rescue yet. After a few minutes, I noticed something disturbing — the water flow seemed to be getting a little faster and deeper. Now I really started to get concerned. Where the hell was everyone else?

I then heard the sound of four-strokes approaching and looked back down the track in the direction I had come. There was my wife and friends riding along the trail, but they turned right instead of going straight ahead as I had done. What? I waved and screamed out, but they didn't see or hear me. By this time I was unable to get back to my bike because the water was really flowing in volume, and the width and depth of the crossing were increasing. I didn't want to leave because I wanted to get my bike out, but I desperately needed some help to do so. I knew my wife and friends would be coming back down that track so I just had to wait. It took about 40 minutes before I heard and saw them returning. I started waving frantically to attract their attention, but again they completely missed seeing me. I couldn't believe it. I'm right here, I thought, right where you said to go, why aren't you looking for me?

As the minutes ticked by, the crossing got wider and wider, and much deeper. My bike was still standing upright, but water was lapping almost to the top of the tyres. Now to add to my anguish it was late in the day and starting to get dark. I was wet, cold, muddy and pissed off when I saw some lights coming down the track. The lights came to the turn in the track and stopped. I waved and yelled out for help. The lights started moving towards me. It was my wife and friend in my 4WD. YES! What a relief it was to see them. After some crazy talk about what had happened to me and my bike, and questions about where they had been, my friend asked why I had ended up there. He told me that I should have realised that I was on a tidal flood plain! 'Well shit, dude, this is where you said to go. I don't live here so I didn't know the ocean flooded in here every afternoon!'

I pulled the winch out of my 4WD and attached it to my bike. All hooked up, it should have been easy! I started gently pulling, taking up the slack on the cable. But the load of the bike, which was still stuck in the mud, pulled the front end of my truck down into the soft ground. I stopped winching and tried to move the 4WD. No way — we were stuck fast. Incredible! Not only was my bike stuck out there in the muddy water, but my ute had joined it in the bog! By this time the language was flying freely as I got more than a little frustrated.

My friend offered to walk back to his house to get his 4WD, so my wife and I had no option but to sit there and wait for his return, forlornly watching my bike and ute surrounded by the swirling water. About half an hour later we saw his vehicle approaching. Thank heavens, out of trouble at last. He stopped a fair way back from my ute and hooked a snatch strap to my vehicle to tow it out. My friend started pulling, but all he achieved was filling our ears with the sound of spinning tyres. Almost unbelievably, we were horrified to realise that he too was stuck. What next? We had run out of vehicles that could help extract us from the mud and it was dark. We had no choice but to abandon the bike and two 4WDs for the night, and come back in the morning daylight to try and sort everything out. Reluctantly, I left my vehicles and headed back to the house with the others.

After a restless night, we were all up early to return to the scene of the previous day's carnage to check the damage. Fortunately and unfortunately, everything was just as we had left it. One bike and two HiLux utes bogged in the soft surface of the flood plain. My friend decided that he would go get the neighbouring farmer to bring his tractor over to get this mess sorted once and for all. Cool.

Nearly an hour later the cavalry arrived. A middle-aged, weather-beaten, lifelong farmer rattled up on his trusty workhorse. He relieved me of $100 for his time, then pulled in behind my friend's 4WD. Throwing out a long chain, he was about ready to tow the first vehicle out. We got it all hooked up, then gave him the 'go' signal, so off he went. But hang on, his giant tractor wheels just started spinning, struggling to gain traction in the soft mud. After some minutes of getting nowhere, he gave it another big rev and down he went, sinking his tractor into the mud to join the growing collection of idiots stuck in the flood plain.

Wow! Where do we go from here? A bike, two 4WD utes and a tractor, all hopelessly bogged. The farmer, who was understandably pissed that his tractor was bogged, said that one of us would have to hike up the road to another farm and get that farmer to bring a much bigger tractor to get us all out of trouble. My friend set off and another hour later we saw this monster vehicle crawling up the track. Damn, that thing was big!

This time the rescue vehicle kept well back from the edge of the mud. We rolled out a couple of huge, long chains that we hooked onto the first farmer's tractor. The monster fired up, pulled effortlessly and bam, the smaller tractor came sliding out. Then my friend's 4WD, then mine, then finally my bike. What a relief, and another $100 well spent.

We thanked the farmers for their help and they chugged off into the distance. Needless to say that by the time we got all our vehicles back to the house that was it for our great weekend away. Not much was said to each other during the packing up and loading process as I think we were all still stunned by the miserable time we had had over the last day and a half. I can laugh about it all now, but I can assure you, there was no laughing there on that fateful day.

Would I go riding down there again?

Hell yeah, just not on the flood plain!

# Ménage à Trois

John Bryant
Bilpin, NSW

It's not all that often that you see overloaded motorcycles on the highways and byways of Australia. I suppose that's because we tend to use our motorcycles strictly for recreation or transport. If we need to carry any sort of load, we grab the car or a ute, unlike parts of Asia where a two-wheeler is often the sole means of family or business transport. Over there it is not uncommon to see a family of five crammed onto a moped, or some old bloke wobbling along with a stack of 44-gallon drums balanced precariously on his 125.

I used to think risky motorcycle acrobatics were confined to Third World countries; that is until my wife started riding pillion on my bike. In the early days of our motorcycle adventures together, it wasn't too bad because the bikes we rode didn't have much in the way of carrying capacity. I mean, how much baggage can you load onto a naked Honda 500? Apart from slinging a small carry bag around the neck, there's simply nowhere to put anything. Even the missus could see that when we were out it was pointless buying anything that needed to be carried unless it fitted in her personal carry bag, which she would then have to hang around her neck until we made it home. But this all changed when I took the big step and upgraded to a motorcycle with a bit of storage capacity.

The first time we did a long trip on my new Honda Gold Wing was when we set out on a two-week tour of Tasmania, taking the bike across Bass Strait on the ferry. Before we left home I thought we had planned the expedition carefully, but I was dismayed when I saw the Little Woman packing a suitcase full of necessities. I tactfully reminded her that we needed to travel light so that we could cram everything into the bike's panniers and top box, which meant that she would have to jettison about 70 per cent of her cargo. She responded by telling me that I should have purchased a bigger motorcycle with decent storage capacity. Yeah right! She found it hard to believe that that wasn't really possible, that there were no bigger bikes available anywhere on the planet. Of course I could have towed a trailer and carried just about everything she had packed, but I had one of those things once and didn't enjoy the experience. Anyway, when we took off on that Tassie trip both panniers, top box and small glove boxes were jam-packed to capacity with clothes, toiletries and other absolute necessities. It didn't matter how much she might come to fancy some little souvenir or knick-knack en route, there simply wasn't room for any extra cargo, not even a toothpick. That first trip was a blast and we arrived back home with pretty well the same amount of gear as we had when we set out.

However, things didn't go quite so well on some of our shorter rides.

She liked visiting open gardens and was always keen for me to accompany her. I wasn't overly fussed about ogling trees and shrubs, so we struck up a deal where I agreed to tag along providing we travelled on the Wing. That way I could enjoy the ride, she could enjoy the gardens. Win-win, or so I thought. Things started to unravel the first time we visited a garden where the owner was offering a range of potted plants for sale. As I waited outside, slouched on the Wing listening to the stereo, I was horrified to see her struggling back to the bike clutching several plastic bags filled with potted plants. 'Where are ya goin' to put THEM?' Regardless of my protestations, she was adamant that the panniers and top box were to be filled with her flowering purchases. Unfortunately, no matter how hard I tried to pack them all in, they simply wouldn't fit, and she refused point-blank to leave anything behind. So after a rather animated kerbside discussion, I pulled all our wet-weather gear out of the panniers to create just enough extra space for her foliage! With nowhere to stow the wet-weather gear we had to wear it; it was no wonder we got funny looks from other motorists, decked out in all our rain gear in the middle of the day in humid summer sunshine, sweating like pigs.

But worse was yet to come, and this time it happened in the middle of winter when we decided to visit the Mudgee Small Farms exhibition. I wasn't all that keen to go, but reconsidered when she said she'd be quite happy biking it. Initially I was wary because I could envisage yet more agro when she spent up big and then expected me to cart a few bales of hay or a dozen trees on the back of the Wing. 'No,' she said when I expressed my reservations, 'I promise you, no plants.'

Like a lamb being led to slaughter, I set off anticipating a pleasant ride with no complications. Maybe I was a little naïve, but I took her 'no plants' promise seriously. So what could go wrong?

We arrived at the show Friday, had a great day with not a plant in sight, and then spent a totally relaxing night at the Mudgee Country Comfort motel. We intended to spend more time at the show the next day, and then head home via the back roads. Life doesn't get much better than this, I remember thinking as I drifted off to sleep.

By mid-afternoon Saturday I had seen enough of the machinery and rural exhibits, but the Little Woman still hadn't checked out the livestock pavilions. Not being a great rabbit, pig and cow fancier, I left her to wander around on her own while I headed back to the bike to listen to a bit of C&W and read the paper. That, I am afraid, was where I made my fatal mistake. I must have been insane to leave her rambling around unescorted, fondling her credit card. About half an hour later, as I was engrossed in the sports section, I heard her voice. I looked up to see her standing there, clutching a large cardboard box under each arm.

'You promised me no flowers,' I almost bawled, tears welling up in my eyes.

'Calm down, I haven't bought any plants.'

She was right; plants don't squawk and make wing-beating noises. Blow me down, she had bought a trio of Faverolle bantams — two hens and a rooster! The ensuing discussion doesn't bear repeating, but when we rode out of the Mudgee Showground that afternoon we had a cardboard box in each pannier, suitably modified with penknife and masking tape so they would fit in the cramped space. When I had tried to close the panniers she went berserk, fearful that the chickens would suffocate from lack of oxygen. I hope they do, I thought to myself, but relented and left both panniers slightly open during the ride home.

By the time we actually got going it was late afternoon and very cold. I abandoned my plan to ride the back roads and decided to head for home as fast as I could, not a particularly happy chappie. When we reached Lithgow it was dark and so cold that it felt like it was about to snow. Our hands and feet were numb, so we decided to break the ride and stop overnight at the Zig Zag Motel, where fortunately there was a vacancy. We checked in, grabbed the room key and headed for a hot shower.

Before settling down for the evening, the Little Woman suggested that I go and get the chooks. 'We can't leave them in the panniers, love, they'll freeze to death.' I hoped she was joking, but she wasn't! She finally convinced me that we could put the two cardboard boxes in the shower recess where it was relatively warm and where the chickens wouldn't freeze overnight. Besides, she argued, they were boxed so couldn't make a mess.

Being one who is forever striving for harmony, I eventually surrendered and carried the clucking cartons into the bathroom. I turned off the light and was pleasantly surprised that in almost no time the squawking noises stopped; the chooks appeared to have fallen asleep. After the cold ride and our hot showers we were pretty whacked, so we turned in early, planning to be up at sunrise to sneak the chooks out of the motel before anyone cottoned on.

I was in a dead sleep when it happened.

At first I thought it was part of a bad dream, the shrill sound of a rooster crowing. The second crow was accompanied by a sharp Karate thump in the ribs, delivered with great precision by the Little Woman. 'Wake up, wake up, the rooster is crowing.'

I rolled over in the pitch dark and peeked at the bedside clock ... 3.58am!

'Quick, go get the rooster before it wakes up the whole motel.'

Panicking, I staggered into the bathroom and grabbed the box, just as the contents were halfway through another piercing shriek. Without hesitating she ripped the top of the box open, grabbed the rooster by the legs and pulled the flapping mound of feathers down under the bedcovers. I stood there staring, freezing, incredulous, open mouthed. Was this woman stark raving insane or what?

'For heaven's sake, get back into bed. If we keep the rooster dark and warm, it'll soon go back to sleep!' She was right, and that is how I came to end up sleeping with two chicks.

# On the Turps

Aldo Anguillesi
Rye, VIC

It was on the way to the Ulysses Club Annual General Meeting in Newcastle several years ago that we got into a little bit of bother. Our group of 15 riders had decided to split up. Eleven elected to take the short and most direct route, while the remaining four of us selected the longer but more scenic road. Our plan was to take it easy — ride for about six hours each day then stop overnight, giving us plenty of time to relax each evening and ready ourselves for the next day's riding.

We old farts had ridden to quite a few AGMs over the years, so we started the journey with great eagerness and enthusiasm. Most of us were seasoned travellers with a love for this beautiful country and its glorious weather. The roads were great with large sweeping bends and almost no wind. The sun beamed down, highlighting the magnificent landscape around us. With cruise controls set we were on our way and living the dream!

We only had an hour or so to ride to our destination when it became obvious that the weather was about to deteriorate; ominous clouds were gathering overhead, proclaiming the arrival of dusk earlier than usual. Alert to the distinct possibility of rain, our ride leader signalled a short stop to don our wet-weather gear. We were back on the road for only a few minutes before the heavens opened and it bucketed down. As the weather worsened, we exercised a heightened level of caution, keeping our eyes peeled in the dangerous riding conditions.

The downpour was huge, forcing us to progressively reduce our speed as visibility diminished. Soon several centimetres of water covered the road and we became concerned that continuing to ride under such conditions could be perilous. Just then I noticed something strange. My steering was getting heavier and heavier. Bloody hell, not a friggin' puncture, that's all I need! I was about to signal my predicament when left-hand indicators started blinking ahead and all four bikes slowly came to a standstill.

I was getting drenched as I examined my front wheel. I ran my gloved hand over both tyres and all I could feel was shiny smooth rubber. The tyres weren't flat, but all the tread had disappeared. What the hell?

I sloshed over to Jim, who was checking his bike. 'I've got a problem,' he said. 'Both my tyres have gone bald.'

There was silence as we tried to comprehend the situation. Soon it was evident that the four of us had exactly the same problem — bald tyres — but how? All four bikes had been serviced in readiness for the big trip and a couple of us had actually fitted new tyres. The rain was pelting down and the light was poor so it was difficult to carry out a detailed inspection. Then Jim yelled out, 'Hey, boys, come 'ave a look at this!'

We congregated around his bike as we watched him flicking shards off his tyre with the aid of a penknife. We were baffled and then almost on cue there was relieved laughter all round as we realised that layers of bitumen had stuck to the tyres, as well as to the underside of our mudguards, a good two centimetres thick.

Several plausible theories were proposed, argued and then discarded. After lots of discussion, we finally came up with the likely answer. We remembered that we had ridden through roadworks where fresh bitumen had been laid just prior to the storm's arrival. The council workers probably saw the water spreading over the road and figured that the bitumen would set quickly. They then simply buggered off and abandoned the work site, thinking, she'll be right, no need to worry.

By this time dusk was upon us and the rain seemed to be getting a lot heavier. With screwdrivers and penknives it took us nearly three hours to remove the bitumen from each of our tyres, or at least sufficient for us to continue to our destination for the night. The next day we got up early to check out the mess. We used over four litres of turps to clean our tyres and bikes.

At Newcastle we related our tale of sorrow to anyone who would listen, only to be laughed at in disbelief.

# The Old Beeza

Dave Garrett
Kurrajong, NSW

At the age of 10 I saved enough dosh to buy my first pushbike and I spent much of my adolescent life on two wheels, of the pedal variety. Having formed a 'Skid Kid' club and built a number of bush tracks on a mate's property for racing around in a hair-raising manner, all without any thought of safety gear such as crash helmets, I became quite adept at manoeuvring two-wheelers. However, the thought of motorising two wheels was never an option as my mother was dead against motorbikes, referring to the riders of such contraptions as 'Temporary Australians'. As a result, under her threat of 'the day you arrive home with a motorbike is the day you leave', I never owned such a machine — at least not while living at home with my parents.

As so often happens when one matures and leaves home, the things that were previously taboo suddenly have a strong attraction, and even more so when the ingredient of necessity is added to the equation. At the age of 23 I married the girl of my dreams. Although at that stage I had two cars, it soon became obvious that one had to go for financial reasons. This caused a dilemma because after we started a family my wife needed the car during the day while I needed a vehicle to get to work, as there was little in the way of public transport where we lived in Frenchs Forest. I was working as a foreman motor mechanic in a service station on the northern beaches when I heard that one of our customers had a son who owned an old 1949 C11 BSA 250 motorbike. He had bought it with the intention of stripping and rebuilding it, but he soon found that he lacked the expertise to complete the task, so he lost interest. For the princely sum of 20 quid I was offered this almost unrecognisable machine, mostly packed in a number of boxes! With necessity my driving force and considering myself a mature thinker no longer under parental constraint, I was confronted with a challenge and an offer too good to refuse.

On one of the days when I had the use of our car to get to work, I hooked up the trailer and arranged to pick up my new machine. I parted with my 20 quid, loaded the bike into the trailer and drove off with a smile on my face — Mum would have been most unimpressed! When I arrived home with this bundle of bits my wife told me I was nuts, because she was unable to visualise how this pile of junk could be transformed into a self-propelled means of transport. Although not overly happy with the prospect of me riding a 'dangerous' motorbike, she soon realised that once I got the thing up and running she would have sole use of our car while I was at work.

The 250 BSA was powered by a single-cylinder 250cc overhead valve engine, which was quite advanced for its era. It boasted a three-speed gearbox, rigid frame, telescopic front forks and drum brakes front and rear. Now began the formidable task of reassembling this old machine into something of its former glory; well at least to a rideable condition anyway. I emptied the boxes of bits and pieces and sorted them into something that resembled an engine, a gearbox, some electrics, a frame and some sprockets and wheels. I had never worked on a motorbike before, but my expertise with motorcars and a general knowledge of things mechanical stood me in good stead as I began to assess just what it would take to bring this whole thing together. I needed a new set of piston rings and a couple of gears to replace the originals which were in very bad shape, but the rest seemed to be in a salvageable condition. Fortunately, just down the road from where I worked there was a motorbike shop run by an old codger who knew the older model bikes and had a reasonable range of new and second-hand parts. I guess I was not very good company for my wife during the next couple of weeks while I had my head and hands buried in the greasy intestines of my new-found toy.

After I got hold of the new set of piston rings and second-hand replacement gears, I began the challenge of assembly. It all went fairly well because most parts were in reasonable condition and I was only aiming to build a reliable means of transport, not a pristine restoration. After chasing around to locate the original specifications, I was able to assemble the engine and grind the valves. The gearbox was a little trickier because everything had to be assembled inside the casing before the outer casing could be attached. The front and rear brake linings were pretty sad, but I managed to adapt some car-type linings I had in my shed. The chain and sprocket were in good condition as were the front and rear tyres. The speedo was mounted in the top right side of the fuel tank, but the ignition switch, headlight switch and ammeter were mounted in the headlamp body, all of which were defunct. I busied myself with some sheet metal and fabricated a small dashboard containing non-genuine versions of the above components and mounted it in the centre of the handlebars. Instead of the original single spring-mounted seat, my machine just happened to have a later model dual seat, which actually made it look newer than it really was. It was also more comfortable.

At last it was time to fuel her up, tickle the carby float bowl, close off the manual choke, turn on the ignition key, get the old boot onto the kick-starter, open the throttle a little and cross the fingers. Much to my delight, following three attempts the old girl roared into life and after a few minor adjustments I was ready to give her a test ride. I didn't have a bike licence and had never ridden a motorbike before, but I assumed it was just like riding a pushbike without having to pedal! I soon felt very comfortable behind the handlebars. At that time a car licence was considered a learner's permit and as soon as I was sufficiently confident I turned up at the Manly police station for my motorbike licence test. After a few brief questions and a riding test that involved a solo ride around the park with the copper watching from the police station steps, I became a fully licensed motorcycle rider.

My motorcycle garb consisted of a surplus store helmet, aviation goggles with interchangeable lenses, my work boots, overalls and my old Canadian jacket. In the wintertime I would stuff a few sheets of newspaper inside the front of the jacket to insulate it and keep the cold wind from penetrating through to my skin.

All went well until one day I set off to work in the rain. As I was heading down through the bends on a wet Allambie Road, just a few metres ahead some school kids ran across the road in front of me. In my mind I knew I shouldn't hit the brakes on a corner, let alone in the wet, but it was hit the anchors or hit the kids, so the kids won and the inevitable happened. The bike and I went down, sliding along the greasy wet road and narrowly missing the kids. By the time I slid to an ungainly halt they were nowhere to be seen. I picked myself and my bike up, cursed the kids, and examined the bike and then myself. Although I was feeling a little sore and sorry for myself, all seemed to be intact apart from a few bent components on the bike. After some swift kicks to straighten what I could, the old Beeza roared into life and I gingerly continued on to work. Upon arrival a quick assessment revealed multiple grazes and bruises but fortunately nothing major, probably due to the road being wet and slippery.

The old Beeza filled a very essential role in meeting my transport needs during those early days, and at a price I could afford too, returning an amazing 75 miles per gallon. Apart from being a handy commuter, she was also an enjoyable way to travel during fine weather, especially in the summertime. While she was no world-beater performance-wise — flat strap she would just make it to 50 miles per hour — she never let me down.

Eventually I replaced the old Beeza with a more family-friendly vehicle, a 1957 FE Holden Sedan. It cost the princely sum of £40, but then that's another story ...

# Growing Old Disgracefully

John 'JohnnyB' Bryant (Ulysses #813)
Bilpin, NSW

Looking back on my life, I am surprised that I can scarcely remember any of my birthdays. One early exception was when I turned six and my parents gave me a Roy Rogers six-shooter that fired caps. The only other anniversary of my arrival on earth that I recall with any clarity is the milestone when I hit the Big Four O. I remember that birthday well because my family threw me a huge surprise birthday party, my first ever.

Superficially, you could say that I had it made. It was 1986, I had a lovely wife, my kids were all doing well at school, my business was booming, and a 1984 BMW K100RT sat winking at me every time I walked into my garage. But although I didn't realise it at the time, there was something happening deep down inside me. With the benefit of hindsight I can now look back almost 30 years and see that I was wrestling with my very own midlife crisis. I had arrived at a point where I had achieved some of my goals, but suddenly I was confronted with that frightening question: 'What next?' I really had no answers. While I couldn't put my finger on it, I felt an undefined yearning to do or be 'something more'.

A few days after my birthday I took a rare day off and jumped onto the BM for a solo midweek run down to Newport Beach. I wanted time alone to think; to think about the now and to think about the future. What was life all about? Where was I headed? What, if anything, was the next challenge?

I grabbed a cappuccino and was heading for a park bench under the trees at the edge of the sand when I passed by a newsagent. A magazine caught my eye. It was a motorcycle magazine, I cannot recall which one, but as I sat sucking my cappuccino and flicking through the pages an article leapt out at me. It was a rundown on a rather unusual motorcycle club that had started a couple of years earlier in Sydney. Membership criteria stipulated only two requirements: possession of a motorcycle licence and a minimum age of 50, although junior members could join at 40. The organisation was called the Ulysses Club and its logo carried the motto 'Grow Old Disgracefully'. I was intrigued.

The article told the entertaining story of a small bunch of blokes who had started this unique social club, attributing its rapid growth in membership to the ethos of the founding fathers. It spoke of the lure of the open road, two-wheeled freedom, goodwill, good old-fashioned mateship and adventures yet to be experienced. The whole concept meshed with what I was feeling down in midlife-crisis-land. Within a month I had submitted my membership application, paid my money and received my membership number. I revelled in the fact that I had joined about 800 other 'oldish' men and women, all dedicated to enjoying their motorcycles, and all committed to giving convention the finger and growing old disgracefully!

I kicked off my Ulysses Club involvement by joining some of the weekend rides in my local area. Anything up to a dozen or more riders and pillions would turn up at a pre-agreed time and place, then set off for a day of riding, eating and socialising. These rides were a great icebreaker, an ideal opportunity to mingle and get to know fellow club members. I quickly noticed that nobody really cared what sort of motorcycle anyone else rode, whether big or small or cheap or expensive. The point was that we were all on two wheels, all intent on hitting the road and enjoying each other's company. Some members were a bit like me in that they had owned motorcycles all their lives. Others had ridden motorcycles during their younger days but had succumbed to the pressures of career, family or whatever, and been forced to spend their middle years on four wheels. After finally throwing off the shackles of responsibility, these folk had climbed back onto two wheels with renewed enthusiasm, ready for any escapade that was going. What better way to kick back, recharge the batteries and have a bit of fun!

There was also another interesting group that found their way into the club, and these were people who had never ventured forth on a motorcycle before. Many of them appeared to have lived disciplined, responsible lives. They had worked hard, brought up the kids, paid off much of the mortgage, but were still relatively young and healthy, and hell-bent on looking for adventure. Maybe there was an air of rebellion in their attitude? Whatever it was, they simply seemed to have a strong desire to ignore convention, unshackle the chains and grow old disgracefully. I could spot them a mile away. Their bikes were often new, big and expensive, proudly exhibiting strategically placed Ulysses Club badges. Their helmets were usually outrageously free of dents and scratches, their arrival heralded by the smell of new leather, and their boots unmarked, looking as though they'd just marched out of the showroom. They wobbled a bit in parking lots, laughed a hell of a lot — it was impossible not to love and admire the lot of them! Anyway, all that started for me about 27 years ago.

In 2013 the Ulysses Club celebrated its 30th birthday, boasting around 23,500 members, making it the biggest and arguably the most successful social club in Australia. To get a handle on the attraction and success of this amazing organisation, it is necessary to go back to the very beginning ... to 1983.

The mid-80s was an exciting time to be a motorcyclist. Intense competition amongst the motorcycle manufacturers in the USA, Japan and Europe resulted in a constant stream of new, innovative, ever larger and more expensive two-wheeled machinery hitting Aussie showrooms. It didn't matter whether your thing was off-road, sports, cruising or touring bikes, there were always many good reasons to open your wallet or sign your life away on a personal loan. This avalanche of enticing equipment was met head-on by a prosperous horde of baby boomers hungrily looking for adventure, excitement and freedom. It was the perfect match. And it was in the midst of this buoyant two-wheeled frenzy that the Ulysses Club was spawned via the pages of a motorcycle magazine called *Bike Australia* (which has since ceased publication).

In his magazine Peter Thoeming (aka The Bear) published a series of letters from readers that tackled issues confronting older motorcyclists. One feisty contributor, a pommy by the name of Stephen Dearnley, suggested that older motorcyclists deserved their own club. Peter responded by proposing that if Stephen wanted to go to the trouble of setting up such a club, he would support it through the pages of *Bike Australia*. Another reader cum motorcycling enthusiast by the name of Rob Hall wrote in support of Stephen's proposed club and suggested the name 'Ulysses Club', drawn from that famous poem written by Lord Tennyson. For those unfamiliar with the poem, it features an old monarch who has successfully fought and won many wars, but in his later years still yearned for adventure and conquest. So in spite of his advancing age the old king set forth yet again with his beloved companions to fight, loot, rape and pillage his way into the sunset. Rob's girlfriend at the time suggested the now famous club motto, 'Grow Old Disgracefully', to define the Ulyssian spirit.

Always one to step up to a challenge, Stephen proceeded to set up a social club for older motorcyclists, while The Bear, true to his word, not only enthusiastically promoted the club in his magazine, but also sketched the badge that has remained the club's logo ever since. The first official meeting of the club took place at the Elizabeth Hotel (since demolished) in Elizabeth Street, Sydney, at 8pm on 6th December 1983. Only Stephen and four others turned up for that historic meeting but, undaunted, the small band of optimists adopted the club name and approved a draft constitution. Perhaps the longevity and success of the organisation can be attributed to the wisdom displayed by the founders when they defined the three basic aims of the club at that initial meeting:

*To provide ways in which older motorcyclists can get together for companionship and mutual support; to show by example that motorcycling can be an enjoyable and practical activity for riders of all ages; to draw the attention of public and private institutions to the needs and views of older riders.*

From these humble beginnings one of Australia's premier social clubs was born, specifically catering to older-aged male and female motorcyclists!

Affectionately known as 'Old Number One' — and usually abbreviated to 'Ol' #1' — founder Stephen Dearnley was not only the driving force behind establishing the club, but he also represented the embodiment of the Ulyssian spirit that has been responsible for attracting more than 60,000 past and present members to the club over the last 30 years.

Stephen was born in England in 1921. When World War II began he was just 18 and too young to join the services, so he spent the next couple of years as a member of the Home Guard until enlisting in the Royal Navy in 1941. After completing his officer training he joined the submarine service, where he almost met his demise when his ship was sunk while minesweeping in the North Sea. He went on to spend a further three years in submarines, during which time he met a young navy signaller, Josephine Irwin. Stephen invited Jo out for their first date while they were both serving on separate ships, Stephen using a Morse code lamp to communicate his invitation for coffee. They were engaged within a fortnight and married within a year. Looking to new horizons after the end of hostilities, Stephen and Jo arrived in Australia in 1947, settling on Sydney's North Shore where they proceeded to raise their four children.

Stephen's love affair with two wheels had started in childhood, with his bicycle morphing into motorised cycling with the purchase of his first motorbike in 1945, an old Indian pre-owned by the US Army. Exuding a keen wit and delicious sense of humour, Stephen was passionate about the club he founded, setting an example of leadership that prompted respect and loyalty from those who came to know him.

One of Stephen's more remarkable exploits took place in 2002 when, during his 80th year, he circumnavigated Australia on a Honda Silver Wing. During his epic 60-day, 16,000-kilometre ride he attended countless functions and media events, raising over $35,000 for the Arthritis Foundation on behalf of the club. Fittingly, in 1999 Stephen was awarded an OAM for services to sailing and motorcycling. Commenting on the award in *The Australian* newspaper, a reporter declared that Stephen's OAM was a 'victory for larrikinism' and nominated him as 'the leader of the largest motorcycle gang in Australia'!

Within a year of its inception, Ulysses Club membership reached 100, with no one more surprised than the founders. Before long the ethos and objectives of the club caught the imagination of older motorcyclists right across the country; they have galloped into membership at an astonishing rate ever since. By 1991 membership had passed the 3,000 mark, quadrupling again to over 13,000 by 1999, and when the club reached its 20th birthday in 2003 it had over 21,000 members on its books.

The growing membership provided a pool of mature men and women with a wide range of professional skills, many of whom were retired with the time to devote to their passion for all things motorcycling. These enthusiastic volunteers contributed to the success of the club by donating their time and expertise to everything from IT to accounting to legal to publishing to engineering to ... you name it.

Since inception, the club kept in touch with its growing but scattered Australia-wide membership via its own regular newsletter. From a simple typed sheet in 1983, the newsletter has evolved into a magazine titled *Riding On*, which is now a professionally produced full-colour publication exceeding 100 pages per issue. The magazine is published quarterly and sent free of any extra cost to all current financial members. With most members owning one or more large machines, motorcycle manufacturers and accessory retailers view *Riding On* as a valuable marketing conduit into a major lucrative market. In fact it has been estimated by one motorcycle journalist that 60 per cent of all large motorcycles sold in Australia are purchased by Ulysses Club members. Apart from serving up a wide variety of interesting information relating to its members and motorcycling, the magazine also features a section called 'Ridden On', which acknowledges the lives of those members who have passed away. Invariably the stories of these ridden-on loved ones record the respect and mateship that lies at the core of this great club.

The Ulysses Club logo, known affectionately as the 'Old Man' logo, has remained unchanged since the first freehand sketch devised back in 1983. Just as all attempts to modify the initial 'three basic aims' of the club have been resisted down the years, so too have efforts to update, modify or change the Old Man logo. Registered as a trademark to prevent its alteration or unauthorised use, the iconic club symbol now appears on club literature and an extensive range of motorcycle-related merchandise.

There are some who say that a member doesn't become a true Ulyssian until he or she has experienced at least a couple of annual general meetings (AGMs). The Ulysses AGM has evolved from the initial short meeting of members in Sydney in 1983, to a weeklong 'party time' attended by anything up to 5,000 members and their motorcycles, depending on the venue.

Very early on it was decided that holding the AGM away from home was a great idea because it gave many members the opportunity to go for a decent ride, as well as to meet up with old friends and participate in the management and decision-making of the club. It has become a well-established tradition to rotate the geographical location of the AGM each year, with meetings having been held at venues as far-flung as Alice Springs (NT), Bunbury (WA), Broken Hill (NSW) and Cairns (QLD).

Those who don't ride a motorcycle often have difficulty appreciating the joys of long-distance riding and the camaraderie that develops amongst those who tackle the road on two wheels. Nothing beats being part of a convoy of dozens or even hundreds of motorcyclists thundering across the Nullarbor or down a major highway to an AGM, heading for a week of partying with mates. Any lone rider with an Old Man patch on his jacket is welcomed into the fold like a long-lost brother.

Over the years an AGM pattern has emerged, with the Friday night developing into a time to catch up with old acquaintances, some of whom meet for the first time face-to-face after communicating on the club's website forum. Saturday morning will traditionally see thousands of motorcycles taking part in a giant street parade, usually escorted by the local police, often taking up to an hour to pass down the main street to the cheers and acclamation of the local populace. The street parade almost always finishes up in a park where the local mayor or other VIP issues a welcome to the visiting motorcyclists and has his or her photograph taken with the bikes. It's worth mentioning that the smile on many of the locals' faces is helped along by the very substantial contribution that the visitors make to the local economy, these days calculated in the millions of dollars.

Also at some stage during a weekend, and often after the street parade, tickets are drawn from a barrel to select the winners of some amazing and very valuable prizes. Several motorcycle manufacturers have got into the habit of generously donating their latest model motorcycles as attendance prizes. Witnessing the emotional gesticulations of the winner of a brand-new motorcycle is something to behold!

Saturday afternoon usually divides all members into one of two groups. Those who have a serious or specific interest in the running of the club will attend the formal AGM to express their point of view and vote on office bearers for the coming year. Those who couldn't give a stuff about administrative issues and just want to cram in as much riding as possible usually join organised rides to local places of interest.

Saturday evening is reserved for the official dinner, which is a logistical challenge of mammoth proportions; staging a sit-down dinner for anything up to 4,000 or more people under one roof is no simple task. After the dinner, members hang out together in a giant party atmosphere with a few beers and plenty of rock'n'roll! It is a time when old mates let their hair down and prove that 'growing old disgracefully' is a lot of fun. Of course defining the limits of disgraceful behaviour, as against objectionable behaviour, can be somewhat difficult at times. Some members are still debating whether the couple that rode through a Saturday night dinner naked on their motorcycle were merely disgraceful, or perhaps offensive. Many others couldn't care less.

On Sunday morning a traditional church service is usually followed by one or more weddings or marriage affirmations; a wonderful and memorable time for those involved, surrounded by friends and well-wishers. The rest of the day usually comprises mass rides to local attractions with many breaking camp and heading for home at some stage.

As the years have rolled on, the AGMs have become bigger, longer and more comprehensive, covering a full week of activities, usually commencing the week before the AGM itself. The addition of motorcycle retailers displaying their new models and offering test rides has added to the appeal, with many new machines purchased by members at 'show special' prices. Add to that the growing army of aftermarket motorcycle accessories and clothing retailers with professionally set-up merchandise tents, and the week becomes an orgy of motorcycles, mates and meetings.

The logistics of staging AGMs has become increasingly challenging as membership numbers continue to grow. For example, in 2003 the Mudgee AGM recorded 4,842 registrations, all of which required undercover seating for the Saturday night dinner. Unable to find such a venue locally, the club hired a 5,000-seat marquee, which was set up in the Mudgee Showground for the week; it was a great hit with members. Even larger numbers were experienced in 2007 at the Coffs Harbour AGM, where an attendance record was established with 6,115 members registering. The complexity of these events now requires three or four years' advance planning, and is a testimony to the dedication and expertise of the large number of local members who volunteer to put on the 'party' for everyone's enjoyment.

Many a legend has grown out of Ulysses AGMs, always exemplifying the spirit that draws older bikers into the club. After the Bunbury AGM, about 1,400 members made the round trip, circumnavigating Australia on Highway 1. Included in the mob was 83-year-old John Shepperd, who took out the 'oldest rider' trophy for his efforts. Then there was the 1996 AGM held in Tasmania, where 1,500 members took themselves and their motorcycles across Bass Strait on the *Spirit of Tasmania*, ending up proudly riding through the streets of Hobart during the Saturday morning parade. Long-distance riding has also become somewhat commonplace, with people like Stan Muller riding his motorcycle a distance of over 5,000 kilometres from Kununurra (WA) to Jindabyne (NSW) to attend the 1992 AGM. And few will forget the unofficial club hymn 'Oh my god I'm over 50, my pubic hair is going grey' sung to the tune of 'What a friend we have in Jesus'!

The club has not been without its challenges, but wisdom and clear thinking at a national level have always prevailed. In 2005, when the AGM was held in Canberra, a local outlaw motorcycle club took issue with a number of Ulysses Club members who were wearing 'rockers' and other badges on their vests, and displaying the Old Man logo on the back of their jackets. The bikies considered that the Ulysses Club patch constituted 'club colours' when worn that way, provoking a number of unpleasant incidents. National committee representatives subsequently met with the national body of the outlaw club, resulting in the Ulysses Club members being instructed not to wear the Old Man logo on the back of their vests or jackets. That solved the problem and allowed members to concentrate on doing what they do best — growing old disgracefully!

Of course the AGMs are only one of many hundreds of events held by Ulysses Club branches all over the country every week of the year. Apart from the ubiquitous weekly rides that can be attended by anything from a couple of riders to literally dozens of bikes, many poker runs, rallies, charity rides and Ulysses Club 'odysseys' have become a permanent part of the motorcycling landscape. In his book *The Ulysses Story*, club founder Stephen Dearnley explained his theory on the mindset that motivated many of the club's activities:

> *Just a few final thoughts about AGMs, Odysseys and motorcycle rallies generally. That more and more members cheerfully ride thousands of kilometres to AGM gatherings that continue to grow bigger each year is a matter of amazement. As I think about this phenomenon, it seems that there could be a parallel with the days of the Middle Ages when folk would travel great distances on pilgrimages to holy places like Rome, Mecca, Jerusalem*

*or Canterbury. I suspect that it was not always religious fervour that drove the pilgrims in those days but an opportunity to take a break from daily village life and to go on a big adventure. An adventure that brought them in touch with people from many different backgrounds, cultures and countries, but all with a common aim and interest. Although the journey might be tough, there would be good companionship and tall tales told along the way and, at the destination itself, much celebration and entertainment. Just like an AGM today, in fact. Perhaps sometime in the future another Chaucer will write down our stories and, even more fancifully, the Ulysses Tales may one day be set as a study text for Leaving Certificate students in 2503 — who knows?*

Every Ulysses Club member claims allegiance to the Australia-wide Ulysses Club, which is governed by a democratically elected national committee. While members are also free to start or join a branch in their local area, participation in branch activities is purely a matter of personal preference. All branches have equal status, none more important than another, all with equal rights and responsibilities. There have been cases where branches have grown large then split up into two or more smaller branches in order to maintain an intimate environment. The club structure has successfully stood the test of time, and it's perhaps one of the reasons the club has enjoyed such peace and prosperity while other social clubs have disintegrated and disappeared. The Ulysses Club has also spread its tentacles internationally with the first overseas branch established in New Zealand in 1987. Expansion into the international arena has not been a considered strategy, but rather a response to demand from older riders around the world. Travellers to countries such as Namibia, South Africa, Zimbabwe, Vietnam, UK, Germany and Norway can expect to see motorcyclists wearing the Ulysses Club Old Man logo patch.

In July 2009 the Ulysses Club Road Safety Committee was formed, emphasising the club's commitment to motorcycle safety. Putting its money where its mouth is, the club offers all members a rebate if they undertake a rider skills and safety course. As long as a member can prove successful attendance at a course run by an accredited motorcycle rider training organisation, he or she can claim a rebate from the club of up to $80 towards the cost.

Where is the Ulysses Club heading?

Currently the average age of Ulysses Club members is around 56, but there are a number of 80- and 90-year-old members still actively participating in the club. The statisticians tell us that Australia has an ageing population, with people in the over 65 age group expecting to double to about 25 per cent of the total population in the next 40 years. Coupled with this growing pool of potential members, motorcycle ownership is also on the increase. While car ownership by men over the age of 45 has jumped 30 per cent in the last decade, motorcycle registrations have leapt 180 per cent in the same period. Surprisingly, this rate of increase is even larger for women in the over 45 age group, with bike registrations jumping a massive 195 per cent. Although some of the increased interest in motorcycles may be attributed to traditional factors such as economics, convenience or manoeuvrability, some psychologists believe that rebellion and the midlife crisis syndrome play an important part. Based on these statistics, and providing the club can remain true to the principles upon which it was founded, its future seems assured.

The club's founder, Stephen Dearnley, continued his active involvement in the Ulysses Club right up until his death on 11th February 2012, when over 1,200 members attended his memorial service at the Mildura AGM in March 2012; a fitting tribute to a man whose legacy lives on in this most iconic social organisation — a club that has given so much joy to so many.

Perhaps Stephen's final words in his book *The Ulysses Story* summarise the secret to the success of the club:

*Many motorcycling clubs have splintered and dissolved in bitterness and acrimony as an individual or clique tries to assert supremacy or use the organisation for selfish purposes. In the case of Ulysses I believe its best safeguard against such self-destruction is the maturity and goodwill of its membership. Certainly there have been and will be those who want to big-note themselves or see the club as a potential power base for their own advancement. Common sense generally prevails because overly ambitious members soon become aware from peer pressure that such behaviour is not acceptable: they either get the message and conform to the ethos of Ulysses or they will look elsewhere to further their ambitions. Unlike the democratic system of government which is based on the adversarial principle of the governing party against the opposition, prosecutor against defendant, Left versus Right, Ulysses is a shining example of government by consensus and goodwill. It often operates in a happy atmosphere of organised anarchy — but it works!*

As older riders most of us no longer have to prove anything.

In Tennyson's own words:

... and tho'
We are not now that strength which in old days
Moved earth and heaven; that which we are,
we are;
One equal temper of heroic hearts.
Made weak by time and fate, but strong in will
To strive, to seek, to find, and not to yield.

# William the Third

Bruce Thorn
Melbourne, VIC

Sometimes what happens on a trip just has to be told.

Bruce and Max were riding with Max's son Mick and their mate Colin in the 2011 'Border Run' from their hometown of Melbourne to Border Village on the South Australian and Western Australian border.

Now Bruce and Max are quite accomplished long-distance riders, being members of the Iron Butt Association. Bruce rides a Harley Ultra Classic and Max a Honda Gold Wing, and between the pair of them they know how to handle a mile or two. Their norm is to ride for a couple of hours, then stop for a snack and a drink out of their on-board tucker boxes, and then continue to the next fuel stop.

Well, their ride to Border Village was progressing according to plan when they pulled into a dirt roadside truck stop for a break. Max parked under the first shady tree, leaving Bruce and the others to travel a little further to the next protected spots. During their travels most of the idle chatter is done over their two-way radios while riding, leaving the few minutes for a rest stop purely for grabbing something to eat and drink and maybe answering the call of nature. However, on this occasion Max was a little puzzled when he glanced at Bruce and saw that he was bent over beside his machine. Max casually wandered over to have a closer look.

He found Bruce distressed, horrified by the fact that he had got off his bike and unwittingly trodden in a rather large 'William the Third' that was lying amongst the sticks and bark strewn around under the tree. Consequently, Bruce spent his rest break using sticks to scrape the evidence of this monster from the sole of his boot. Needless to say, Bruce didn't get much time to enjoy his snack and drink; nor did Max, who was circling the scene laughing his head off, much to the entertainment of Mick and Colin.

The group headed off again, but there was no pleasant chatter over the radio, just Max laughing and Bruce telling him to shut up. The next stop was for fuel, then they took off again and headed for the next break, which would be in a designated roadside rest area.

As they pulled in, Max once again took the first shady tree with Mick and Colin following suit, grabbing the next couple of sheltered spots. Bruce came in last and was about to pull up under a tree when he noticed a few ominous-looking tissues on the ground, so he bypassed that tree and continued on to the next. That last tree, providing the only remaining cool parking space, was a rather large bottlebrush. As Bruce headed for the shade, he was very wary of the old bottlebrush cones scattered all over the ground. He concentrated on avoiding them because they could have caused him some grief if he ran over them at slow speed on his heavy Ultra Classic.

Having finally come to rest under the shade of the bottlebrush, Bruce stepped off his bike onto what at first he thought was just an old rotten bottlebrush cone. But, oh no, it was another 'William the Third', cunningly camouflaged amongst the fallen cones and leaf litter. He couldn't decide what irritated him the most — the heat, the flies, the smell, his soiled boot or Max circling the scene laughing his head off. Bruce was decidedly unimpressed while he once again poked away with an assortment of bark and sticks as he attempted to remove the filthy residue from his boot.

As the ride progressed and the rest stops accumulated, Bruce was very wary of suffering a repeat performance. Fortunately, he was in the company of good mates who were there to look after his welfare and remind him to be careful. As Max said several hundred times before Bruce made it home: 'You've stepped on two, mate — don't step on a turd!'

# Indian Love Story

## Ken Hager, Indian 'One-Eleven Original' #1
## Macedon Ranges, VIC

Over the last couple of decades the motorcycling world has witnessed a parade of born-again motorbike marques. Famous brands from the first half of last century, such as Voxan, Triumph, Hesketh, Excelsior-Henderson, Brough, Matchless, Norton, Manx, Atlas, Commando and Dominator, were killed off by competition, mostly by newcomers from the Land of the Rising Sun. But many of these legendary brands have since made their comeback, soaring aloft like the phoenix, to tantalise and delight baby boomers like me. I haven't bought them all, but heaven knows I've been tempted after watching the launch of yet another nostalgic brand from yesteryear. With the benefit of hindsight I suppose I am responsible for the death of some of those brands, as well as their subsequent resurrection many years later, simply based on my own motorcycle purchase decisions.

Born and reared in Woodstock, Illinois, about 120 kilometres southwest of Milwaukee, Wisconsin, my earliest motorcycle was a new 1971 Triumph Bonneville. This bike tried very hard to self-destruct, so after just two years I had had enough and sold it. In its place was my first Japanese bike, a 1973 CB500F Honda Four, which I sold in 1975 to immigrate to Australia the following year. After a few years of indecision about whether to live in the USA or Australia, 1981 found me aboard another Nipponese machine, a new 1981 Yamaha XJ650, which I hung onto for 20 years. Great bikes both of them — super reliable and representing fantastic value for money. I didn't get back onto a more traditional brand motorcycle until I was converted at a demo ride day put on by the local Harley-Davidson dealer. Consequently, I bought a 2002 XLH Sportster, followed six years later by a Dyna-Glide. I enjoyed those two machines, chalking up a total of over 125,000 kilometres in 10 years.

I stuck with the Harley-Davidson brand after attending the Sturgis rally in 2004, where the USA-made Victory range of motorcycles was being offered for test rides. I was attracted to the Victory Vegas model in particular, but was not likely to get one as they were not for sale in Australia at the time or in the foreseeable future. In 2011 I bought a second-hand Vegas and rode it from Carson City, Nevada, to Watertown, New York State, while on holidays. That motorcycle still remains in the care of my brother, who thinks he owns it because it's in his garage. It's a beautiful arrangement; he pays all the costs of maintaining and insuring the bike, and I get to ride it whenever I visit him over there. Then in 2012 when I saw a second-hand Victory Vegas for sale in Melbourne I just had to have it, and have been riding it ever since. In the years I have owned the Vegas bikes in both the USA and Australia I've been very impressed with their build excellence and their ride quality. So when I subsequently heard that Victory manufacturer, Polaris Industries, was about to reincarnate a famous old American brand, it had my immediate attention.

The news that the Indian motorcycle brand was about to be resurrected reached my ears back in 2011. Although there had been previous attempts by small companies to relaunch that brand, the thing that really grabbed my attention was the profile of the latest corporation to buy the rights to the trademark and designs: Polaris Industries. Not only was it a successful multi-billion-dollar American company, but in my opinion it had already proven itself in the motorcycle market by designing, manufacturing and distributing the Victory range of motorcycles. However, at that time I didn't get too excited because I figured that it would take many years for the born-again Indians to arrive in the Australian marketplace. If the Indian product followed the same route as the Victory range, it could take four to five years in product development, followed by a decade of sales in the US domestic market before being released to the rest of the world. I figured that we would be lucky if Indian bikes arrived in Australia much before 2025. On top of that, I was suspicious that the pile of dollars that may be required to land one's bum on an Indian seat could be higher than Mt Everest, or at least Mt Kosciuszko.

All that changed in April 2013 when I and five of my mates decided to travel from Yea, Victoria, to the Ulysses Club Fraser Coast AGM at Maryborough, Queensland. Upon arrival we were delighted to be confronted with the usual conglomeration of motorcycle manufacturers and accessory purveyors, all trying desperately to flog us their products. I booked in for demo rides on the new Yamaha FJR 1300 as well as the CanAm Spider ST. They were both great machines, but not attractive enough to entice me to jettison my Victory.

Having inspected the displays of the major players, I then noticed two more exhibits in a remote corner of the AGM showground: Kawasaki and Indian. Indian had a range of branded clothing and associated knick-knacks for sale, but no motorcycles. I was vaguely aware that Indian was close to releasing a new motorcycle, as I had seen teaser advertisements in motorcycle magazines revealing only a silhouette of a V-twin motor, but the full release was some way off, or so I believed. Also, in early 2013 I had listened to the rumble of their new engine on the internet, but was still left wondering, though not really all that interested. In retrospect Indian has conducted a marvellous marketing campaign, slowly dribbling out bits and pieces of information to raise brand awareness in the marketplace prior to the release of the actual motorcycle.

As I wandered around the Indian display tent at the AGM, I was captivated by a presentation that heralded the introduction of their new motorcycle that they said was soon to be on its way to Australia. There, in pride of place under the spotlights, was the new V-twin 'Thunder Stroke' 111 cubic inch (1810cc) engine that would power the machine. And that was it — no complete motorcycle and no other details. The veiled engine display was a spectacular surprise and shot my theory to bits about having to wait decades for an Indian motorcycle. Not only did the new Thunder Stroke 111 motor remind me of a gorgeous piece of art deco from yesteryear, it also incorporated a host of modern technological features. To top it off, it looked like it had been assembled with the precision of a Swiss watch. I felt myself strongly attracted, if not starting to fall in love!

As I stood there drooling over the engine and trying to imagine what the rest of the bike may look like, a smooth-talking, silver-tongued Indian representative encouraged me to consider becoming one of the 'One-Eleven Originals'. It was 'a chance in a lifetime', he said. In a nutshell, the first 111 bikes released by Indian in Australia were going to each bear a plaque numbered from 1 to 111. The people buying these 111 motorcycles would become known as the 'One-Eleven Originals'. In addition to the numbered bike, each Original would receive a kit containing a T-shirt, an Indian glass Warbonnet paperweight, an Indian belt and buckle, an Indian original print and a Bell helmet decorated with One-Eleven Original livery.

My saliva was dripping on the floor as I asked the rep how I could become a One-Eleven Original. He said that all I had to do was to be one of the first 111 people to put down a $1,000 cash deposit, sight unseen. That would entitle me to attend the launch, where I would see the full motorcycle for the first time, but that I could cancel my purchase at any time up until then. And if I wasn't impressed by the bike and decided to pull out, I would receive a full refund of my deposit. After thinking about the proposition for fully 30 seconds, I thought, what the heck, and plonked down my deposit, guaranteeing myself a place in the history of the reborn Indian motorcycle marque. Although I hadn't seen the bike or its specifications, and although I didn't have any clue as to the ultimate price, I figured I could jump ship and get my deposit back if the sausage didn't live up to the sizzle! Before I had walked into the Indian display tent, my heartbeat was normal at about 68 beats per minute, but by the time I walked out it had shot well past 100!

As I rode home from the AGM, the image of the Thunder Stroke 111 motor was burned into my brain. Try as hard as I could, I just couldn't visualise the whole motorcycle, so I spent the following two months in a state of suspended excitement. Then in early July I received a letter from Indian Australia advising that there would be a worldwide release of the new bike the following month. The unveiling event was to take place simultaneously in Sydney and Sturgis, South Dakota, which is the home of the world's largest motorcycle rally, started in 1936 by the Jackpine Gypsies, an Indian motorcycle club. All the One-Eleven Originals were invited to attend the Sydney launch, and following the unveiling they would have the opportunity to either confirm their bike purchase, or have a last chance to cancel the transaction and receive their $1,000 deposit refund.

I was on a knife edge. Attending the launch in Sydney would involve only the expense of the airfare, because accommodation and food were to be supplied by Indian. To be honest, I did consider backing out and claiming my refund at that stage. On the other side of the ledger, I reckoned I had lost a lot more than $1,000 on other motorcycle-related activities over the years, so in the end I decided to go along for the ride. I booked my airfare. After all, Indian is a 111-year-old brand that's gone through a long and fitful series of deaths and rebirths, and I wanted to be a part of this one.

I arrived in Sydney on Saturday 4th August 2013 and

checked into the Four Seasons in the heart of the city where the out-of-town One-Eleven Originals were staying. At the appointed time buses arrived to transport us from the hotel to the Victory dealership premises on Parramatta Road at Ashfield. As I tumbled out of the bus and marched into the Indian showroom, I could hardly contain my excitement; it was like entering one of those arranged marriages where you are about to see your new bride face-to-face for the first time! However, I was sorely disappointed because apart from the Victory motorcycles sitting in the display windows of the dealership, there were only several old vintage Indian motorcycles scattered around the showroom floor. 'Where are the new models?' was the question on the lips of the 300-odd people who had turned up for the event. As we indulged ourselves in the free food and drinks, we learned that the actual debut of the new model was scheduled for the following day, timed to coincide with a similar unveiling in South Dakota. The suspense was killing me!

Then came the main event for that evening: the allocation of the first 111 sequentially numbered 'original' Indian motorcycles. It was organised so that each of the people who had put down their $1,000 deposit would draw a number from a barrel containing Indian key rings numbered from 1 to 111, which corresponded with the commemorative plaques that would be affixed to the first 111 motorcycles sold in Australia. The drawing would take place in the same sequence that deposits had been placed with Indian. I learned that I was the 19th person to place a deposit, so that meant that I would be the 19th person to draw a numbered key ring from the barrel. Obviously like everybody else I was eager to draw one of the most highly coveted key rings, either #1 or #111. The place was electric with anticipation as I noticed a few familiar faces from the Ulysses AGM, clearly fellow club members who had also succumbed to temptation and placed their deposits back in April.

Fortunately for me, as the draw proceeded, the first 18 people failed to extract either of the two most highly prized numbers, so key rings #1 and #111 were still in the barrel when my turn came. Statistically, the probability of drawing one of these two numbers had improved considerably, but it was still a long shot. I held my breath as I dipped into the barrel, grabbed a key ring and handed it to the MC, Shane Jacobson. Shane looked at the key ring, looked at me, squinted at the crowd, and then announced somewhat incredulously that I had drawn key ring #1. I could hardly believe it! I was to become the owner of the first ever Indian motorcycle sold into the Australian marketplace, manufactured by Polaris Industries.

Following the allocation of the 111 key rings, there were lots of photos, several interviews and much backslapping while the video cameras were rolling. Perhaps the most bizarre addition to this epic experience was an approach I received from a fellow riding enthusiast just before the evening concluded. He stunned me by offering $10,000 for the privilege of taking over my #1 key ring and position.

As I boarded the bus for the return trip to the Four Seasons that evening, my mind was in overload. Here I was holding the #1 key to the most coveted, newly released American motorcycle in several decades, considering an offer that was almost too good to be true. But, I hadn't even seen the machine that was the subject of all the excitement! I figured that my best strategy was to wait for the unveiling of the motorcycles the following day. If I wasn't impressed, I would grab the $10,000 and continue to enjoy my Victory Vegas. Needless to say, I didn't get much sleep that night.

I was up early Sunday morning, perhaps one of the more memorable days of my life, ready for the final unveiling. Walking around The Rocks, I tried to contain my excitement, but found it hard to concentrate. Breakfast, checkout, and then the bus ride back to Ashfield to eat more food and indulge in a couple more drinks.

When I walked into the showroom things had changed. The vintage Indian motorcycles were no longer centre stage, but had been shuffled into a line-up at the entrance. In the centre of the showroom were six large turntables, each shrouded with a tipi that was obviously concealing a large object that could reasonably be expected to be a motorcycle. The level of collective anticipation made conversation difficult for many of us. Ian Moss was performing when suddenly the music was interrupted by Peter Harvey, the head of Indian Motorcycle Australia, who announced that we were switching to a TV link to Sturgis in South Dakota for the live unveiling. I think Ian Moss might have been a bit peeved to be interrupted mid-song, but what could he expect? We were there to witness the launch of a motorcycle, not listen to music.

The BIG MOMENT had finally arrived!

With a fanfare that would have made Barnum and Bailey Circus envious, the bikes in Sturgis were revealed at the very same moment that the tipi covers were lifted from the six turntables in Ashfield. As the cameras flashed, the crowd let out a stunned gasp. Not one new model, not two, but three different Indian motorcycles! A naked cruiser called the 'Chief Classic', a soft bagger designated the 'Chief Vintage' and a faired hard bagger aptly named the 'Chieftain', all available in a choice of either Thunder Black or Indian Motorcycle Red or Springfield Blue. What a closely held secret — nobody anticipated the range and colour variations!

Almost immediately the staff wheeled out additional bikes so that we could all get up close and personal; sit on them, caress them, eyeball their intimate parts, all the while trying to figure out which of the models and colours we might buy. I suddenly realised that I had absolutely no intention of cancelling my order or accepting the amazing offer of a $10,000 windfall.

Goodbye, Victory Vegas — long live my new Indian Chief Vintage in Springfield Blue!

After the excited crowd were given a good long opportunity to peruse the bikes and ask all their questions, the Indian staff set about completing the paperwork for those who had decided to confirm their purchases. I was amused to note that one bloke, clutching a single-digit key ring number, was still trying to decide which colour he wanted long after the staff had completed the paperwork for the 100 other bikes. I suggested that since he liked all the colours so much perhaps he should buy one of each, to which he replied, 'That's not a bad idea, but now you have given me even more to think about!' I still don't know what he decided.

As the euphoria of the August launch subsided, I arrived home feeling excited but impatient; the delivery of my new bike was still a couple of months away. I felt as though I had signed the marriage licence but still had to endure further delay before I could embark on the honeymoon and sweep my new bride off her feet. It wasn't until 2nd December that my dream became a reality and I was finally united with my long-awaited Indian Chief Vintage bride. She looked gorgeous, smothered in chrome, decked out with virginal whitewalls, resplendent in her Springfield Blue!

I organised to have the first 800-kilometre service one week later. Racking up the kilometres was easily achieved, but due to inclement weather I moved the service to the following week. My Thunder Stroke engine had developed a noticeable ticking sound and this was also to be checked while in for the service. Victory, in the past, had always been good at providing a replacement vehicle, when available, for customers having their motorcycles serviced. I didn't need one for that day as I went to the movies while the service was being performed.

When I returned the service was completed, but the mechanics couldn't determine the cause of the ticking. It was agreed that I would leave the bike so they could identify and repair the defect, so they gave me a Victory Cross Roads LE from their demo fleet to use. I was happy enough with this arrangement as they didn't have any spare Indians in stock and I had been loaned this bike previously when getting my Victory Vegas serviced. It is very similar to the Vintage in concept, and in reality it is a very good bike. It would definitely be my choice for ownership had it not been for the arrival of the Indian.

Two weeks later I was still riding the loaned Cross Roads, mainly because my Indian repairs were interrupted by the workshop being closed over the Christmas holiday period. Then, while out riding in the country one sunny day, I stopped for lunch, checked my phone and noticed a message from Indian. Yay, the bike had been repaired, or so I thought. I returned the call and found that no, the bike wasn't ready. Instead, they urgently needed the Cross Roads back so a potential buyer could take it for a test ride. Okay, but I was two hours away and needed to be at work in two and a half hours. Indian then informed me that they had organised a different loan bike for me to use and it would be ready when I arrived.

Two hours later I finally pulled into the dealership on the Victory, and there sitting winking at me was a brand-spanking-new, unused Thunder Black Chieftain!

Unbelievable!

Not only had I bought the number one bike of my dreams, but while it was being serviced I got to ride another brand-new Indian, the top of the range with all the bells and whistles. Two new Indians to break in and enjoy within a month — fantastic — and by the time I picked up my Vintage I had chalked up over 1,900 kilometres on the beautiful new Chieftain!

So where to from here for Indian?

Polaris CEO Scott Wine, who has gambled $100 million on rebirthing Indian in a bid to unseat Harley-Davidson, the entrenched market leader, put his finger on it when he told Businessweek.com, 'It occurred to me that bringing this business back to life is quite similar to the birth of a child:

tremendous excitement and anticipation, followed by great joy and adulation and then years of really, really hard work.'

Time will tell, but what I do know for dead sure is that I am the owner of the first new Indian motorcycle to be sold in Australia in over 60 years!

# Surfing in Leathers

John Bryant
Bilpin, NSW

Like many motorcyclists, I have a couple of different groups of riding buddies. There's the mob I ride with regularly, and then there is the once-in-a-while riding group that has become known as the 'Kiwi Blokes'. There are seven of us in this group, six Aussies and an En Zedder. The reason for the group's name is that every year or two we get together, book flights to New Zealand, hire off-road bikes over there and have a ball. Apart from these irregular biking adventures, we rarely see each other.

There are two key Kiwi Blokes. Perhaps the most important is Clive, without whom the group wouldn't exist. He's a Kiwi who lives in Auckland, and who just happens to have won their national motocross championships several years in a row back last century when he still had hair. Now well into his 70s, he can still outride anyone on dirt, thrashing blokes a third his age! Apart from being a bloody good bloke with a stable of very nice dirt bikes, Clive has always planned the itinerary for our trips. He knows the Kiwi landscape back-to-front because he's ridden it all his life, both on road and off. We rarely ride on bitumen; the public roads simply represent a convenient way of getting from one off-road location to the next, fast. Clive has led us up mountains, into volcanoes, along beaches, through forests, down abandoned tunnels, beside disused railway tracks, into underground mine shafts and to scores of other interesting places that most locals, let alone tourists, have never seen.

Clive has been married to Queenie longer than either of them can remember. She has tongue-lashed him mercilessly for the best part of half a century, contributing to his amazing endurance and poor hearing. Queenie is well loved by the Kiwi Blokes because of her culinary skills, lavish hospitality, generosity and hatred of anything to do with motorcycles, which she articulates in a snorting sing-song voice after a few bubblies. She's very funny! Every NZ adventure starts and finishes with a sumptuous feast at Queenie and Clive's, usually highlighted by Queenie dancing the night away with anyone whose leg or back hasn't been injured in a motorcycle get-off. Clive doesn't dance due to the limitations imposed by his back brace, which he stiffly climbs into each morning, usually while hanging onto one of us for stability. He swears his back injury was caused by falling out of bed during an overly active love tryst, not falling off a motorcycle. Queenie always chimes in with 'lying old bastard' ...

The other key bloke is Bazza, an Aussie who owns a management consulting business in Sydney. He rides a RT100 at home but also revels in getting off road and into serious dirt. He is an organisational freak who started Kiwi Blokes by drawing together a number of his Aussie mates, most of whom hadn't met each other before our first trip away. Bazza is related to Queenie by marriage, which is how he knows Clive. It was Bazza who suggested the first of our motorcycle adventures to New Zealand and followed up by making all the arrangements, including coordinating the trip times, arranging all the flights, booking accommodation and, most importantly, negotiating the hire of our motorcycles. He always takes care of every last detail, including the provision of a van to transport the group directly from the airport to the motorcycle hire shop.

Between them, Clive and Bazza do the hard work and all the rest of us have to do is turn up with our riding gear and pocket money. We don't spend all that much cash while we're away because we usually bunk down for free with one of Clive's many mates at various locations en route. In places where he hasn't any friends worthy of exploitation, we stay at caravan parks or cheap cabins. Everywhere we go people seem to know the bloke and usually offer us 'Clive's discount prices' without being pushed. On one occasion we were in the middle of nowhere when we came across a caravan blocking a narrow dirt track. As soon as we pulled up, a very large and aggressive-looking tattooed Maori came out of the caravan and glared at us, arms folded. A huge hand-painted sign on the van said 'Tribal Land, No Whites'. Clive removed his helmet and the Maori broke into a toothless grin, embraced him and rubbed noses. We rode off into the tribal territory with the Maori's words of farewell ringing in our ears: 'Stay as long as you like, men.'

Clive loves spending time with our group when we go over on our trips, and it isn't just because we are the worst off-road riders he has ever come across. It gives him an opportunity to get away from Queenie for a week or so and catch up with what has become a group of really good friends. Clive is particularly fond of another Kiwi Bloke, Boris, a Sydneysider who has an MBA and PhD, and rides a Fat Boy back home. Clive constantly pesters Boris to perform his party trick, which involves taking a swig of wine then spraying it out both nostrils. Even though Clive has seen him do it a dozen times, he still collapses with laughter, followed by a coughing fit.

Another rider in our group who intrigues Clive is 'the Kid', a 20-something Tasmanian kelp farmer who has been riding motorbikes on his family's property since he was tiny. He is the most talented off-roader amongst us, but he has a strange habit of sleep walking. One night on our first trip the seven of us were bedded down in a single-room cabin on four double bunk beds, sound asleep after a hard day's riding. In the early hours of the morning the Kid started shouting in his sleep, waking us all up. It was pitch black so his blood-curdling incoherent screams scared the hell out of us, and being in a strange place we thought someone was being murdered. In the dark we heard the sound of running. Someone switched on the light just in time to see the Kid, naked, run full bore into the wall and then crumple on the floor, still screaming and thrashing his legs. I looked across at Clive in the opposite bunk. His eyes were as wide as saucers as he pulled a blanket up over his head and muttered, 'You really are a crazy bunch of bastards.'

Of all the memorable experiences we have enjoyed in the Land of the Long White Cloud, one in particular stands out because it could so easily have turned into a monumental tragedy. It happened on our second time over there in 1998 when, for the first time, we were riding the full length of the North Island, mostly off road. Five of us were on single-cylinder Honda XR650Ls and the other two on BMW R100GSs. These weren't bikes of choice, but simply reflected the best we could scrounge up from the most conveniently located motorcycle hire shop. The Hondas, which we found to be pretty capable off-road machines, were fitted with large aluminium panniers and matching top boxes. Although our hire agreements didn't permit us to take the bikes onto any beaches, Clive said it would be okay, providing we washed them down afterwards to get rid of the 'evidence'. Who were we to argue with our expert tour guide?

On the morning of the incident we arose and packed early then headed for Ninety Mile Beach, anticipating a great day of riding based on the glowing descriptions provided by Clive the night before. When we arrived at the beach it was even better than he had described it. The tide was on the way out, leaving a huge expanse of flat white sand running as far as the eye could see, right to the horizon in both directions. The sand nearest the waterline was very hard packed, which made it perfect for riding at full speed. As soon as we made it onto the beach, we were like kids let loose in motorbike heaven, riding seven abreast absolutely flat chat, screaming and whooping it up. The only obstacles were the odd 4WD and occasional bunch of other motorcyclists doing exactly what we were. When we'd had our fill of the high-speed antics we ventured into the softer sand to see who could do the longest broadsides, tightest doughnuts and fastest figure eights. There were countless spills, some quite spectacular, but nobody got seriously hurt.

By early afternoon we'd had enough thrashing about so we set off to travel along the length of the beach in a northerly direction. As the name suggests, the beach stretched for some 90 miles so there was plenty to experience as we rode along the coastline on the hard-packed sand at the water's edge. The tide had gone right out and was about to turn when we came across a narrow sandy track leading from the beach to a small raised island just offshore; it had been left exposed by the receding water. Eager to explore, we followed the sandy bridge out onto the island and pulled up. We'd been riding for several hours at that stage and decided to take a break, peeling off our helmets and riding gear to enjoy the cool breeze coming off the ocean. A couple of the blokes had a snooze in the sun while others walked around, looking in rock pools and throwing stones at seagulls.

After about two hours we decided it was time to get going again, so we retraced our steps, following along the raised sand bridge as we rode back towards the main beach. As we got closer to the beach, we were horrified to see that the incoming tide was causing the rising water to overlap parts of the track, potentially cutting off our only access route back to dry land. The implications were terrifying!

We rode along as quickly as we could and were relieved when it appeared as though we would make it back onto the main beach just before the track was inundated with water. Then, with only 50 metres between us and the beach, we came to a deep trench cutting across the path that we had to take. As the waves surged in, they filled the trench to a depth of a metre or two with foaming, boiling water. Then as the waves drew back out again, they left the trench almost empty, to the point where it looked possible to ride through the shallow water. It became obvious that our only means of escape would be to ride across the trench, one at a time, during the 10 to 20 seconds when the waters receded. Either that, or leave our bikes to the mercy of the waves and swim across as best we could. This was hairy stuff and I must admit we were all pretty worried, but there was no time to sit around discussing the situation because the tide was coming in quite quickly. We had to act immediately or the trench would disappear under deep water, leaving us stranded in the midst of the rising ocean.

We lined our bikes up, ready to take off across the trench. Being the most experienced and accomplished rider in our group, Clive said that he would go first. If he could make it, then the rest of us could emulate his effort. The six of us sat on our bikes watching anxiously as the next big wave came in, then slowly sucked itself back out again, leaving a watery trench about 20 metres wide. As soon as the water appeared to have fallen to its shallowest level, Clive's bike exploded in a cloud of blue smoke and he charged his way across, his back wheel spewing up an arc of water and sand. He reached the safety of the beach okay, stopped, turned around, and gave us a big grin and the thumbs up.

The Kid went next. Like Clive he waited until the surf had receded and the trench was at its shallowest, then he took off like a rocket. His entry and exit didn't look nearly as neat as Clive's, but he too arrived triumphantly on the beach, completely drenched but safe and sound. Another big grin.

Now it was Boris's turn. He was sitting on his bike next to me, revving it up and waiting for the right moment. Just before he took off he glanced sideways at me, winked and said, 'Mate, if I don't make it, tell Sonia I love her!' With that he was off, standing on the pegs as the heavier but more powerful BMW kicked around underneath him, trying to buck him off, throwing up an arc of salty slush as he hacked his way across the trench. With clouds of steam rising from his big twin he hit the beach and raised his fists in triumph — he too had made it!

I was next. I don't think I've ever been more scared in my whole life. I was deafened by the sound of my own heart pounding in my chest. I waited, intensely watching the foaming swirling water. Then as the next wave reached its lowest point, I grabbed a handful of throttle and accelerated into the trench. In hindsight I realised that I hadn't followed the exact same trajectory as the three previous motorcycles. Because I was a few metres to their right when I started my run, I was perhaps a metre or so off to one side of the route that the other three had taken. I got about halfway across the trench when suddenly my front wheel nose-dived, falling into an invisible hole underneath the waterline. My back wheel bucked up into the air as the motorcycle cartwheeled, throwing me over the handlebars and into the surf. Within seconds a huge wall of water surged over me as the next wave came barrelling down the trench. I coughed and spluttered as I tried to disgorge the huge gob-full of salt water that had forced itself up my nose and into my mouth. Somehow I had retained my grip on the Honda's handlebars and to my surprise the motorcycle was floating. I later worked out that the fuel tank was probably half full of air, plus both the panniers and top box were fairly airtight as well, so in sum total the machine was reasonably buoyant.

But my troubles had just begun because I then realised that I was clinging to a floating motorcycle that was being rapidly sucked along a trench parallel to the beach and would then head out towards the open sea. I have never been in such a life-threatening situation before or since; I seriously thought that this was it, I wasn't going to survive. I remember yelling, 'Help!' at the top of my lungs, but that wasn't necessary because my six mates were all standing there, three on the beach and the other three waiting to take their turn across the trench, fully aware of my predicament.

To their enormous credit, the two youngest and strongest blokes, Boris and the Kid, who had already crossed the trench, ran along parallel to the shore until they were close to where I was being swept along. They both immediately stripped off their riding gear, jumped into the water and swam out in the frothing surf to where I was struggling for dear life. I have no idea how they did it, but they dragged me and the bike to the shallows, through the pounding surf. Even though I finally managed to get my feet down onto the sand and start struggling up onto dry land, I found the going very difficult because I was clad in a full leather outfit, crash helmet, leather gloves and a pair of Johnny Reb riding boots. I reached the beach and looked around. I was horrified to see that my two young mates were still struggling with the floating Honda in the raging surf. I kept yelling at them to forget the bike, leave it there and get out, but the silly buggers persisted until they managed to drag the bike out of the water. By this time they were both thoroughly exhausted and threw themselves down on the sand, panting for breath next to the bike.

While this whole drama unfolded the other three had made their dash across the trench, avoiding the route that had been my downfall. Finally the whole seven of us were safe and sound on dry land, somewhat chastened by what could have turned out to be a very tragic disaster indeed.

But it wasn't over yet; attention now turned to my drowned Honda. We were on a very remote section of the beach which was literally miles from anywhere, so it was vital that we get the bike started. We did all the usual things, including turning it upside down, emptying water out of the single cylinder and pulling the carby apart and drying it out. We took a chance on the fuel tank, pushed the starter a few times and the thing fired up! Unbelievable! However, our joy was short lived. After revving it and letting it warm up for a few minutes, it suddenly stopped, never to start again. It turned out that everything, including all my riding gear as well as the insides of the Honda, had been invaded by incredibly fine particles of sand. We figured the bike had suffered a serious internal haemorrhage, so we gave up trying to resurrect it and focused on how to get out of our predicament.

By this time my adrenaline production had subsided to a normal level and I suddenly realised that my leg was hurting. I peeled off my leather pants to behold a hole in the muscle of my right leg, probably caused by a protrusion on the bike, maybe the foot peg. It was hardly bleeding at all, but very painful.

After discussing the alternatives, we all agreed that I should ride the Kid's bike, while Boris would try to tow the Kid on my defunct Honda using the only tow rope available, a pair of Clive's jumper leads. We figured that we would have to ride at least five to 10 kilometres along the beach to a point where we could leave the sand and get onto a sealed road. The other blokes suggested that I take off immediately, while they mucked about trying to tow the dead Honda, which promised to be a pretty slow trip. We agreed that I would take the first exit off the beach and wait for them there if they hadn't already caught up with me.

I took off by myself, taking it easy because my leg was really throbbing. As I continued along the beach, it started to narrow quite dramatically. On my left was the pounding surf and on my right was an increasingly vertical sand dune, almost too steep to ride even if I had been in good enough shape to give it a try. I became gradually more alarmed as the beach got ever narrower, with the waves crashing right up onto the sand, closer and closer to the base of the sand dune. And then disaster struck.

Without warning a very large wave crashed up onto the beach and came surging along the sand like a tsunami wall of water, knocking me off my bike. It wasn't deep enough to suck me back into the ocean again, but I stalled the bike and lay there on the wet sand, feeling like a stunned mullet. Fortunately, it seemed as though I had been hit by a freak wave because subsequent breakers didn't quite make it far enough up the beach to reach me. I struggled to my feet, managed to wrestle the bike back onto its wheels, said a quick prayer and hit the starter button. My prayer was answered — thankfully it fired. I got back on and rode as quickly as I could, looking desperately for a pathway through the dunes and back onto the sealed road that I was told ran parallel to the beach. Within another few hundred metres I was greatly relieved when I saw a small canyon open up through the sand dunes. I rode off the beach onto the track, which wound its way through 100 metres or so of scrub, onto the main road.

I pulled up under a tree and slumped down to await the arrival of the others, but didn't have to wait long. About 20 minutes later four of them pulled in, followed not long after by Boris towing the Kid on my extinct Honda. Clive ran straight out onto the road, hailed a passing car which gave him a lift to the nearest house, where he borrowed their phone and called a mate who came and picked up myself and the Honda with his ute. Two hours later we were all showered and sitting in the bar of a local pub eating steak and chips, reminiscing on a day of riding that none of us will ever forget.

After another couple of days we arrived safely back at Clive's home in Auckland, indulging ourselves in the farewell dinner, cooked to perfection by Queenie herself. With the beer flowing and Old Port cigars glowing, Clive tapped his glass, called for order, then presented me with an utterly buggered pair of jumper leads as a memento of one of the Kiwi Blokes' greatest adventures.

'And in closing,' chuckled Clive, 'I'd like to propose a toast to the only mad bastard I've ever seen go surfing in his helmet and leathers.'

# Skipping Bail

## As told to John Bryant by Martin Kimber
## Cranebrook, NSW

When I got to the final year of my mining engineering degree at the University of New South Wales, I was required to spend the first six months studying, followed by a further six months getting some practical experience at a mine site. During my time at uni I had developed a couple of close mates, so we decided to try and arrange for us all to go to the same place for our mining experience. After casting around for alternatives, we all applied for mining positions at Mt Isa Mines, one of the few Australian mines big enough to take us all in one hit. Fortunately, they agreed to take all four of us, including my best mate, Alan John Jones.

Although I had lived in Sydney all my life, I embraced the rugged Mt Isa landscape and the mine lifestyle in an instant, especially in the company of a bunch of good mates. Once I surveyed my new surroundings, I realised that my most pressing challenge was 'transport'; the barracks where I was living were a considerable distance from the mine site where I would be working underground. I mentioned the problem to my father during one of my weekly telephone calls to home and he came up with an immediate solution. Dad reminded me that he had an old Yamaha Deluxe 100cc motorcycle in the back shed doing nothing, so he said he'd ship it up to me so I could use it for daily transport. Sure enough about two weeks later the machine turned up as cargo on an aeroplane. Looking back at the experience now, I am particularly surprised that the bike hit the tarmac ready to ride away. Not only was the battery installed and connected, but the tank had petrol in it!

The bike was an immediate success, enabling me not only to commute to work and back, but it also gave me the wheels to start exploring the vast Queensland outback. Meanwhile my mate Alan John Jones decided he needed a motorcycle too, so he bought a Honda 360G from one of the workers who was leaving the mine. I must confess I was a little jealous when I saw Alan's bike — it was a monster compared to my mosquito-like Yammy. The first time I threw my leg over the 360G for a test ride, I couldn't believe the power. The 356cc engine was tuned for broad-range torque, and coupled with a six-speed gearbox it felt like a Ferrari. It was obvious that my tiny single-cylinder Yamaha had some severe limitations when it came to covering any sort of distance, so I looked around for an upgrade.

I found what I was looking for when I came across a new Yamaha DT250 at the local Yamaha dealer. It handled the daily commuting like a breeze, but had the added advantage of being a reasonably competent dirt bike as well. This was a great bonus when it came to poking about off road, investigating some of the dirt tracks that led to old mine workings, billabongs and riverbeds. I loved the crackle of the two-stroke exhaust and the knobby tyres gave me confidence on off-road surfaces where road tyres would probably have killed me. Over the next few months Alan and I did a heap of recreational motorcycling, visiting places as far afield as Camooweal, Winton and even one marathon epic to Tennant Creek and back.

Life was pretty sweet in those days before we had any real responsibilities. We worked hard but loved our jobs, with plenty of time to party and get out amongst it on our beloved bikes. Like most young blokes on two wheels, we had our fair share of spills, but nothing that was serious enough to keep us off work in the sick bay.

When it came time to taking holidays we would always fly out, usually to Sydney or Brisbane, sometimes via Townsville.

On one of these flights I recognised a hostie, a girl who happened to be an old friend from high-school days. Sue said she was a regular on the TAA routes around Queensland so we arranged that next time she had a stopover in Mt Isa we would get together. This culminated about six weeks later in a big night out at the Barkly Hotel to celebrate Al's and my birthdays. When I told Alan that Sue and another hostie were looking for a night on the town he was only too willing to oblige. We both turned up on our respective motorbikes, scrubbed clean and ready to rock'n'roll. Someone later said that they knew we were in town due to the pervasive aroma of Californian Poppy!

The night was a rip-roaring success, especially when measured in litres of Tia Maria, which was one of Al's favourite weaknesses. Towards the end of the evening it became pretty obvious that none of us were in a fit state to drive, which didn't matter for the girls because they were staying at the hotel. I was able to bludge a lift back to the barracks with a less inebriated driver, but Alan was keen to party on to see if he could drink the hotel out of Tia Maria. Before I left I made the girls promise that they wouldn't let Alan get on his motorcycle when it came time for him to leave — it would probably have been his last ride if he did.

The next morning I was awakened by a severe throbbing in my temple. My first thought was whether Alan had made it back to the barracks in one piece. I stumbled out into the daylight and made my way around the corner to Alan's room, but after banging loudly on the door there was no answer. When I went around to the window and peeked through the curtains I could see that his bed was still made. Al was not fond of housework, so it obviously hadn't been slept in. That sobered me up pretty quickly. He may have been in an accident on the way home, ending up in hospital or worse.

Jumping on my bike, I headed off to the Barkly Hotel to see if I could pick up his trail and find out where he was. When I arrived, there in the car park was his Honda, in one piece, so obviously he hadn't had a motorcycle accident.

Relieved, I went back to the barracks to get ready for work. I had just pulled up and was taking off my helmet when Alan walked up as though nothing had happened, although he did look pretty seedy. 'What happened? How the hell did you get home? Where did you spend the night?'

According to Alan, with some of the details filled in later by eyewitnesses, he was about to leave the hotel when a Falcon sedan, which he took for a taxi, pulled up next to the group of revellers. The fact that the 'taxi' was populated by two uniformed police officers didn't impress Alan one bit, so he proceeded to give them a piece of his mind, using extremely colourful language which had obviously been fuelled by his record-breaking binge on Tia Maria. After being told to 'move on' and ignoring the instruction, he was taken into custody and chauffeur-driven to the local lock-up where he had spent the night.

The next morning when he'd sobered up, the police told him he would have to appear before the circuit magistrate who would hear the 'drunk and disorderly conduct' charges that had been laid against him. But there was a snag — the magistrate wasn't due for another month. So since the police wanted to get him out of the lock-up, they decided to offer their prisoner bail. Luckily for Al he had only 10 cents in his pocket, so bail was set at 10 cents and he was released. The only part of the story that didn't come out at that time was that Alan had given the police a false name and address. Somewhat intoxicated, the name he gave them was Alan John Kimba, 'Kimba' being a very small variation on my own surname of Kimber.

Perhaps because Alan didn't really need that 10 cents, or perhaps because he didn't relish the prospect of appearing before the magistrate, he sort of forgot about the whole incident and failed to turn up for the hearing. Unknown to him, a warrant was issued for his arrest, but because of the false name and address and the relatively minor nature of the charges, the police didn't get too serious about looking for him.

All of this would have quietly faded into history had it not been for a dramatic event that occurred in the Top End on Christmas Day 1974. That was the day that caught the whole of Australia's attention when a cataclysmic cyclone devastated Darwin. Immediately after the news of the cyclone hit the airwaves, worried relatives and friends scrambled to try and find out whether their loved ones were safe and well. A number of Darwin residents, their homes badly damaged or destroyed, started driving south towards safer territory. In Mt Isa we met a lot of these people, and we also got phone calls from some of our own friends in the southern states to see if we could find out more about their friends and relatives who had been in Darwin at the time. The best source of information about the survivors was the Mt Isa police station, where the authorities had set up an operation to coordinate information about the movement of survivors through that part of the country.

Alan and I had a list of people we were trying to locate, so we rode our motorcycles down to the police station to see what we could find out. When we got there I went to the counter to make enquiries while Alan stood well back near the entrance, arms folded, straight as a telegraph pole, with his full-face helmet on and tinted visor in the down position. He was also wearing his standard motorcycle gear, which included boots, trousers and shirt that closely resembled the standard police-issue uniform. I had always assumed he dressed this way as a tribute to his father, who had been a Crown Sergeant at Fairfield police station in Sydney.

As I completed my enquiry about the Darwin survivors, the police officer on duty asked me for my name, to which I replied Martin Kimber. The cop looked up quizzically and asked me if my surname was spelt Kimber or Kimba. I assured him that it was Kimber with an 'er' and enquired as to why he wanted to know. He said, 'A few months ago we arrested a drunk with a similar surname, Kimba, but the bastard skipped bail and failed to show for the hearing. We don't enjoy being treated like idiots — we'll find the prick if it's the last thing we do.' I assured him that I had never been arrested for drunk and disorderly conduct, but as I turned to leave I heard a motorcycle accelerate away from the police station.

Alan Jones, alias Alan Kimba, alias 'the bastard', had disappeared!

* Names changed to protect the guilty!

# Dog in a Box

Mick Beltrame
Canberra, ACT

'Does he travel with you on the bike?'

It's a question I get asked often, usually by lovely young ladies of the fair-haired persuasion at some out-of-the-way rest stop or small-town cafe by the side of the road. I have two stock answers to that most perplexing question: 'No, but I have a long leash and he runs really fast' and 'Yes, but I sit in the box and read the map while he rides the bike'. It gets a laugh, proves that they really are blonde, and is usually the prompt for me to gear up and get moving again.

My dog is a Border Collie named Kipper. He is a chick-magnet without the bike, and doubly so when dressed in his riding gear. I'm just the scruffy old biker who leads his pack.

Kipper had a rough start to life as a working dog. He 'failed sheep' as a pup and spent his first three years wandering the grassy fields around Grenfell, New South Wales, hiding from the farmer and playing games of tag or chasings with his woolly mates. Or so it seemed. 'Free to good home' was what the advertisement said, so I took a punt on a young dog that had failed miserably as a worker and had never known the delights of living in the city. I carted him back to Canberra and he settled into his new life as a much-loved pet without blinking an eye. He is a fast learner and will try anything that looks interesting to him. Chasing balls and Frisbees is not interesting. Being around people is, apparently.

It was on a bright sunny day while I was washing my BMW R1150R that it happened. Kipper was doing what Kipper does best: hanging around, chilling out and piddling on the garden while I was working. He wandered over and looked at me while

I was drying the bike's seat, so I gave it a pat and invited him up. Quick as a flash he was there, peering over the screen and wanting to go somewhere. That's how it all started. From then on, it was not a matter of if he would be riding with me, but how to make it work.

My first tentative steps into the world of carting a dog on a motorcycle involved fitting an old travel-crate to the back of the bike, using the pillion seat and luggage rack for support. It worked, but it meant that Kipper could only see a sideways view of passing scenery. We embarked on many test runs as I tried to ensure that he really liked motorcycling and was not just playing around. He always seemed keen to get back in his crate and moving again, so I knew that I would need a longer-term solution. I purchased another crate and progressively modified it to give Kipper a forward view and a little more room to move about. His welfare has always been a concern, and a safety harness and quality dog coat are a mandatory part of his attire. The harness prevents inadvertent sheep chasing, and the coat keeps the cold air off his back and chest. Kipper never took to wearing 'doggles', so he rides without them, but sits low enough behind me to be protected from the stones and bugs that might otherwise cause problems with his eyes. My desire to travel further afield also meant that the bike would change from a low R1150R to a taller and heavier R1150GS Adventure. This would bring a new level of excitement to both our lives, but not always in a positive way.

In most states it is illegal to carry a dog on the front of a motorcycle where the dog can impede control or obstruct the rider's vision. I have no such issues with Kipper harnessed into his travel-crate behind me. He has enough room to move about and rest if tired, but he prefers to spend his time with his head in the breeze and will often lean as far forward as his harness allows in order to peer over my shoulder. He loves the twisties, but cannot be relied upon to lean to the inside of the corner, so I am always mindful of that. Dog and box weigh in at 25 kilograms, so he is less of a problem than a fidgety child pillion. I've been pulled up at random breath stations twice in my travels and the boys in blue have never questioned my setup, so I guess I'm legal.

It's a pleasant way to see the country when your best mate is with you. The rides we do are often long, sometimes covering a thousand kilometres or more in a weekend. The biggest ride Kipper has completed was a trip from Canberra to Port Augusta and back over three days. We averaged 900 kilometres a day for all three days and slept rough. We had an absolute blast on deserted roads in empty country.

I've learned that Kipper hates to stop, but when we do he's off the bike in a flash to find a bush or tree or wayward lizard to piddle on. He likes to quickly inhale a small snack biscuit and take a slurp of water, then he's ready and waiting at the bike, often before I've removed the lid from my own drink. He's a complete nutter when it comes to bike travel and that's why we can do such big distances with relative ease. In all our thousands of kilometres of travel there has never been a problem with him. I carry his food and water and stop for him rather than for me, but it's always best to avoid the crowded places and the inevitable questions. We are clearly a novelty act and are often photographed on the run or during our stops. I tolerate the attention as it is somewhat inevitable, but Kipper doesn't care and usually looks with disdain at the camera sticking out the window of the car alongside us.

One time a girl about 12 years of age and her younger sibling approached us at a stop and asked the usual question. I looked at her and shook my head, turning so that she could see that there was no other form of transport at the roadside rest stop, other than my bike and her parent's car. She laughed as she suddenly realised the silliness of what she had asked, and then asked if she could pat Kipper. I couldn't refuse. I delayed my departure for a while as I chatted with the family about travelling with my dog. Why do I do it? Where do I go? Is it fun for the dog? Does he ever get travel-sick? Is it hard work for me? Do I have trouble getting him back on the bike? That last one's a beauty and is often asked. It's answered when I've packed the battered water bowl and biscuits away and I tell Kipper that it's time to go. He races to the bike, leaps up onto the seat and into his box, spins around and is ready and raring to hit the road again. Is he trouble? Not likely!

My travels with Kipper haven't always been beer and skittles. One of our trips involved roughing it, so the bike was loaded with light, but bulky, camping gear. This was not a problem from a weight perspective, but it upset the balance of the bike just a little bit. I normally camp off the road in a quiet rest stop near the grey nomads, so that I can get a free coffee or beer, or sneak down some farmer's open driveway to some trees where I won't get run over. But this time I decided that a radio transmission tower a few kilometres from the main road traffic was a better option. I had almost made it when the front wheel rolled off the side of a large stone near the tower and down we went. Oops. No animals were harmed in the dropping of the bike, but getting it back on two wheels was an effort I won't forget. Kipper was not impressed of course. He stayed well away from the bike until it was back upright and then wandered over to offer some help! You're too late, boy. Relax. Chill out and have a biscuit. Good boy.

Kipper is now 10 years old and still travels with me. He doesn't do every trip as I'm finding it harder to manage the balance of the bike when it's heavily loaded, especially as Kipper and I get older. We tried a sidecar for a while, but that had its own problems and was soon discarded. I don't know how many kilometres we have ridden together. Maybe we've travelled around 30,000 kilometres across two bikes and the sidecar; but maybe it's a lot more than that. We are considering a new setup for the remaining years we have to travel as a team. I'd like something with more stability. Shiny and new would be nice, so watch out for the old bloke with the

Border Collie riding shotgun, coming down your road soon. Funnily enough, it doesn't seem to matter where we travel, the question never changes: 'Does he travel with you on the bike?'

Kipper gets quite upset now if he sees me putting on my riding gear when I can't bring him with me on a ride. I've taken to hiding my riding gear in the garage the night before, so that I can sneak out without him. It's a sad state of affairs when you have to hide from a bloody dog! But he's not just a dog, is he? He's my best mate.

Looking back, taking on a failed sheep dog as a pet was a gamble that paid off big-time. Being able to travel with Kipper by motorbike is one of the best things about my life with motorcycles and it fits neatly with many other personal achievements and wonderful events that have made me who I am. We've even done an Iron Butt Association ride together, so he has a spot in my heart that is irreplaceable.

I dread the day when age or illness puts an end to our travels together. There is nothing like the friendship of a good dog to bring peace into your world and unconditional love into your life. The joy he brings to the kids and oldies alike that we meet on our travels will also be missed. While I'm the guy they spotted riding out on some deserted road or travelling a freeway, it was the Border Collie riding pillion that made them smile, laugh or scream with delight. Yes, the day will come when I'll have to bury my mate in the backyard alongside the other family pets and companions. He'll wear his well-used travel coat and take his beaten-up water bowl to wherever it is that dog spirits go.

He will be missed.

But I'll still have my fading memories of our travels and funny photos to show people. They will look at the photos in wonder and ask the same old question. 'Does he travel with you on the bike?' No. Not any more. But he used to.

# Thanks, Dad

## Matthew Menzies
## Paringa, SA

My father passed away six years ago, but he never knew how he saved me, or that he even saved me at all. I never had the guts to tell him.

About 11 years ago I was working for a grape harvesting mob out near where I live in a small rural town with a population of around 2,000. On this particular day I was heading down the main highway to the local pub to cash my pay cheque. I was riding an old junker: an antiquated CB200 road bike, no mirrors, no front light, wiring hanging out all over the place and obviously no rego because it would never have qualified for a roadworthiness certificate. Since I didn't have a car licence at the time, the bike was my only mode of transport.

So there I was, casually spluttering down the road, no helmet, when I spied a couple of cops on motorcycles and a police paddy wagon coming towards me. Unfortunately, I just happened to be driving on a section of the highway where there were no turn-offs or other means of escape. I had that horrible sinking feeling in my stomach and my bum hole clenched tight — I knew I was screwed. With gritted teeth I remained looking straight ahead, head up, feigning innocence, and just kept riding. I glanced back after they passed and sure enough I saw brake lights; they were all turning around. I slammed the old clunker down two gears and took off, flat strap, scrap metal spewing out the exhaust pipe! The tears in my eyes clouded my view of my speedo, but I reckon I must have been pushing the poor old girl to at least a dollar 15.

I decided to try for the first turn-off to the right, but I was travelling way too fast. All I could do to avert disaster was, at the very last moment, swing onto a side road that ran parallel to the highway. As I was halfway into the turn, I clipped the gutter, but somehow just managed to hold it together to avoid a big get-off. Back on the gas, I could hear the sirens closing behind me as I saw the next turn looming. I banked it right over hard as I went into the corner, just grazing the gutter on the outside of the bend, doing the Superman while sliding a good 10 metres with the throttle cranked wider than wide open. Miraculously I somehow stayed on the bike.

The coppers were gaining fast and would soon be sitting on my clacker. The sealed bitumen was a no-contest zone, so I figured one of the adjacent paddocks was probably my best option. The wail of the sirens deafened my ears as I screamed through a give-way sign, just missing an old ute that flashed past me in a blur. By this time I could feel the thunder of motorbike engines pounding directly behind me. Three more houses flashed past at the speed of light when I decided it was now time to up the ante. With the hairs on my head standing up in a full mohawk despite the lashing wind, I gritted my teeth and smashed the decrepit CB across a drainage ditch and into the paddock. Standing on the pegs, I tap-danced and slithered my way across the rabbit-warren-infested long grass at maybe 70 kilometres per hour, shaking off a number of unwanted motorcycle accessories in the process.

I was amazed that somehow I was still on two wheels by the time I reached the end of the paddock. With only one more turn to negotiate, I was almost within sight of my house. Just as I was about to make my final turn, and before losing sight of the coppers, I looked back. Sure enough they had baulked at riding into the rough stuff, but I had enough sense to realise that they wouldn't give up that easily.

I kept it at full noise until I rounded the corner into my driveway then laid the bike down, hard. It broadsided across the grass and came to a stop behind an old bus that was parked in the yard, front end spinning like a roulette wheel.

I lay there in the long grass panting, adrenaline squirting out all my orifices, as I watched the police troll slowly down the street, looking into each of the properties. As soon as the police had gone, I jumped up and casually walked inside, kissed the missus and acted like nothing had happened. About 10 minutes later, when my hands had almost stopped shaking, the phone rang. It was my dad.

'Hi, son, did you hear all the commotion? It was a motorbike chase!'

I was stunned. I lied: 'Nah, heard nothing. How do you know it was a bike chase?'

His answer blew me away.

'I was just driving to the pub to put some bets on, half cut of course, when some stupid dickhead on an old trashed road bike ran a give-way sign. I almost hit the wanker but then almost took out the cops who were chasing behind him — slowed 'em up good and proper. Thank god they were busy chasing that idiot or I would've got done for drink drivin'. Lucky, eh?'

To the day my father passed away I didn't have the courage to tell him that I was the wanker on the trashed road bike. So Dad, if you can see this — THANKS HEAPS!

# Saved

John Bryant
Bilpin, NSW

I had allowed myself four hours to ride from Sydney to Cowra, where I was booked as dinner speaker for a group of about 40 Christian businessmen. If the weather had remained fine, I may have just about made it, but as I climbed the mountains I rode into cloud. Then the temperature dropped sharply and very strong wind gusts began buffeting my bike. Riding with me was my mate Mark, both of us mounted on separate Gold Wings.

As we travelled the Mid Western Highway, the weather conditions went from bad to atrocious. The combination of the midwinter sun dropping below the horizon and the heavy cloud cover resulted in premature nightfall, even though it was not much past 5pm. But worst of all was the wind. As we headed west, it cut across our trajectory at right angles, causing us to ride with our bikes slanted at an angle to counter the icy blasts.

Common sense dictated that we should have slowed up and taken it easy in the deteriorating conditions, but anxious not to arrive late for the meeting, I foolishly pushed ahead at the speed limit, and then some. We were almost at our destination, somewhere between Woodstock and Cowra, when I should have become a road fatality statistic!

We were in an open stretch of country where the cross wind was gusting in extremely strong bursts, and we were sitting on about 110 kilometres per hour. A very large Pantech-style truck, pulling an equally large enclosed trailer, came thundering towards me from the opposite direction. I recall thinking to myself, here comes another driver that's not slowing up for the conditions; we were closing on each other at well over 200 kilometres per hour.

As we passed one another, the truck and trailer momentarily blocked the cross wind, but after it had moved on I was instantly hit with a massive, and I mean massive, wind blast. The shock wave knocked my bike at least two metres to my left, off the bitumen, and I found myself still upright, but riding at 110 kilometres per hour in the road shoulder slush. Not only that, the bike was gradually tracking away from the road and further into the never-never. I instinctively stood up on the foot pegs to exercise greater control, an automatic response from my old off-road riding days. Fortunately, I had enough presence of mind not to hit the brakes or try any dramatic changes in direction. I remember three of those low white plastic guideposts flashing past. They are usually positioned about 100 metres apart, so in no time at all I had travelled 200 or more metres along in the muck.

In the few seconds that all this took place, I immediately knew that I was in dire trouble. I was going way too fast to be able to stop the bike before running off further into the scrub, which undoubtedly would have had a fence or drainage ditch hiding in there somewhere. The steering was useless on the boggy surface; if I tried to change direction, I would undoubtedly have flipped the bike. Standing on the pegs, hurtling into the bush at over 100 kilometres per hour, I exercised my only remaining option. I screamed at the top of my lungs, 'Lord help me ... Lord help me!'

Although at that very moment I was heading away from the bitumen, I instantaneously found myself back on the blacktop! I have no memory of steering the bike out of the slush and back onto the road. I am not that talented a rider, and anyway, I believe that would have been an impossibility considering the weight of the bike and the wet, windy conditions.

I can offer no rational explanation as to how I escaped my hopeless predicament, other than to attribute the miracle to a supernatural response to my call for help. I have never experienced any other type of 'unexplained' event either before or since.

My mate Mark, who was riding about 100 metres behind me when all this happened, later gave me his account of what he saw:

> When that truck passed you I saw your bike get pushed off onto the side of the road, into the dirt, and start gradually heading into the bush. My immediate thoughts were 'how far is the nearest hospital' and 'I wonder how badly he's going to be hurt'. I cannot believe that you didn't come off, and I can't believe that you got it back onto the road. One moment you were in all sorts of trouble heading for disaster, and suddenly you were back on the road as if nothing had happened. How did you do that? If I hadn't seen it with my own two eyes, I simply wouldn't believe it. Incredible!

I later came across something written in the Old Testament nearly 3,000 years ago. Perhaps it provides a clue:

> And it shall come to pass that everyone who calls on the name of the Lord shall be saved. (Joel 2.32)

It worked for me!

# I'll be Doggone

Mike 'The Bike' Warren
Dunsborough, WA

Almost everyone I know has a dog story. Not the kind of story where your pet dog got run over, or when your dad said, 'Buddy has gone to sleep' — I always hated that one — what bullshit, dogs die, they don't go to sleep! I'm talking about a dog experience that leaves a lasting impression. An encounter that has instant recall and you say, 'Hell, that's nothing. I remember once when ...' I've always liked and respected dogs. That is, I like small dogs and respect large ones. I especially respect large dogs that don't wag their tails and have a nasty habit of curling their top lip to reveal a row of jagged teeth the size of a picket fence.

My dog story is hinged to the swinging doors of the 1970s, at a time when we were immortal, invincible and impressionable. However, apart from dogs, my real love in the 70s was motorcycles. Not those little buzz-box types, no, a big thumping 900cc Kawasaki. That bike was a billboard for testosterone; loud, brash and uncompromising. A twist of the throttle produced the bark of a Rottweiler and acceleration like a thief in the night. The Kwaka was my immortal time machine from *Doctor Who*. It had the ability to cross time zones, awaken the dead and put fear into the heart of every daughter's mother.

The Kwaka had a certain rhythm that became hypnotic at around 140 kilometres per hour. The bike 'got on song' and an ethereal flow pulsated through the mind and body. There was no time to focus on the countryside as it all became a blurring mass of greens, browns, blues and the smell of cow shit. It was the cow shit that kept you in tune with the countryside, not the colours, and there was no distinction between Aberdeen Angus, Hereford or Jersey. Same grass, different rear ends, same smell.

One day I was riding along when a loud metallic sound suddenly penetrated my psyche in a plaintive attempt to warn me of an impending mechanical failure. 'Shit, what the hell's that?' I said out loud. 'Bloody chain guard,' I surmised and quickly checked ahead in the hope of discovering a garage, or shed, or repair shop, or anything.

I throttled back and there, just over the brow of the hill, I spotted sunlight bouncing off the tin roof of a large farm shed. Nursing the clanking bike along, I finally parked it near the corner of the shed where I saw an old farmer leaning over a bench with a grinder going full bore, showering him with sparks. Every now and then he jumped back, shouting, 'Bugger, bugger!' while madly brushing smoking embers of metal from his thin checked shirt.

He wasn't aware of my presence, but something else was. It erupted in a massive ball of fury, snapping and snarling, and with a throaty roar that I assumed came from some primitive source. I reeled back in terror. What the hell was happening? It was almost impossible to distinguish its form. There was no time for a reality check; self-preservation erupted through every pore of my body. 'Bloody hell!' I screamed, at which point the shower of sparks stopped and a gruff voice said, 'Stay away from that dog.'

I started to focus on a thick rope, straining and vibrating. Attached to the end of this rope was the most vicious, bull-headed dog on earth. I froze in my tracks. The dog was straining to rip at any part of my body that may have protruded into its space, but thankfully the rope held. The dog continued to dance on its back legs to the accompaniment of snarling and ferocious barking, with the farmer yelling.

'Shut up, ya bastard!' he screamed. The dog slackened off a millimetre, stopped barking and sat.

'Wow, what a wild bastard,' I said, trying for a brave face and a cool demeanour.

'I reckon,' the old farmer said, casually brushing some fragments of dust and embers from the front of his shirt as if he was getting ready to receive a visitor. The old boy had an engaging smile, but I could hardly take my eyes off the dog.

'Sorry to trouble you,' I said. 'Got a bit of a problem with the bike and I need some wire and pliers.'

'No problem,' he obliged. 'Come over to the bench and we'll see what we can find.'

It was a typical farmer's bench; a thick blanket of dust covered everything. There were old tractor parts, a bicycle wheel and bell, nuts and bolts, electrical fittings, pipes, PVC elbows and joiners, broken drills, hammers, screwdrivers, old newspapers and magazines, and thankfully, some tie-wire and a pair of pliers.

'There we are,' he said, obviously proud of his uncanny ability to remember exactly where everything was.

We headed back towards the motorcycle, avoiding such topics of conversation as the weather, politics and the price of fuel. Nearing the corner of the shed, I began to feel a little apprehensive; this was tiger territory. I could hear the dog getting ready for another lunge, a supreme test of the rope and my nerves.

'That bloody dog is mad,' the old boy muttered. 'Damn good watch dog though. Look at this.' And in a moment of supreme madness the old farmer stuck his leg into the dog's face, straight into its open jaws.

'Holy shit!' I yelled and jumped backwards as the dog savaged the old boy's leg and ripped into his ankle with incredible force. This was becoming a horror movie of Stephen King proportions. I was momentarily frozen with fear. I needed a stick, an axe, a gun, a weapon, something to ward off the dog. Kill it, immobilise it, render it useless; I had to save the farmer.

I have read how some people, in moments of imminent danger, can call upon great reserves of strength and courage to help them through. Unfortunately, I have never experienced this and even then felt nothing but an urge to escape, leaving the dog to its lunch of shin bone and ankle, courtesy of the crazy old man.

I looked at the farmer's face. I tried to hear his screams of anguish above the snarling and ripping, but there was nothing but smiles and laughter. The old fella's totally crazy, I thought to myself.

'Ha, ha, ha, got ya, I got ya,' babbled the farmer. I looked in total astonishment as the old boy pulled up a tattered trouser leg to reveal the chomped remains of a wooden leg.

'You old bastard!' I yelled in total disbelief. 'You fairly sucked me in!'

The old boy was beside himself with laughter. Tears rolled down his face, his chest heaved and wallowed like an asthmatic. He kept slapping his thigh and shaking his head.

'I got ya good and proper!' he roared through his wheezing laughter. 'Got ya good and proper.'

By the look of his leg I'd say quite a few have been 'got'. The dog was smiling — I think it was in on the scam.

# The 13

Name and address withheld
(to protect the Wimp!)

I bought a new Kawasaki Z1300 in 1982, an awesome in-line six-cylinder water-cooled beast with shaft drive, and still get as much satisfaction as when I first threw my leg over her. Although I've been tempted to trade her for other bikes that have caught my fancy over the years, the snag has always been the memories. That, and the fact she still goes like a bat out of hell. She may be heavy, she may look a bit old-fashioned, and she may chew through the juice, but man she GOES!

Last Christmas I decided to take The 13 for a run from Melbourne to Sydney to our traditional family get-together. Julie and the kids drove, I rode.

I was poking along the Hume Highway, thoroughly enjoying the passing countryside and looking forward to every minute of the trip. Somewhere between Albury and Ettamogah, sitting a tad under the speed limit, I glanced in my rear-view mirror and noticed a squadron of bikes slowly approaching from behind. I watched them for a while as they gradually caught up with me; they must have been sitting just over the speed limit.

When they got to me they roared past, aggressively close, almost touching, about a dozen tattooed blokes on very loud Harleys, all with outlaw patches on their backs. Then once they had passed they dropped their speed back down, forcing me to slow down and sit behind them. This annoyed me, but I sat there for about 15 minutes, hoping they'd pick up speed again and leave me in clean air. But they didn't, they just sat there, as though they were trying to intimidate me. I'm pretty sure The 13 resented being corralled like that!

I finally got fed up. These blokes were ruining my ride so I decided to blast past at speed. I planned to get well ahead and leave them to their silly games.

I crossed my fingers, hoping that there were no cops or radar traps in the area, especially as it was a double-demerit holiday period. With a twist of the throttle I swooped past them in an instant. I assumed I had escaped, maintaining about 140 kilometres per hour, but was horrified to glance in my mirrors and see that the whole mob had accelerated and were sitting immediately behind me again, in grim-faced formation.

Fortunately, I was pretty comfortable wearing my full-face helmet and tucked down behind a bikini fairing, protected from the wind. The outlaws were all wearing open-faced helmets, riding in a laid-back cruiser-style position, their bodies acting as wind socks!

Even though I was already doing well over the speed limit, I decided I had to get rid of these blokes, so I sped up: 145, 155, 160. The outlaws stuck with me for several minutes, but the wind, grit and bug splat were obviously starting to take their toll, so one by one they dropped back, until there was just one lone bikie sitting on my back mudguard, probably the leader of the pack. I very slowly edged my speed up further ... 165, 170. The 13 loved it!

The remaining bikie then made a supreme effort and pulled alongside me. Even with my helmet, ear plugs and the wind noise, I could still hear his V-twin screaming for mercy. I peeked sideways to look at him; I'll never forget his comical appearance. The flesh on his cheeks was flapping like flags in a cyclone. His sunnies were pressed so hard into his face that he would probably need to have them surgically removed. Both his arms were stretched like rubber bands, knuckles white from gripping the handlebars, and no wonder — my speedo said we were doing just on 175 kilometres per hour. Then he made a fatal mistake; he opened his mouth, probably to shout an obscenity. Once the wind got between his lips, it popped his mouth wide open, leaving him frozen with an expression that looked like a Howler monkey in full mating mode.

I didn't hang about to hear his message, I just gave The 13 her head and took off. How fast did I go? I have no idea. I was nervously watching the rear-vision mirror, half expecting him to pull out a rifle and pick me off. The 13 was probably near red line as the bikies slowly shrank into a tiny speck in my mirror. When I finally lost visual contact with the mob I dropped The 13 back to just over the speed limit, assuming that the pack would also drop back once I was out of sight.

About an hour or so later I was near empty, but I didn't want to risk stopping at a servo on the main road in case the bikies happened to pull in too. I took the bypass into Gundagai and quickly filled up, keeping an anxious eye on the passing traffic. I then donned my bright yellow wet-weather gear over the top of my black leathers, dramatically changing my appearance.

When I arrived at my destination my brother asked me why I was riding in my rain gear, especially in view of the bright sunny weather and the muggy Christmas heat. I jokingly told him that the wet-weather gear created less air friction than leathers, thereby increasing The 13's fuel efficiency. That was the end of that.

I'm still riding The 13, but I must admit we both get nervous whenever we unexpectedly hear the burble of a bunch of big V-twins!

# Our Dear Davidson

As told to John Bryant by A Lord
Hunter Valley, NSW

Charlie Lane was the runt of the litter according to his father, even though at birth he was only a couple of ounces lighter and 90 seconds behind his twin brother. But only his mother called him Charlie, or Charl when she was being affectionate; everyone else simply knew him as 'Shorty'. Shorty himself never gave it a second thought; his dad had lumbered his 11 siblings with colourful nicknames too, some of them less endearing than his.

Being the youngest and smallest of 12 children meant that Shorty grew up in a competitive environment at the tail end of the Lane dynasty. He saw himself as a small, clever and capable underdog, which compelled him to devote 110 per cent effort to everything he tackled. First at school, then later in his working life, his mental outlook was so positive and his perseverance so dogged that he rarely failed. It was no wonder that he carried his small wiry frame with a pugnacious air of humble self-confidence.

Although his dad never actually expressed it in so many words, he knew that when the chips were down he could rely on Shorty. Like most men of his generation, he rarely discussed his innermost thoughts and feelings with anyone, not even his spouse. Yet the affection he felt for his youngest son allowed him to sometimes draw him into his confidence, especially when he was worried about something. And so it was, in the winter of 1936, just after Shorty had celebrated his 19th birthday, that he followed his youngest son into the feed shed and confessed, 'I'm a bit worried about Old Dick. I doubt 'e's gonna make it through winter.'

Old Dick was the Lane family's one and only horse, a draught horse. He was a giant, weighing close to 800 kilograms and standing about 18 hands, but blessed with the strength, patience and docile temperament that so endeared his species to generations of pre-industrial farmers. Everyone loved Old Dick; he was as much a part of the family as each of the kids. They all rode him, sometimes up to six of them at a time when they were little. He dragged the plough, pulled tree stumps and got hitched to a dray every Sunday to take Grandma to church. No one was too sure exactly how old he was; he'd been bought second-hand by Shorty's grandfather at an auction 20 years earlier, so it was no real surprise that he could be approaching his use-by date. In later years horses were to become the playthings of the rich, but back in '36 Old Dick represented the only horse power on the Lane family's 154-acre farm, as well as the family's sole means of transport apart from a couple of old bicycles.

As Shorty processed his dad's sombre words, he immediately grasped the gravity of the situation. If they lost Old Dick, productivity on the farm would grind to a standstill. They would have no way to get around the district or collect supplies from town. In short, not only would Old Dick's demise represent the loss of a dearly beloved member of the family, but economic disaster would surely follow.

Over the next two weeks the whole family watched with increasing alarm as Old Dick coughed himself hoarse, almost stopped eating and became too weak to do any work. The vet sold them a bottle of stinking green slop to mix into Old Dick's oats, but he reckoned the real problem was old age and he didn't have a cure for that. Then one morning Shorty awoke to the sound of wailing. He and his twin brother, Sprocket, raced outside, and there in the middle of the house paddock were three of his sisters gathered around Old Dick's stiff carcass. That day was the only time the family ever saw their dad cry. He didn't make a sound, but he couldn't hide the tears that spilled from his eyes and trickled down his weather-beaten cheeks. Was it the financial loss or simply his love for an old workmate? No one knew.

Doing his best to regain his composure, Dad declared that Old Dick would have to be buried where he fell. He was too heavy to move, so the simplest solution was to dig a whopping great hole right next to the body and roll him into it. Dad announced that a 'prior commitment' would prevent him from participating in the burial operation, so Shorty was more than chuffed when he was put in charge, with full authority to 'do what it takes, son'. As Shorty started planning the operation, the family members peeled off one by one, offering excuses as to why they couldn't get involved. Finally it came down to just Shorty and Sprocket, a couple of shovels and a crowbar. Undaunted, they pegged out the gravesite and started digging, quickly passing through topsoil and clay but slowing up considerably when they hit shale. All day they toiled, hitting the crowbar with a sledgehammer to penetrate the shale. By late afternoon they hit bedrock, but they'd completed a waist-deep hole a bit larger than Old Dick. They debated whether they needed to go deeper, but Sprocket estimated that they could pop Old Dick in, fold up any loose bits and drag some logs across the top of the mound to prevent anything from digging up the corpse. Respecting his older brother's opinion and too tired to debate the point, Shorty agreed.

As the sun sank slowly in the west, with the help of a block and tackle anchored to a nearby apple tree together with a couple of timber fence posts for leverage, the lads finally rolled Old Dick's mammoth carcass into his eternal resting place. There he lay on his back in the grave, his four stiff legs majestically pointing skywards, with something close to a smile on his taut green lips. Lying on the grass, panting from his exertions, Shorty surveyed their handiwork with a sense of satisfaction, until he suddenly noticed that the hole wasn't quite deep enough — Old Dick's extended legs were protruding well above ground level.

'Just fold 'em up,' suggested Sprocket from his supine position, never having previously attempted to bend a dead horse's legs. Although Shorty gave it his best shot, he was unable to bend Old Dick's knees and hocks. He was completely rigid now that rigor mortis had set in — those mighty legs seemed destined to stand aloft forever. By this time it was getting dark and dinner was on the table, so Shorty suggested they backfill the hole until he could come up with a solution. As they went in for their meal, the only evidence that Old Dick had ever existed were his four legs standing upside down, bolt upright, in the middle of the deserted paddock.

Later that night, true to his word, Shorty implemented his solution. He snuck into the shed, grabbed his dad's very sharp competition wood-chopping axe and very quietly hacked off those parts of Old Dick's legs that were protruding above ground level. The quadruple amputation successfully completed, he retired for the evening.

The next morning the family gathered around the breakfast table to discuss their options now that Old Dick was gone. A ripple of excitement ran around the table when Dad said that they wouldn't be getting another horse, but that they would be following the example of some of the other farms in the district and investing in machinery. He revealed that he still had the proceeds from Grandpa's estate, so he was going to use some of the cash to buy a second-hand Vickers Aussie tractor (a British-built unit based on the US-designed McCormick-Deering 15-30). And then he dropped the bombshell. Since the tractor couldn't be used for running into town for supplies or for carting Grandma to church on Sundays, the family needed a road-going vehicle. A motorcar was out of reach financially, but he'd given it a lot of thought and reckoned that an economically viable alternative was a motorcycle, a motorcycle with a sidecar.

Shorty could hardly believe his ears! For the past five years he had been watching a growing number of local men thundering around town on their Triumphs, Velocettes, Indians and Harleys, but didn't dare dream that he would ever be able to ride one, let alone belong to a family that owned one. Later that day, still trembling with excitement, he caught up with his dad in the feed shed. With the two of them alone, his dad confided that he had no desire to ride a motorcycle himself, but that he was counting on Shorty to learn to ride it and act as the family chauffeur.

The budding motorcyclist had trouble sleeping for the next couple of weeks, sitting up most evenings by the light of his kerosene lamp, poring over the 'for sale' columns and checking the specifications of the various alternatives. Then he found it — an ad in the *Sydney Morning Herald*, 29th August 1936 edition, which was two weeks old by the time the paper reached him. It read 'Harley-Davidson 1928 with sidebox, well shod, splendid order, overhauled at cost £12, good as new, £42 cash or near, MA2977'. After calling the number, Shorty, accompanied by Sprocket who loved watching his brother in action, hitched a ride into town to do battle. He had just £35, the amount budgeted for the purchase of the motorcycle, tucked securely in his pocket.

When they arrived at the bike's address, they found the seller was a bald-headed old bloke who had several other bikes for sale, obviously a backyard dealer making a few extra quid on the side. The bike looked magnificent, or so thought Shorty, squinting through untrained eyes. The monkey-crap-brown duco was complemented by a whopping chrome-plated headlight mounted high above the handlebars, with a polished timber box attached to the left-hand side of the bike. The sidebox resembled a coffin and had the brothers looked underneath they would have seen that it had no suspension, just a home-made steel frame bent out of leftover water pipe. All Shorty knew about motorbikes was what he had learned the previous day by grilling a local mechanic, who had outlined the main things to check. Does it start easily when cold? Are there any oil leaks? Compression? Tyre tread? Oil dirty? Engine noises?

After a quick inspection and listening to the bike start up and run, it seemed to check out on all points. Shorty slipped into negotiating mode and spun the seller a line about this being one of many machines that he would be checking that day. Without making an offer he pretended that he was about to leave to look at some of the other bikes for sale. The old bloke could see his £42 disappearing out the door, so he suggested they negotiate, proposing £40. Shorty laughed and told him the Harley was a dog, that he would be flat out getting £30 for it. The old bloke acted insulted, so Shorty headed for the door. The dealer grabbed his arm and whined that £38 was his lowest offer. Shorty countered by dropping his offer from £30 to £28.

'But that's lower than your first offer,' his adversary cried indignantly.

'Well, sir, you should have grabbed the big money when it was on the table,' chortled Shorty, now running on high-octane adrenaline.

'£35 and that's it!' shouted the dealer, nervously winking at Sprocket, who interpreted the wink as an involuntary facial twitch caused by stress.

Inwardly Shorty was squirming with joy now that the negotiation had reached a point that matched the £35 in his pocket. But he knew he could do better, so he calmly feigned another walkout.

'What do you want then?' pleaded the old fella. 'I can't go below cost. The bike's rebuilt like new, cost me a package. Give me your best offer, sir.'

'Okay, I'll tell you what I'm going to do,' said Shorty as he propped in the doorway. 'I'll jump it back up to £30 and you've got yourself a deal, but if you want to play silly games I'm off.'

Ten minutes later the old bloke had finished writing a receipt for the finally agreed £31-5-6 and was filling the tank with fuel from a rusty five-gallon drum. After a crash course on how to start the bike and operate the clutch, gears and brakes, the boys were off, Shorty driving, Sprocket clinging desperately to the sidebox. If it had been a solo, Shorty surely would have killed both himself and Sprocket on the way home, but being an outfit he didn't have to worry about balance, instead concentrating his full attention on operating the controls. He stalled it once after narrowly missing a horse and cart yet managed to kick-start it again, but then almost came to grief on his first tight left-hander as the sidebox started to lift off the ground. Fortunately, he was only going slowly, but his heart was in his mouth before the sidebox touched down again. He also discovered the joys of being able to barrel into right-hand corners without fear of capsizing.

When he finally pulled up in front of his house he executed an impressive right-hander under brakes, broadsiding on the grass, drawing a wild cheer from his parents, his grandma and a couple of neighbours who were enjoying afternoon tea under the grey gum. Shorty felt like a world-class motorcycle ace as well as the world's greatest negotiator as he handed his dad the £3-14-6 in change.

The arrival of the tractor and motorcycle marked a turning point for the whole Lane family, especially Shorty. His dad often boasted that the Vickers Aussie tractor and its monstrous 15-horsepower engine could do the work of dozens of Old Dicks, but the truth was that he always got nostalgic when he walked into the feed shed, where drums of fuel and oil had replaced the bags of oats and bales of hay. It just didn't smell the same.

Although Shorty also missed Old Dick, he was too caught up in the excitement of the new motorcycle to dwell on the past. Officially the Harley belonged to the whole family, but since he was the only one who could ride it, it was essentially his own. To everyone's astonishment, Grandma also claimed a degree of ownership as she always referred to the bike as 'our dear Davidson' and she was the first one to go for a ride after Shorty arrived home. He had barely come to a standstill after his broadside across the grass when Grandma clambered into the sidebox, her gummy grin indicating she was ready to go. Only too eager to show off his new toy, Shorty took off, executing a tentative left-hander into the street. To his surprise, there was not even a hint that the sidebox wanted to lift off the ground, so he quickly realised that with Grandma acting as ballast, the outfit could negotiate left-handers almost as quickly as right-handers. He couldn't help thinking that maybe there was a practical use for grandmothers after all.

That first joyride took them around the perimeter of the town on dirt roads, Grandma squealing with delight as the unsprung sidebox crunched over large potholes, doing its best to buck her out. 'Geedy whiz!' she screamed above the thumping of the big V-twin.

Trailed by a dense cloud of dust, Shorty finally wheeled back into his front yard, where an even larger crowd of neighbours had gathered to applaud their return. But he hadn't turned off the engine before the yells of approval suddenly died down to an eerie silence. He happened to glance across at Grandma and was horrified to see her face was covered in blood; no wonder everyone, except Grandma, looked horrified. She obviously didn't realise anything was wrong, her ear-to-ear grin fuelled by the gallons of adrenaline that were still pumping through her veins. What had happened? She hadn't fallen out or been hit by anything. It wasn't until Shorty's mum had cleaned up Grandma's face with her hanky that the mystery was solved; the culprit was Grandma's one remaining tooth that protruded from her lower jaw. That tooth stood out like an alabaster gravestone in a gloomy cemetery, all its brethren having rotted from their sockets years ago due to Grandma's lifelong love affair with sweet home-made ice cream, fizzy drinks and crystallised ginger. Her tooth had obviously penetrated her top lip a number of times due to the lurching and bucking of the sidebox. Grandma, who had been through a World War and the Great Depression, was undaunted. She was hooked. There was no way a minor disaster was going to dampen her enthusiasm for her new-found love of hooning around in 'our dear Davidson'.

The next day Shorty realised that motorcycle ownership involved a couple of responsibilities. The first was that he had heard that he needed a licence to ride on public streets, so he rumbled down to the local police station to enquire. Scotty, the local constable and his father's occasional drinking partner, said not to worry too much about it, that he should come back after he had some riding experience and he would see about conducting a test.

The second problem was solved almost as easily.

Shorty loved his bike and wanted only the best for her, and that included providing some sort of garage to keep her out of the weather as well as somewhere to work on her. There was no room in the feed shed since his dad had knocked out one end wall to provide tractor parking, and there was no money for building materials. Fortunately, the family had developed a very creative attitude towards their housing needs over the years, because they always came up with a novel solution each time one of the 12 children arrived on the scene. Initially they resorted to bunk beds, but when the two bedrooms were chock-a-block they resorted to canvas army cots, which they trotted out each evening and set up in the living room. By the time baby number nine arrived the house was bulging at the seams and the only space left was in the ferret cages in the backyard, but they had family planning problems of their own.

Undaunted, Shorty's dad had demolished the front porch and used the timber and tin to construct a small lean-to on the side of the house, which ultimately housed Shorty, Sprocket and two of their older sisters, all in bunk beds. The beds took up 99 per cent of the floor space, leaving no room for a swinging door, so Dad cut an access hole in the side of the house to connect the new bedroom to the main structure. His mum fitted a red velvet curtain to the unfinished hole, which Shorty felt added an exotic Asian ambience to his cosy bedroom. The downside with this arrangement was that the access door opened into the house via a tiny bathroom, which somewhat annoyed the more modest members of the family, who had to suffer the indignity of family members trekking through to Shorty's bedroom while they were sitting starkers in the bath. The upside was that Shorty was one of the few people in his town to enjoy his own ensuite, even though he still had to visit the long-drop dunny outside like everybody else.

By the time the Harley arrived six of the 12 kids had left home so the family's housing pressures had eased considerably. Dad was sympathetic when Shorty approached him for somewhere to house the bike; since he had paid for it he was keen to protect his investment. As he stood in the front yard, chin in hand, surveying the exterior of his family home, he considered possible solutions. The house still looked a bit odd with the front porch missing. Apart from a set of stone steps leading up to nowhere, the imprint of the front porch still surrounded the front door, which he had nailed shut. The last thing he wanted was for someone to stumble out that door during the night and fall three or four feet to the ground where the porch had been. He considered excavating a small garage for the bike under the front door, but that involved real work. Finally he decided the easiest option was to transfer Shorty and Sprocket to another room inside the house, then knock a hole in the end of the lean-to bedroom, large enough for the outfit to drive straight in, up a small ramp. Simple! An instant garage without cost or effort; a perfect solution. And so it was that Shorty got to work on his Harley in his own garage, with immediate access to an en-suite bath tub, which, when not populated by naked relatives, was ideal for washing bike parts in kerosene.

Almost as soon as the new 'garage' was commissioned, Shorty started adding refinements. A bank of old army ammunition boxes stored his growing collection of spare parts, a couple of rows of shelving housed instruction manuals and motorcycle-related literature, and with a home-made hoist consisting of a block and tackle swinging from a steel tripod he could lift almost anything. Since the white ants had eaten out the timber piers that held up one side of the garage's foundations, the floor sloped to the northeast, which meant that any bike parts inadvertently dropped usually rolled down to the end of the garage where they could be retrieved.

Shorty's reputation quickly spread throughout the local community. Not only did he have the only dedicated motorcycle workshop in the district, but it became apparent that he also had a natural aptitude for mechanics. He could pull down an engine or split a gearbox almost by instinct and was nearly always able to diagnose and fix problems that baffled others. Coupled with his ownership of a highly desirable Harley-Davidson outfit, it was no wonder he attracted a crowd of fanatics who either owned motorcycles, or dreamed of doing so. Most evenings there were almost as many pimple-faced adolescents crammed in his garage as there were moths committing suicide as they dive-bombed the kerosene pressure lamp that burned until all hours.

With the arrival of his new motorcycle came one of his first mechanical challenges: fixing the beast's atrocious handling. He found that he needed the strength of an orang-utan to wrestle his outfit around corners, leaving his shoulders sore after only short rides. He didn't need to be a mechanical genius to work out that a big part of the problem was the unsprung steel frame that sat underneath his bike's sidebox. Not only had the rough ride sent Grandma's tooth through her lip, but the violent vibrations had also caused a near tragedy when Sprocket accidentally discharged his 12-gauge shotgun while riding in the sidebox. The calamity had happened the first time the brothers decided it would be fun to use the outfit for a motorised rabbit-hunting expedition. Because the V-twin made so much racket it was impossible to sneak up on their prey, but they found that if they went hunting at night and caught a bunny in the headlight it would usually sit still, staring at them, until they bagged it. In the excitement leading up to their first nocturnal rabbit kill Sprocket, seated in the sidebox with his 12 gauge, had fumbled and discharged his weapon, blowing out the front end of the box and also taking out the front tip of one of his boots. Dad reckoned that it was a miracle that he still had two feet and 10 toes!

Grandma also started to whinge about the sidebox. Every Sunday after her ride to church she would whine about how unpleasant it was with the wind whistling up her skirts through the gaping hole that Sprocket had blown in the front end of the box, especially when it rained. Fortunately, she couldn't complain during the actual trip because she had to clench a rolled-up hanky between her gums to prevent her one remaining tooth from giving her another bloody lip.

The pressure to fix the suspension further escalated around the time of Grandma's 80th birthday party. Shorty had used the Harley to fetch a case of cheap champagne for the party, which was being held in the local town hall. The bubbly pink wine endured a 15-mile trip from the winery over potholed dirt roads in the suspension-free sidebox, well and truly shaken to bits by the time it arrived on the tables at the birthday party. Grandma was sitting at the official table on the elevated stage, in full view of the entire town, as Uncle Athol prepared to uncork the first magnum for the purpose of charging their glasses and proposing a toast. Always the joker, Uncle Athol removed the wire restraint from the top of the bottle, placed both thumbs under the cork and started to ease it out of the magnum, all the while pointing the bottle at the guests assembled on the floor of the hall below. There was pandemonium as women squealed, scrambling to get out of the way in anticipation of the cork letting go. But before the expected eruption, the bubbly's frantic ride in the sidebox had generated so much pressure in the bottle that the bottom suddenly blew out, showering three pints of bubbly over the guests at the official table, including Grandma. The noise of the explosion coupled with Uncle Athol's stunned facial expression caused the guests' hilarity level to ratchet up into overdrive. Without warning several inebriated townsfolk started a food fight with some of the leftover king prawns that were scattered around the tables. Then everybody else joined in, throwing anything and everything within reach. The entire town talked about the event for years afterwards, agreeing that it was one of the best shindigs ever held in the town hall. The normally affable Grandma, her new party dress ruined by the shower of champagne, didn't quite remember it that way. Blaming the whole debacle on 'our dear Davidson's' rough cartage of the bubbly, she harangued Shorty every time she came across him. 'Gotta fix our dear Davidson, Shorty, quick smart!'

It wouldn't have been a month after Grandma's party that a newcomer pulled up outside Shorty's garage late one afternoon, riding a BSA fitted with a Steib sidecar. He had just arrived in town to take on a security job at the local jail and needed some work done on his motorcycle, so one of the local lads had directed him to Shorty's garage. Tired of wrestling with his outfit, he wanted the chair removed to convert his BSA back to a solo. Shorty held his breath as he asked him what he was going to do with the factory-built Steib, which featured luxurious leather upholstery, a windscreen, a wire spoked wheel nestled under a full mudguard, a fully integrated leather lap blanket and, last but not least, a sophisticated suspension system. After exercising his prodigious negotiating skills, Shorty agreed to disconnect the sidecar, do a decoke, valve grind and tune-up on the BSA, then service it for the next year, all in exchange for the Steib.

Three weeks later Shorty rumbled out into the front yard on his born-again Harley.

The whole family had assembled in the expectation of witnessing 'something exciting', and they were not disappointed. They gasped in unison as they took in the legendary and altogether fabulously luxurious Steib chair. To cap it off, Shorty had resprayed the Steib black, converting it from its previous drab watermelon-green appearance. While he was at it he had also sprayed the bike to match, finally ridding it of its sombre monkey-crap-brown hues. During the conversion process he had fallen in love with the motorcycle all over again. He took a few paces back and surveyed his jet-black machine, now a streamlined and superbly integrated colour-matched outfit, sitting there winking at him in the sunlight, just begging to hit the open road.

Shorty's reverie was interrupted by a very loud 'geedy whiz' as Grandma rushed forward, laying her eyes on her renovated conveyance for the very first time. Gone was that horrible windy coffin-shaped torture chamber, and in its place a carriage of almost unbelievable comfort, fit for a queen. Lifting the leather lap blanket, she clambered aboard, sank into the plush leather seat and nestled expectantly behind the tall windscreen, ready for the road. She was about to pop her rolled-up hanky between her gums for protection when it occurred to her that maybe the ride wouldn't be so rough now. Perhaps her sole remaining tooth would no longer threaten her top lip?

As they accelerated out the front gate, the chair seemed to float along like a schooner on a gentle ocean swell; to Grandma it felt like it was at least a yard off the ground. With the suspension soaking up the bumps and the upholstered seat cushioning Grandma's considerable buttocks, her lips were free to exclaim 'geedy whiz' every time Shorty cracked the throttle. She couldn't help thinking that this was heaven on earth, making a mental note to include Shorty in her will. At last, Grandma was happy!

His motorcycle make-over completed, Shorty now rode the best-looking outfit in the district, which didn't go unnoticed by a number of people including those of the female gender. Added to that he had thrown in his job as a sales assistant at the local grocery store and was now running his motorcycle repair business on a full-time basis, having extended the lean-to with new materials he had actually purchased with cash. Mothers of marriageable daughters referred to him as a 'good prospect' whereas the girls themselves called him a 'cool cat'. Shorty liked girls, but he was too focused on his business to pay them all that much attention. That changed dramatically in early 1939 when the Dawson house caught fire.

It was early one morning just after Shorty had unlocked the workshop when he heard the clanging of the fire bell. He ran outside in time to see the town's fire engine come careering around the corner, heading out of town, one of the firemen madly smashing the clapper against the bell housing. It must have been urgent because old Tommy Whitfield was hanging off the back of the truck in his pyjama shirt, with a very long hank of hair from his sweep-over, together with his unfastened braces, flapping wildly in the breeze.

Thinking that maybe he could help the fire crew, Shorty quickly pushed his outfit out of the garage, fired her up at first kick and headed for the gate. Before he got there he almost smacked into Grandma, who had run around the side of the house to investigate the commotion. When she saw the fire truck disappearing into a cloud of dust she quickly concluded that Shorty was heading for the action, so she yelled that she wanted to go on 'our dear Davidson' too. He didn't really want to take the old lady to the fire, but in a split second he decided that some ballast in the sidecar would speed up his trip, so he pulled over while she scrambled aboard, then took off.

They were a good two minutes behind the fire truck and Shorty had no idea where they were heading. He couldn't see the truck and he couldn't follow the sound of the fire bell as it was drowned out by his howling V-twin. Fortunately, there was no breeze, which allowed him to follow the trail of dust that was hanging in the air in the truck's wake. Desperate to catch up, Shorty really put the hammer down, much to Grandma's delight. He caught snatches of 'geedy whiz' above the din as she hung onto the floating Steib for dear life, loving every minute of it.

After several minutes of frantic riding, he figured he must be gaining on the truck because the pall of dust seemed to be getting heavier. Anticipating a glimpse of the fire truck at every turn, he was gathering speed, fast approaching a left-hand bend that ran around the perimeter of the cricket ground.

Perhaps he wasn't paying enough attention, or maybe he was travelling just a little too quickly, or possibly he had overestimated Grandma's value as ballast, but whatever the cause Shorty found himself in serious trouble as he rapidly approached the apex of the left-hander. With his handlebars on left lock Shorty instinctively hit the anchors, but without a brake on the sidecar wheel, the Steib pulled aggressively towards the bike, suddenly lifting the chair off the ground. Grandma, by this time her single tooth clenched firmly through her top lip, sat staring down at Shorty from on high. It was the first time he'd ever seen fear written across her wrinkled old face. 'Geedy ...'

Shorty frantically wrestled with the handlebars, all thoughts of fires and trucks replaced by his will to survive. The chair had lifted so high that it was about to capsize. He tried to correct by accelerating, hoping to pull the sidecar back towards the bike, but it made little difference. The outfit shot across to the wrong side of the road as he straightened the handlebars in a desperate attempt to bring the chair back to earth — he may have been prepared to kill himself, but he was buggered if he was going to take Grandma out as well! With centrifugal forces now dissipated, Grandma came back to earth with a resounding thump, but all hope of steering the bike out of trouble was lost. All he could do was cling to the outfit with the back wheel locked up, teeth gritted and eyes closed, anxiously hoping he could wash off enough speed to soften the inevitable impact. The last thing he heard before the crash was 'GEEDY WHIZ'.

When he opened his eyes, peering through the dense cloud of dust, he was amazed to find himself still in the saddle with Grandma firmly ensconced in the chair. The only injury appeared to be the dribble of blood on Grandma's lip. He was shocked by the eerie silence, but then realised that the bike had stalled when it had hit something that was now lying crumpled underneath it. A quick inspection revealed that it was a pushbike, a lady's pushbike, which must have been lying on the nature strip outside an adjacent house. After quickly assuring Grandma that they were both okay, Shorty knocked on the front door of the house to confess his sin, seek forgiveness and offer restitution, because he was that sort of bloke.

The door opened and there before him stood the prettiest girl he had ever seen. He introduced himself to Vera, who was only 17, slender and dimpled, and the owner of the demolished Malvern Star bicycle. Although he didn't find out until much later, Vera had been his secret admirer ever since observing him thundering around the district on his outfit. She readily accepted a ride into town the next day to buy a new bicycle, and that was the start of a steady relationship that developed quickly into love, culminating in their marriage a year and a half later.

By this time World War II was in full swing and many of the blokes in the district had already left to do their duty. Shorty was dead keen to join them but was torn between enlisting and staying home to help run the farm after his dad had been partially incapacitated by a stroke. Finally patriotism and his sense of duty to his country overrode his more immediate family concerns, so he volunteered for the army and followed his mates into the unknown. During basic training his superiors recognised his mechanical skills and he ended up in a General Transport Company, which saw action in the Middle East before being deployed in Port Moresby, Papua, in 1943.

In the last letter that Vera received in 1945, three months before the war ended, Shorty wrote that he was desperately looking forward to getting home, not only to pick up where they had left off, but also to hold baby Annette for the first time; she had been born six months after he had left to go to the war.

That was the last time anybody heard from Shorty.

The official army report stated that he had volunteered to carry vital dispatches through the jungle to an isolated command post on his army-issue WLA Harley, but he never returned. No trace of him, or his bike, was ever found.

Shorty's grandma died in 1947, and by 1964 his mum and dad had passed away too. Since all the other kids had moved out of the district, a local real-estate agent was engaged to put the old family home up for auction. During his first inspection the agent was intrigued to find that a rough lean-to on the side of the house had both its internal and external doors nailed shut. Using a jemmy, he prised one of the doors open to find a large object covered by a sheet of stiff canvas; the canvas was covered in water marks, spider webs, bird droppings and dust. He pulled the canvas off, and there sat a pristine jet-black Harley with colour-matching chair, perched up on blocks.

The word 'Vera' was airbrushed on the black nose of the Steib in gold paint.

# Acknowledgements

While riding a motorcycle is a unique recreational activity providing an incredible sense of freedom, it's the camaraderie with fellow riders that puts the icing on the cake. Over the years I've been blessed with a wide variety of travelling companions, sometimes just one or two, sometimes hundreds on our way to a rally or charity ride. While there are far too many to name, I'd like to pay tribute to a few who stand out in my memory.

Early on it was my Uncle Perce. Even before I was old enough to hold a licence, he unwittingly kick-started my lifelong interest in motorcycles when he helped me rip a small Ducati engine off a motorised wheelchair to fit to my bicycle.

Then in 1976 along came Dave 'Flash' Lane, waving his brand-new Gold Wing under my nose, forever infecting me with new-motorcycle-lust.

On my longest rides I have been responsible for Pete Rosenhain, famous for spraying an occasional white wine from his nostrils during fits of laughter.

Putting most of us to shame with his natural riding ability (or was it sheer good luck?) is Johnny Taylor, who has always ridden it like he stole it.

When it comes to an impressively high pain threshold, old mate Steve Drury comes to mind; usually back in the saddle ready to ride no matter how severe his get-off or injury.

In terms of spectacular stacks, I still don't know how Geoff 'Nigel' Nippard survived leaping off the escarpment at the top of Kangaroo Valley on a Kawasaki 250. How did he miss the gum trees as he crashed off the road and down the mountainside through the thick bush?

I cannot forget Gordon Hooker, a truly supportive Ulyssian mate and a worthy fellow seeker of the meaning of life.

And finally Graeme 'St Clem' Eggins, simply the funniest and most compassionate bloke on two wheels today.

Thank you, one and all, I've enjoyed the journeys immensely. It is your souls that live on in the spirit of this book.

# GOT A STORY TO TELL?

Have you got a story about
your motorcycling adventures?

Drop John Bryant an email at
motorbikelegends@gmail.com